Sports Management and Administration
2nd Edition

Sport is a growing industry with enormous numbers of people now involved in the management and administration of sports, fitness and exercise. Whether voluntary, public or commercial sectors, all can benefit by improving the practice and delivery of the management of sport and its organizations. This text is designed to help all those delivering sport to deliver it better and includes:

* What's different and special about sports management?
* The voluntary sector
* Event management and marketing
* Marketing, fundraising and sponsorship
* Managing staff and volunteers
* Organizational management principles
* Legal issues including health and safety
* Case studies – both local and national

Full of practical examples, this book reveals sports management in action, showing how good management helps us to deliver better sports participation, at all levels.

This book is a must for undergraduates as well as an invaluable tool for professionals in sports management and administration in the private, public and voluntary sectors.

David C. Watt has worked in sports administration for over 35 years, in both the private and voluntary sectors. He is a director of sports and leisure consultancy Organising Leisure, and also of Leisuretraining.com.

Sports Management and Administration

2nd Edition

David C. Watt

Routledge
Taylor & Francis Group

LONDON AND NEW YORK

First published 1998
by Routledge
11 New Fetter Lane, London EC4P 4EE

Simultaneously published in the USA and Canada
by Routledge
29 West 35th Street, New York, NY 10001

Second edition first published 2003

Routledge is an imprint of the Taylor & Francis Group

Typeset in Goudy by
Florence Production Ltd, Stoodleigh, Devon
Printed and bound in Great Britain by
Biddles Ltd, Guildford and King's Lynn

British Library Cataloguing in Publication Data
A catalogue record for this book is available
from the British Library

Library of Congress Cataloguing in Publication Data
Watt, David C., 1951–
Sports management and administration/David C. Watt. – 2nd ed.
    p. cm.
Includes bibliographical references (p.   ) and index.
1. Sports–Great Britain–Management.   2. Sports administration–
Great Britain.   I. Title
GV713.W358 2003
796´06´9–dc21   2003046545

ISBN 0-415-27456-7 (hbk)
ISBN 0-415-27457-5 (pbk)

Contents

Figures and Table

Case studies

Acknowledgements

Sincere appreciation is expressed to the following organizations and individuals who helped in the compiling of this book. Their advice, guidance and comments proved most beneficial.

Colin Billyard; Peter Bilsborough (University of Stirling); Phil Collier (Sport England); Slava Corn (Canada); Penny Crisfield (formerly National Coaching Foundation); Kees DeKonning (Netherlands); Amanda Killingback, Edith Henry, Claudia Campisi and Simon Whitmore at E & FN Spon; Jayne Ford (Sport Scotland); Fiona Grossart (University of Edinburgh); John R. Hinton; Institute of Leisure and Amenity Management – Information Centre staff and past staff Nigel Benton and Ian Fleming; Jan Klumer (Juliana Welzijn Fonds); Dr Jozsef Leitner (Hungarian School and University Sports Federation); Anthea McWatt; Ralph Riley (Institute of Sport and Recreation Management); Graham Ross (formerly Scottish Athletics Federation, now Sport England); Sports Council for Wales; Brian Stocks (National Indoor Arena, Birmingham City Council and Manchester 2002); Tony White (Sport Scotland); Ian Whyte (Bell College). Angela Tan and all her students (past and present) in Singapore have also been an encouragement to press on.

To all the typists who listened to lengthy mumbling tapes and helped produce the text – Joyce, Yvonne and in particular Kelly and Donna; and not to mention Maggie who, as ever, helped push, tidy and ensure it all came together.

About the author

David C. Watt has over 35 years' experience in sports administration, having started as a willing volunteer even before leaving school and having continued that commitment in a variety of voluntary and public organizations, within a number of different sporting organizations right up to the present day.

He has held a number of different posts in a range of bodies, including six years as president of one national governing body, two as chairman of another and two and a half as an employee of a third.

Like many others, he became involved in sports organization and administration as a volunteer who was identified as having some ability (or at least being willing) and then had an increasing number of tasks piled upon him. Also, like others, he had no formal training in sports administration or management, although he has a background in physical education, enhanced by a degree in social sciences and an advanced diploma in educational management.

Ten years ago, he established his own business in sports and leisure, specializing in staff training and general consultancy, particularly in event organization, organizational management and strategic reviews. This work has allowed him to take a wider look at provision in the field of sports management and to get involved in programmes such as Running Sport, which focus on training for sports administrators and managers.

With this background and experience he felt that a book dealing with some of the practical issues would be of benefit to others interested in the field of sports management and administration – so this text was written, hopefully, to assist others involved and raise the standard of sports organizations to match the growing standards of participant performance and coach education.

David is a Fellow of the Institute of Leisure and Amenity Management and the British Institute of Sports Administrators.

His latest venture – leisuretraining.com – is a members' website devised to support the professional development of those working in sport and leisure, paid or unpaid. It develops many of the ideas featured in this book about management and leadership in the sports setting.

Introduction

Sport, like so many other areas of life and business, changes radically and very quickly in this modern age. Since the first edition of this book, many of the structures and organizations governing sport in the UK have altered quite significantly in terms of structure and delivery mechanisms.

The Sydney Olympics have had a major impact on the profile of sport worldwide, and have left a massive 'feelgood' factor which has influenced governments worldwide.

In the UK, the government has had much more impact on the delivery of sport through various initiatives and guidance like how lottery and other funding should be focused and delivered. There is a massive new emphasis on sport in schools, and the government has begun to see sport as a tool in tackling social problems.

These changes can often seem remote to people operating at local level, but in truth they have a major impact across all levels of sports delivery in the country. A change in focus for the lottery, for example, can mean that access to sports funding at a local level can change quite radically.

This new edition reflects on all such changes and has a new section to include website addresses as well as an extended bibliography to reflect the sizeable growth in relevant information and publications on sport and its delivery. Sports management and administration is truly a growth business.

The text also looks at specific current issues, including Best Value and technological developments, and includes a larger section on sports development planning and the input of volunteers.

The contents reflect the current trends in the growing and dynamic sport scene in the UK, and provide information to help the practitioner and the student understand the key issues more clearly, and ultimately deliver improved sports management and administration.

Now is an exciting time to be involved in sport and the future looks just as promising – if not more so!

Background

> Sport is the unalienable right of every person.
>
> *European Sports Conference*

> Sport is the most precious commodity we can hand on to the next generation.
>
> *Ron Pickering (1930–91), BBC commentator and sports coach*

> The level of participation and degree of excellence attained within a given sport is dependent, at least in part, on how that sport is organized. Sport has traditionally been organized in an *ad hoc* way, relying on volunteers who are committed to their particular sport. It is now clear that to encourage higher levels of participation and international excellence, new ideas about organizing need to be diffused to those involved in the management of sport.
>
> *Newell and Swan (1995)*

It is to be emphasized in this introduction and throughout the book that this text is written from a practitioner's point of view. The contents are meant to be of assistance to the student and practitioner of the business of sports administration and management – it is to be hoped that all practitioners continue to be students of their business as well.

The contents cover a number of areas selected by the author from his considerable experience in sport. They are a personal selection of issues thought to be important and relevant to sports administration in the United Kingdom and beyond. It is felt that UK lessons apply in most other countries of the world as far as management and organization are concerned, even though some countries are more advanced than the UK in sports participation levels and standards of performance. No list of contents would be comprehensive enough to cover such a large area in a relatively new occupation or study as diverse as sport, which has well over a hundred governing bodies and many thousands and millions of participants, at a wide variety of levels.

The author has been involved in sport as a volunteer, an employee, a participant, a coach, a local authority official, a national governing body official, a tutor, a trainer, an official, an administrator for a national organization, an administrator for a local league, a co-ordinator for an industry training organization, a member of a professional institute – almost every conceivable role available. Such experience has led to a fairly accurate impression of what knowledge is useful to people involved in delivering sport in the UK at this time.

While it could be seen as a movable feast, certain common requirements are likely to persist over the next decade or more as sport undergoes major changes influenced by television, money and increasing professionalism, as well as the increasing pressure on volunteers in terms of time and our societal changes in terms of job roles and commitments.

Someone else coming from a specific interest area or from an academic viewpoint might well come up with quite different contents and emphasis in a book on the same subject, but this does not invalidate this text, which offers a personal preference and rank of importance of the subjects included.

> Sport has the power to change the world, the power to inspire, the power to unite people in a way that little else can.
>
> *Nelson Mandela, in a speech at the Rugby World Cup, 1995*

As stated, this book is written by a practitioner to be of practical help to practitioners working in the field of sport and physical recreation, as well as of benefit to students of sports management and administration. It is intended to be an academic support, as well as a managers' handbook applied to the sports management and administration business. Very little has previously been written in the UK on the subject, and many people come to the work with little prior specific knowledge and little direct guidance – merely a great deal of the essential ingredients, enthusiasm and energy, or administrative experience gained elsewhere.

It is hoped that this book will cover many of the significant issues in this enormous and varied area. However, inevitably certain items will not be covered as fully as some people (including the author) would like.

The consideration of the history and the social structural context of sport in the UK is merely to give a background to the situation in which the sports manager or administrator works. As in any practical management situation, it is essential for the practitioner to be aware of his or her environment.

> Sport is a preserver of health.
>
> *Hippocrates*

A manager who ignores this environment and the specific setting is in danger of producing unrealistic practices unsuited to the situation in which they operate. This contextual understanding is vital but need not be a theoretical concept – rather, it entails a realistic analysis of the organizational and external environment which guides good practice.

It is also to be hoped that a good manager will be able to apply the suggested practices, procedures and thinking to a variety of situations. For example, an identified weakness in the implementation of the Compulsory Competitive Tendering process within local authorities was that many operating direct services organizations saw their role as being solely to manage their facilities, while the client side was regarded as the agency which would develop sport and consequently increase the usage and numbers using the facilities. This approach has proved to be flawed and it is clear that facility managers must allocate time to developing usage, and consequently the development of sport, if they are to see a sustained increase in user figures. It is quite wrong for sports facility managers to concern themselves only with the present and solely with facility and procedural management, forgetting about the developmental role. They must think more broadly and take a longer term strategic view if substantial progress is to be achieved and sustained.

As we move forward, there is no doubt that the base of sport is still very much in the hands of the volunteer. However, the situation must change if we are genuinely to treat our sport more like a business – in a more professional and full-time manner. This surely is the only recipe for success. The administrators and managers of sport must take it as seriously as the participants, have the same full-time commitment, and receive payment if they are to progress to the proper level of administrative support and managerial practice. This book aims to assist in this area and be a step towards the achievement of better standards in the management and administration of sport, so that the participants can benefit from effective back-up service, whoever the supplier.

A massive voluntary effort is put into sport. Its importance should not be diminished; rather, it should be boosted by a growth in the numbers of full-time professional managers supporting the effort.

On some occasions, in this text, specific reference may not be made to the voluntary sector but it is assumed and believed that the principles of good management practice can correctly be applied to the voluntary sector in sport and that, while volunteers bring their own commitments and technical expertise to the field, they will benefit hugely by following proper business practices, adopted from other industrial sectors.

This book will constantly recognize and emphasize that the ethos of sport is the fundamental background to beneficial management practice within it, and this should never be forgotten. This, however, is not a reason for not following business practices; rather an even stronger reason for grasping such ideas. If such practices are not followed then the ultimate sufferers will be the participants – who are, after all, what the business of sport is all about.

> Sport is our lifeblood.
>
> *John Major*

This book will also cover a range of issues related to the knowledge required for the National/Scottish Vocational qualifications and, in particular, will attempt to cover the key areas identified for the sports administration vocational qualification. The information will hopefully give some increased knowledge and understanding to those interested in proceeding with the workplace assessment required for this qualification.

The past years have seen significant growth in the area of Sports Council(s) initiatives, as well as a rapid increase in the number of local authority development officers being appointed to promote and administer sport. It is likely that the next 20 years will see a significant growth of professional sports administration, at a national and local level (this trend has already started), and that the training of these professionals, coupled (hopefully) with a constantly growing band of volunteers, will be crucial to improving the performance of our sports people throughout the world at all levels of competition.

The development of vocational qualifications will mean that practitioners will be able to become qualified in sports administration as well as sports development, facility management and operations, and coaching. This will mean a considerable improvement in the potential for on-the-job training and assessment leading to a qualification. This initiative will help fuel the growth of a strong qualified profession of people employed in managing and administering sport and recreation.

This book is written at a level which will hopefully prove useful to practising managers and administrators and help them in their work – after all, there is plenty for all such personnel to do.

Sports administration will never be the highest paid occupation, and it will always require a tremendous amount of commitment and energy, but it can be very rewarding and will be done better by people given necessary training and support, as well as all the background knowledge that is available. This book is a step along the road to help the hard-pressed individuals and organizations involved in sports administration, with a view ultimately to making things more efficient and effective for the sports performer.

This text does not deal specifically with facility management in sport and recreation, although many of the principles outlined will be of value to facility managers and relate to management in almost every sporting situation, because, while the details may differ in specific instances, the principles and guidance offered will remain the same.

The emphasis of this publication is to look at the management of the sporting process in the UK, and the people, structures and practices involved in it (or at least those who should be involved in it). In particular, management of the voluntary sector is an integral part of the target market, as well as the management of professionals working within their own operation or, as often happens, in close partnership with the voluntary sector. Indeed, the management of the relationship between the paid professional and the volunteer is referred to on many occasions. The dynamic of this relationship can be fundamentally improved if everyone involved takes a professional attitude (regardless of payment) and adheres to the principles outlined in this text.

The object of this book is to encourage a rise in management and administrative standards, bringing an increased standard of facility and opportunity provision for everyone participating in sport regardless of the context in which this provision is made. The benefits to everyone involved in sport will be enormous if serious consideration is given to the processes suggested.

Ultimately everyone involved will be able to increase their enjoyment and, if they wish, their standard of participation significantly, due to improved organization.

Sport has been defined as the institutionalization of skill and prowess. Sport is also about personal development, team development, community and society development. In recent years the government has also become keen to use it as a tool for social change. Sport has further been defined (Coakley, 1994) as 'an institutionalized competition that involves vigorous physical exertion or the use of relatively complex physical skills by individuals whose participation is motivated by a combination of intrinsic and extrinsic factors'.

Such definitions go to some lengths to distinguish sport from recreation, play and spectacle. This book does not make such a fine definition, feeling that many aspects of sports participation are for recreation, play and spectacle, and sheer fun and enjoyment often come long before any form of institutional competitive activity for performers at many levels.

Certainly sports administrators and managers (aside from team managers) should not see their role and input as limited to 'competitive' sport, at least in the narrow sense.

Sport and politics

There have been many famous examples over the years of sport being involved in politics, and of major international conflicts or controversies affecting sport. For example, the Soviet invasion of Afghanistan in 1979 led to the boycott, by many countries, of the Olympic Games in Moscow in 1980. Further, and perhaps more famously, there has been the boycott of South Africa at national sporting level, even in traditional sports such as cricket and rugby, in order to influence its policy on apartheid. There can be little doubt that ultimately this, allied with sanctions, had a fundamental impact in changing South African policy. It is intriguing to venture that the white population of South Africa had such a desire for sports involvement that they would eventually cede the exclusive 'right' to govern their country in order to take part in sport at the highest level.

It is also quite ironic that events such as South Africa winning the World Rugby Cup in 1995 have proved to be unifying factors in identifying the soul of the new South Africa. The appearance of Nelson Mandela in a Springbok jersey was, in itself, a remarkable statement about the change in political and social attitudes in South Africa.

The recent Cricket World Cup controversy ('should England play in Zimbabwe or not?') is a further illustration of the strong link between politics and sport. It seems ironic that the Prime Minister could appear on the same platform as Robert Mugabe at a conference, but the cricket team couldn't visit his country. In this case, is appeared that sport was the only weapon being used.

Many more traditional sports thinkers and participants have felt that politics should not be involved in sport because sport is about some of the more idealistic aspirations of the human race, whereas the activities of politicians and politics are less than tasteful. However, since both affect humankind so fundamentally, it is difficult to separate them. This is proved true from Olympic to local level.

The role of local authority politicians in the UK should not be underestimated in terms of the control they have over a significant spend in the support of sport, in terms of facilities, staffing and performance. Local authority funding is crucial to sport in the UK, and ultimately the decisions as to where this funding is allocated are made by local politicians for political reasons. It is naïve to believe that at a local level sport is not tied up with politics.

Equally, there are some 'political issues' that need to be considered in terms of relationships with sponsors or other funding sources. For example, certain sponsors might not be happy to be associated with a sport where drug-taking was thought to be prevalent, or where there was the potential for child abuse, or, indeed, in past days where some performers, e.g. the occasional rogue rugby player, would go and play in South Africa.

There is also a significant debate in the UK about the relationships between sports and within sports themselves. This is certainly non-party-political, but there can be major clashes between lobbies or interest groups over how sport as a whole, or particular sports, should be run.

On a number of occasions such behaviour has been seen in paid and voluntary situations to the severe detriment of the particular sport and its participants. One government minister told the author confidentially that 'sport is more political than politics itself' – a statement born of bitter experience of trying to keep the sports fraternity in Britain happy.

Additionally, issues such as gender equality and racism are political issues in society as a whole and therefore become significant issues within sport.

Funding from the National Lottery is now being used as another weapon to encourage clubs (especially the more traditional ones, such as bowling and golf clubs) to introduce an equal opportunities policy, and not to display traditional discriminatory positions, particularly against women.

The issue of racism in sport is perhaps most clearly seen on the football pitch and on the terracing, but is often used by groups with other interests as a vehicle to display their bigotry – shouting abuse at particular individuals or devising racist chants where they feel they are hidden by the mass of the crowd.

Issues such as nationalism and patriotism can also be linked substantially to sport, sometimes positively and sometimes negatively. There can be no more classic case of negative nationalism affecting sport than the 1936 Olympics, which Hitler tried to make a vehicle for his Aryan superiority views.

Equally, as mentioned earlier, South Africa's Rugby World Cup victory (and Scotland's Grand Slam title in 1990) had a unifying effect. The feelgood factor generated in Sunderland by the team's FA Cup win in 1973 was significant for the whole community at a time of economic recession.

The role of central government in sport in the UK is principally concerned with providing the policy framework and establishing financial guidelines. It does not concern itself with direct service delivery, leaving that to the local authorities and sports bodies, with the sports councils setting the strategic direction.

The UK is one of the few countries in Europe (and indeed beyond) that does not have the full post of Minister for Sport, although there is within the Department of Culture, Media and Sport (DCMS) a post for a junior minister with this title. Most other countries have this post clearly identified and given cabinet rank, perhaps linked with education, youth or culture.

The devolved governments in Scotland, Wales and Northern Ireland also have a junior minister with sport as part of their responsibility. This leaves the DCMS junior minister effectively only responsible for sport in England, and can cause some confusion in implementing policies across the UK where appropriate.

It is interesting to note that after the arrival of John Major in Downing Street, the policy involvement of the top rank of government, i.e. the Prime Minister, altered significantly. Through his personal interest in sport he had some influence on the national curriculum in schools through the Department of Education and Employment, where he felt that team games were not sufficiently included – a belief he shared with the then Minister of Sport, Ian Sproat. This led to several initiatives throughout the UK, such as the Youth Sports Trust, where significant government policy and resource direction were involved – although often no additional funding was granted, except through the National Lottery.

The election of a Labour government in May 1997 brought about significant changes in sports policy. They have continued John Major's enthusiasm for sport and, in the year 2000, increased the allocation of money into the revenue funding of the National Sports Councils in the UK – the first significant increase for many years.

Allied to this funding increase, however, is an underlying change of policy emphasis – towards 'sport for all' and participation, especially through schools. The government also sees sport as an important agent in delivering some of its key policy objectives:

- social inclusion and justice
- community planning
- anti-drugs initiatives
- economic regeneration
- after-school care
- individual and community capacity-building
- its overall 'quality of life' agenda.

1   Sport – what it's all about

This chapter sets out to define sport, giving it a setting in a UK environment, with afterthoughts on how this perspective guides modern-day thinking and practice. It proceeds to consider sports participation trends and costs, before moving on to assess the economic impact of sport and how spending trends are moving. Sports clubs are then examined – their operation, style and effectiveness.

Parameters and definitions

> Sport was born of a man's highest ideals and has been around for 33 centuries, which is longer than any other religion, culture or sub-culture; and must be defended and harnessed for its values.
>
> *Ron Pickering*

The council of Europe's *European Sports Charter*, adopted in 1992, defines sport as 'all forms of physical activity which, through casual or organized participation, aim at expressing or improving physical activity fitness and mental wellbeing, forming social relationships or obtaining results in competition at all levels' (Council of Europe, 1992).

It is important to be clear about what is meant by the key terms used in this text. As with almost any word or concept, contrasting meanings and interpretations can be adopted by different individuals or groups on varying occasions. For the purposes of this text the following definitions and meanings will be adopted.

- Where the term **recreation** is used, it is understood that the recreation is of a physical nature.
- **Recreation** is seen as the physical (when related to sport and usually the allied mental) re-creating (renewing) of the body and the person.
- **Sport** is seen as a physically active pastime participated in at a wide variety of levels, under agreed rules; not necessarily, but often, in a competitive setting; at the very least competing against oneself.
- **Activity** is the specific thing which is done to exert the energy – in this text its use will be a sport of some sort.

According to Elvin (1993), sport includes:

1   elements of competition
2   physical activity
3   aspects of organization
4   the influence of outcome on quality of experience.

He further differentiates between sport and recreation by stating that in recreation:

1   the focus is on activity *per se*
2   satisfaction is gained primarily from the quality of the experience.

Such a distinction as Elvin makes may be of some interest in certain areas of operation and perhaps should be recognized, but for managers and administrators the exact definitions are not crucial. It is, however, clearly important to recognize the level of commitment, 'seriousness' and performance at which people are involved in their sport. Their demands may not be as high if they merely want to participate for the sake of participation and enjoyment as opposed to seeking some type of improvement in performance and some sort of specific outcome.

It is vital that the level of provision that managers and administrators provide is the same in terms of standard and consideration for everyone concerned, regardless of level. But it is helpful to understand what the participants' perceptions and expectations are.

There may be some who think that a sports provider can lessen the quality of thought going into the process, or reduce the standard of provision, merely because it is concerned that the sports people are there to participate rather than perform to a high level. It is the job of a professional administrator to provide to the highest level at all times for all groups of customers, regardless of standard, ability or objectives.

The *European Sport for All Charter* (Council of Europe, 1990) gives the following classification. A great range and variety of activities is covered by the term 'sport', which they subdivide into four broad categories.

1   Competitive games and sports which are characterized by the acceptance of rules and a response to an opposing challenge.
2   Outdoor pursuits in which participants seek to negotiate some particular terrain (signifying in this context an area of open country, forest, mountain, stretch of water or sky). The challenges derive from the manner of negotiation adopted and are modified by the particular terrain selected and the conditions of wind and weather prevailing.
3   Aesthetic movement which includes activity in the performance of which the individual is not so much looking beyond himself and responding to man-made or natural challenges, as looking inward and responding to the

sensuous pleasure of patterned bodily movement, for example dance, figure skating, forms of rhythmic gymnastics and recreational swimming.
4   Conditioning activity, i.e. forms of exercise or movement undertaken less for any immediate sense of kinaesthetic pleasure than for long-term effects that the exercise may have in improving or maintaining physical working capacity and rendering subsequently a feeling of general wellbeing.

Another example is given by Rodgers (1978): 'Ideally, all the four following elements are present in a sport, and the first two are always present. Any sport involves physical activity, it is practised for a recreational purpose, there is an element of competition and a framework of institutional organization.'

It is generally difficult to categorize sport and recreation (for the purposes of this book it is probably better to say physical recreation) definitively. To some extent, like beauty, sport is in the eye of the beholder, and in addition some of the beliefs expressed and feelings held come from the perspective of the viewer.

In essence, the theoretical definition of sport and physical recreation is not key to the administrator or manager; their concern is the support of the efficient involvement of others in their chosen activity. Some type of restrictive definition is not helpful and does not assist anyone. The aim of sports administration is to involve people efficiently, effectively and enjoyably, and to avoid excluding them through administrative bureaucracy, or indeed through any restrictive definition of the activity involved.

The history of sport

This is not the appropriate place for an in-depth study of sports history, but history in every situation is very important in guiding present and future practice – setting it in a realistic context and perspective. This is as true of sports administration and management as it is of other areas of activity.

A great deal is said about the history of sport in the UK, but there has been limited study of the area, especially in the less well-known 'minority' sports. There is a great deal of conjecture and supposition over sports participation and development in some quarters, without a great deal of factual information to back this up. Sports officials are famous for sweeping statements!

At the time of writing there is only one Professor of Sports History in the UK and only a relatively small band of people, around 250, who have enough interest to join the Association of Sports Historians. This band has certainly grown and there is an increasing awareness that the future of sport and its development must be soundly rooted in a knowledge and awareness of the past and the lessons it has to offer.

It is interesting, for example, to note that the current much-debated commercialization of sport first appeared a long time ago. The late Victorian era, for example, saw 70,000–80,000 people at a race meeting and a situation where top jockeys such as Fred Archer could earn the equivalent of over £1,000,000 in today's money during their career. During the period 1906–14 there were never fewer than 100,000 spectators at a Scotland versus England soccer match, so there was a demand and a commercial aspect to many sports, especially the major ones.

There had been, in the earlier Victorian era, some significant changes in the format of some sports to bring them into line with the desires of the population and the challenges facing them. Horse races, for example, had been shortened to enhance interest and increase the number of races that could be staged on each race day. Rugby union and rugby league had split in conflict over the issue of payment, and professional sport was beginning to develop. In 1890 the players of Glasgow Celtic went on strike for more money at a time when soccer was officially an amateur game.

While this professionalism brought about some pressures in sport which led, for example, to saliva tests for drugs in 1910 and various other accompanying problems which continue to the present day, it would be wrong to suggest that there was a relaxed or happy state in such sports before they became professional. Before professionalism many sports were violent, disorganized and strongly sexist as well as unethical, with, for example, W.G. Grace – a supposed amateur – ending up as a millionaire. The real need for a study of sport's history is to challenge these myths and relate it more closely to the social and economic history of the country. Much more could be done to examine the economic effect of sport and to look at the effects of sport on society historically. As Professor Grant Jarvie said at a talk at Stirling University in 1995, it is important that 'we use historical evidence to modify theory and concept; realize that sport is a part of our popular culture, economic strata and political life. Sports history prevents myths from becoming facts and while doing this, study must never remove the excitement or thrill of sport.'

There are also some well-supported, if possibly flawed, arguments that, during the middle of the nineteenth century, sport was used as an instrument of social control to indoctrinate and pacify the working classes. This argument has some inherent weaknesses, since in most situations the actual exchange and interaction between the upper and lower classes is limited. While there was a significant participation of a variety of classes in sport they tended to be in different sports and, even where they did play together, this was usually limited to the playing fields and did not extend to the clubhouse – in the case, for example, of golf and cricket.

Many working-class people did take part in sport but these tended to be the more traditional sports such as quoiting, while the upper classes continued to have their own sports to participate in and dominate. If there was to be real social control then there would have had to be close contact and this, in large part, did not take place.

Any real student of sport should also be a student of sports history and be aware of the background of sport in general and specific sports in particular. There is room for a great deal of further study in a wide variety of sporting texts (some are listed in the bibliography). Such a study would be useful to improve the guidance of present and future practice in sports administration and management as in many other areas such as sports performance and coaching. It is genuinely beneficial for everyone involved in a specific sport to have an awareness of its history and traditions, while never being a slave to either. Such knowledge allows even participants to put all their effort into perspective; to realize that others have done it before them and that there is a strong tradition of sport behind them and supporting them. It is somewhat humbling and very useful in getting our present commitment into context to examine the past of any sport and to understand that there is a background of participation, commitment and involvement that stretches back for many years – in some cases many hundreds of years.

Additionally, it helps modern-day participants and administrators put their performances in perspective when they realize that many achievements were made by their predecessors with much less suitable equipment and facilities. A historical understanding can also make many performers have more confidence in themselves when they realize that there has been a great deal of activity in their sport before them and often there is a strong history of participation. For example, gymnastics and table tennis in the UK, which now may not seem major sports, have significant past participation levels and in some cases very successful histories.

For all the participants in a competition at the grass-roots level of sport, it is inspiring to know they are joining a select band of performers who have performed successfully in a variety of arenas worldwide over many years. Such a context is meaningful for everyone involved in the sport and helps encourage a commitment for the future. Far too often sport is seen only in its modern setting and not for the considerable history it has given to the nation, the individual and many different communities.

The setting of history can also help individuals in realizing their relative unimportance in any given sports setting, perhaps bringing in a little much-needed humility and supporting the belief that no individual or team can ever be bigger than the sport itself – a key value which must underpin all successful and effective sporting participation and administration.

To ignore history is stupid but to rely on it too much is dangerous – learn from it; don't live in it.

Trends in sports participation

Sports administrators must always be aware of trends in sports and the resulting effects on participation. Change can be rapid, e.g. the onset of many people retiring early; or predictable, e.g. the reduction in numbers of young people. In any such instance, sports management must react or, better still, anticipate.

Published research by Gratton and Tice (1994) indicates that 'between 1977 and 1987 indoor sport has shown the fastest rate of increase in participation, with 60 per cent more adults taking part in at least one indoor sport compared to a 13 per cent increase in those taking part in at least one outdoor sport. The average frequency of participation is also steadily increasing.'

This published research also mentions that:

- the average age of participants increased across all activity groups
- the percentage of retired participants increased dramatically for virtually all activity groups
- the percentage of female participants increased in all activity groups except those taking part in only outdoor sport.

Part of this information was produced through study of the General Household Survey and, although this takes only a sample of the population, it gives a general indication of trends that appear to be prevalent in sport participation and the related habits of the population at that time.

The main trends identified by an analysis done by Sport England (1999) reveal that a number of sports, such as snooker and darts are on the decline while a significant number of sports, such as walking, swimming, cycling and golf are increasing in popularity and participation levels.

- The 1996 figures for sports participation (as revealed by the General Household Survey) indicate that from 1990 there was a slight fall from 65 to 64 per cent.
- A greater proportion of men (71 per cent) than women (58 per cent) take part in sport, but since 1987 women's participation has risen while men's has fallen.
- There has been a significant increase in participation in the fitness- and health-related areas and sports.
- Activities such as cycling, keep fit, aerobics and walking have seen increases.
- The fact that these are individualized sports (not necessarily requiring colleagues to facilitate participation) is an interesting trend (perhaps a reflection of more independent individuals in society).
- There has been a decrease in interest in marathons and road running.
- Countryside and water recreation have seen a significant growth.
- There has been the advent of what might be called 'trendy' activities, e.g. mountain biking.

Interestingly, the administrative base of organized sport continues to be under national governing bodies, whereas the growth of participation centres on informal and casual sports. Activities and sports such as walking, swimming and golf have large participation levels outside any recognized organizational base. Even where there is a significant governing body in any sport, e.g. athletics, there is only a minority of participants in formal membership of the governing body.

It is also interesting to note that while governing-body membership has remained static in recent years there continues to be a growing number of small clubs coming into existence. These clubs are still dependent on a large voluntary support basis but indicate a significant existence of sporting interest which is not allied to either local authorities or national governing bodies. This raises the issue of how such more formalized organizations relate to mass participation and involvement on the informal basis.

Another interesting trend has been the rise in overall participation by women, though just to state that would be simplistic, because, within this overall trend, there has been a continuing change towards female participation in keep fit and aerobics, which have seen a 33 per cent increase in a three-year period. Meanwhile there has been some decline in other, more traditional, outdoor activities, to the benefit of indoor sports where women appear to be participating in larger numbers. Women do seem still to be constrained by their lack of uncommitted time and money in comparison to men, and sport still seems in many situations to be dominated by men and not yet seen as a significant part of women's role in our society.

Almost inevitably, with changing demographic trends, the fastest growing area of sports participation is that of middle-aged and older people. This ties in with the growth in activities such as walking, swimming, bowls and golf. People under 30 tend to participate in the more active and team sports where there are still some problems such as school/club gaps, leading perhaps to lower-than-desired levels of participation and poor standards in some sports. There is, however, a significant participation at an even younger age group – for example, under 16 in sports such as basketball and volleyball.

In terms of social class it would appear that there has been a narrowing of the gap between participation by unskilled manual workers and the professional group in recent years. There is still the issue that some lower social class groups remain relatively disadvantaged and have low participation rates, particularly women in the semi-skilled and unskilled groups. It is interesting to note that this variation is not true across sports as, for example, soccer reflects little difference while golf and squash do.

There also seems to be a small but noticeable difference in participation in the southern parts of Great Britain and particularly greater female participation in the most southerly parts of England – from the east Midlands down. The difference is not enormous but is noticeable, and perhaps is some reflection of the social class factors mentioned above, as well as perhaps reflecting the economic wellbeing of certain areas and the sports facilities provided.

Research such as the General Household Survey means that administrators are now better able to identify participation trends in sport in the UK, and it is important that they look at these trends on a regular basis.

Pricing of sports participation

Research by Coalter (1993) indicated that the cost of entrance into sports facilities is a relative, rather than an absolute, determinant in deciding participation.

Relatively speaking, the costs of entrance to a range of common sport–physical recreation facilities are low. This would seem to indicate that the high subsidy culture which exists in the UK is comparatively successful in supporting participation levels.

Coalter concludes by saying:

> It is more useful to view the decision to participate not as a simple economic one, but as indicating an order of priorities, in which the major enabling facility and resource is not just money but time. Decisions to participate are taken within the context of the relationship between values, attitudes and lifestyle factors. It would seem that for most people the actual and perceived cost of sports participation is not simply money but time.

The economic impact of sport

> Clearly sport rests on an economic foundation.
>
> *Harry Edwards in* Sociology of Sport Journal, *1973*

Information published by the GB Sports Council and researched by the Henley Centre indicates that sport has a significant impact on the economic activity of the UK. In 1990 the gross figure generated by sports activity was £8.27 billion, equal to 1.7 per cent of the UK gross domestic product. This indicates an increase from 1.4 per cent in 1985.

Estimates around that time suggested that just over 457,000 jobs were generated in sport-related economic activity, which is just above 2 per cent of the employment market in the UK. Such a study does not include the large number of unpaid hours put in by the voluntary people involved in sport. It was suggested that, in 1990, this input could equate to over 70 million hours.

Paid employment seems to be split fairly evenly between males and females, while 25.6 per cent was professional/managerial, with routine non-manual accounting for a further 26.5 per cent. The largest category is semi-skilled and unskilled work, with over one-third of the jobs, while skilled jobs account for the remaining 13.4 per cent. Overall occupational distribution is somewhat similar to the national picture, though the skill component is somewhat lower than in some industries.

In terms of gross domestic product, impact and employment the commercial sports activity sector with £1.77 billion came second to the commercial (not directly sport-related) activity, which saw a spend of £4.99 million.

To clarify, this distinction is related to wages, rates, building maintenance, fitment maintenance, clothing, and personal purchases by people for the purpose of pursuing their sport. Obviously sports goods and equipment expenditure illustrate that there is a significant spend generated by sports participation, as well as by direct employment in sport.

The voluntary sector saw a spend of £0.83 billion, with local government spending £0.6 billion. The voluntary sector employed 79,000 people, with local authorities employing 48,200 people, throughout the UK.

The trend in spending indicated by the General Household Survey information suggests an increased participation in sport and implies a significant impact of spending on sport for the economy as a whole. Fashion can also have an effect; recently, for example, baseball hats have become trendy, and for many years sports trainers have been popular footwear for daily use.

Other implications are raised, e.g. the ability of local authorities to maintain their contribution to sport with the changes in their powers, the current reorganization and cutbacks in central government support for local government. The lottery, however, has seen a significant increase in spending throughout the country, particularly in the construction industry, architecture and various other project-related spin-offs to the funding raised through the lottery and spent through the Lottery Sports Fund.

The lottery trends are positive but there are threats to spending and it is interesting to set it in context; for the same period, the spending on gambling was £2.84 billion and on cigarettes £7.7 billion. Such a comparison means that sport, while a significant economic factor, has some way to go to be one of the major players in the economy. The economic impact, however, is certainly an argument in support of sport and the growth it continues to foster for the economic health of the nation.

The other key point is that such studies did not attempt to gauge or evaluate the benefits to the productivity of the nation as a whole, of a population made fitter by their participation in sport; nor, indeed, do they tend to look at the contribution of sport to the welfare of society. An investigation into both these items would be interesting and perhaps would provide another argument for central government to increase support of sport.

Sports clubs

Arguably the most crucial factor in the operation and survival of sport in the UK is the sports club. The nature of these clubs varies in different sports, geographical locations, facility bases and traditions, but typically they are localized, single-sport clubs organized by volunteers and living almost hand to mouth from a limited contribution of members' subscriptions, local authority support and other income raised through the contacts or efforts of club members.

Some clubs are quite affluent due to recreational play income and relatively high fees – such as golf clubs. Some survive quite healthily through income from bars or other social activities, e.g. bowling clubs or tennis clubs. One of the most difficult areas of sport to fund is that of youth sport, especially developing talent, due to the necessity to look to many members to provide the large part of the funds to support the development of future excellence in a few.

The club base is very often made up of a group of parents, friends or experienced performers who administer the club for the benefit of the participants, which they will probably be themselves. There may be support from the local authority, local sports council or other agency. There will be some requirement to affiliate to the local sports council, join the national body to participate fully in the widest range of sports opportunities, and while this may bring some benefits – technical advice, coaching support, competitive outlets – there will also be some cost implications.

The typical model for sports clubs in the UK has very much tended to be single sport, while sports not necessarily independent (especially in facility use), e.g. many athletics clubs and swimming clubs, use a variety of facilities for their training. This model is not typical of much of western Europe, where community-based multi-sports clubs are much more common. Throughout Holland, Scandinavia, Spain, Germany and France, clubs such as hockey, football and rugby share changing and social facilities as well as playing fields, and there may also be allied indoor facilities for basketball, volleyball, handball, etc.

This type of multi-sport club is rare in the UK and is much envied by a number of clubs who would see such an amalgamation as quite healthy. It should be noted that there have been some, mostly unsuccessful, attempts at amalgamation in the UK on a local basis, but it would appear that differing histories, social traditions and expectations have caused some practical problems in drawing clubs together effectively. This is a model, however, favoured by many and it is quite likely to be pursued in the future, especially as economic demands place additional difficulties on clubs. Current lottery funding arrangements tend to favour such logical facility developments, which are often beyond the means of one club on its own.

The multi-sport club does appeal in the sense of combining all resources – not just physical or social, but also in terms of personnel and joint fundraising efforts, etc. The difficulties arise when any funds raised have to be disbursed and significant debate can take place as to how this should be done, pitting one sport against another or one group against another.

The voluntary nature of sports clubs in the UK has been their strength for many years but looking at the fast-changing sporting scene, both domestically and internationally, one has to debate whether the small club units functioning on a voluntary basis can continue to support the development of sport at a time when individual performers can aspire to be paid tens of thousands of pounds for one appearance. This dichotomy of individual wealth set against club (and indeed governing body) poverty seems to identify an issue which will cause significant problems for sports in the next ten years at least. The professionalization of athletics and rugby union among others will necessitate serious reconsideration of how such sports are administered at local and national level.

The scale of the finance available will mean substantial changes in the operation of the volunteer as opposed to the paid administrator at all levels of sport. Individuals or teams, paid thousands of pounds, even up to hundreds of thousands of pounds, will not easily coexist with spare-time volunteers in delivery terms. The response time required by paid top performers is short and rightly demands appropriate efficiency from the sport's administration.

This debate will evolve and develop but it seems likely to be performer- and finance-led rather than dictated by the sport administrators or lower-level participants. For example, the greater funds available have already meant that individuals have been attracted to larger clubs through financial inducements and this trend will continue, further endangering the smaller clubs by removing the cream of the players and encouraging the player to look for (at the very least) substantial expenses packages. It will not seem much of a reward to hard-working volunteers in the local rugby club if every-one they encourage and develop through the early stages (in a voluntary capacity) departs as soon as they show any serious promise, to look for substantial sums of money in a more lucrative club setting. The movement towards buying success even at club level must be a major disincentive to volunteers in the other 'feeder' clubs.

Sports clubs' effectiveness

Some interesting lessons can be drawn from research by Koski (1995), who studied 835 Finnish sports clubs in an attempt to analyse their organizational openness and effectiveness. Koski examined five dimensions of effectiveness:

- ability to obtain resources
- internal atmosphere
- efficiency of the throughput process
- realization of aims
- general level of activity.

He felt that all dimensions except internal atmosphere were interrelated, and his findings indicated that many of the features of effectiveness were largely linked to the size of membership, ideological orientation and organizational environment. Perhaps more worryingly, he found that success orientation was incompatible with a relaxed atmosphere.

Finnish sports clubs are similarly independent and voluntary organizations; they are not connected with the school system as happens, for example, in

North America. Koski examined a wide range of clubs – some having only ten members, others having more than 5,000. Some are based on social considerations and social interaction, while others are highly commercial organizations where the main concern is entertainment. Koski feels that sports clubs differ significantly from organizations such as firms or entrepreneurial organizations. He defines effectiveness in relation to the achievement of the functions of the sports club.

Many are moving towards a service of business organization from being based on a non-commercial purpose. Increasing commercialization and business planning are the key developments identified, while there must still be a commitment to the basic ethos of sport and sports participation. While the dimensions discussed in relation to sports clubs were the ability to obtain resources, internal atmosphere, the efficiency of the throughput process and the realization of aims, these must be underpinned by a high level of general activity, and club operation should be about input in terms of participation as well as financial outcomes.

At the end of his research Koski found that the number of sports disciplines supported by the club was associated with the ability to obtain income and the number of participants. Specifically, clubs specializing in fewer disciplines were more effective than those catering for many disciplines – specialist clubs were able to generate more income. In addition, members of these specialized clubs were more active in their participation in club activities. This movement towards specialized clubs with fewer sport disciplines is a recent one in Finland – 70 per cent of the clubs founded in the 1980s specialized in only one sport, whereas the comparative figure in the 1930s was only 30 per cent. Koski found that, in general, clubs with clear values underlining their activities were more effective, particularly in their ability to obtain resources and in displaying a high general level of activity. He also found that the size of the club in terms of the numbers of members had a considerable influence in almost every dimension of its effectiveness. The power of the voluntary organization rests on its members – the more members the club has, and the greater the support, the more potential for action the club will have. In large organizations official positions are more sought after, therefore more competent and motivated people are available.

Koski felt that the most important factor of his research as it related to the development of sports clubs was that they must have a broader definition of effectiveness. Other organizations may be satisfied with a narrow set of goals as the means to assess their effectiveness, but voluntary organizations need to broaden their definition of effectiveness and measure it accordingly. Such a broad definition may require further research to generate easily quantifiable indicators of performance, though these may be adapted from effectiveness measures used by others, such as those used by non-profit-making firms.

Issues facing sport

Elvin (1993) highlights a number of issues that the Central Council for Physical Recreation (CCPR) has previously identified as management-related concerns or challenges for sport. These include:

- the sale and subsequent loss of school playing fields
- the competitive tendering, contract management and the effect on public facilities
- the national non-domestic rates
- the taxation on national governing bodies of sport
- the development of a coherent role for sports sponsorship
- the availability of central government funds
- the structure of sport within the UK.

Although these issues were first highlighted ten years ago, most of them still seem live. Perhaps now the following issues could be added:

- the impact of the National Lottery
- the potential of the UK Institute of Sport and the mechanisms for implementing this
- the potential change in government policy from excellence to participation
- the apparent lack of volunteers coming through to administer sport
- the continuing development of international sporting standards of countries other than the UK and how the UK keeps up
- the level of underskilled staff administering sport (and indeed coaching it) in the UK
- the continuing difficulties in delivering through the new UK Sports Councils' structures
- the restriction of local government spending and its impact on sport and recreation.
- the considerable problems the UK seems to have over international sporting events (e.g. soccer World Cup, athletics World Championships and the Olympics).

As you can see, this list is lengthy and could probably grow daily. There are many problems – actual, perceived and potential – facing sport, but as ever if they are faced up to in an aggressive and active way then achievements will be made.

Trends affecting sport

Being involved in sport creates attention and, while some in smaller sports may complain about the lack of publicity and image, there is a significant public interest in many things (sometimes unpredictable) that affect sport. The most recent, perhaps, has been the phenomenal impact of sports clothing (from shoes to hats) on general fashion trends, and this has fed back into sport, making goods such as training shoes extremely expensive. It has also brought international fame and fortune for major trading names such as Nike, adidas, LA Gear and Reebok, which have become the significant players in the sports game. The amount of money being made by these companies is mind-boggling, and the pressures they can impose are significant in terms of both the fashion market and the influence they can exert commercially in the sports world.

To quote some figures, in 1987 Nike's sales amounted to $887,000,000, producing a net income of $35,211,000. By 1991, only four years later, sales had grown to $3,000,000,000 and the net income to $279,400,000. Such enormous growth in the profits of many companies has come through massive advertising campaigns, close involvement with sport (even down to the local level) and the employment of big names such as Michael Jordan and Andre Aggassi to publicize training shoes and clothing.

This has made a huge difference to the return, as illustrated. In the case of LA Gear, the sales were $36,000,000 in 1986 and over $902,000,000 in 1990. Growth is spectacular, and this market has been typical as T-shirts, sweatshirts, etc., have developed in a radical way.

The signing of Tiger Woods by Nike in 1999 for $20 million led to a profit of over $200 million in the relatively new area of golf for the company. Indeed, it has moved into club manufacture as a result of this success. This exemplifies the power as well as the commercial impact of the star individual.

However, recent troubles with ITV Digital and NTL, the telecommunications company, largely caused by over-investment in football, show that such investment is hazardous. Sport's popularity and personalities can be transitory and should be treated with some caution. Obviously, sports organizations should exploit this popularity while they are on the top, but be aware that it won't last forever.

In the UK, a lot of sports provision has traditionally been leased in the public sector and a continual government drive to reduce public spending has curtailed the level of provision that many local authorities, in particular, have been able to make. The situation eased just a little as the new century dawned, but given the demands of health, education and social services on public spending, it seems unlikely that sport will get a great deal more public finance in the foreseeable future.

Self-assessment question

Consider sport in your area and suggest the key issues facing its operation and development at present. Draw on the history of sport in the area and make comparisons with 50 and 100 years ago.

2 The sporting context

This chapter starts by referring to the importance put on sport by politicians and states – from the ancient Greeks and Romans right through to current governments. It moves on to consider the diversity of settings and the nature of provision. The various benefits of sport to society, communities, organizations and individuals are then considered, followed by some debate over the aims and objectives of sport in various situations.

The second half of the chapter examines a number of the key current issues facing sport, including women in sport, professionalism and commitment, team spirit, political context, sport and health, the European dimension, and sports venues and facilities.

> I think we have undervalued sport and the place of it in our national life . . . You watch the morale rise in any sport when we get a good team. People like sport and they enjoy it; it is part of our national psychology.
> *John Major, BBC TV Interview, August 1993*

It can be argued that sport has always preoccupied the mind of humans, perhaps inordinately given its importance. Going back to the ancient Greeks and Romans, physical prowess in relevant sporting fields was seen as important and a mark of someone's characteristics and worth. This perceived status has always put it in the public eye and made it subject to scrutiny, comment and criticism.

Even in modern times, apart from the period of the two world wars, the role of sport and its importance in our society has been a matter of debate in the media and in all forums of society. The social meeting places (including public houses) of our culture constantly reverberate to animated discussions on the sporting prowess and success, or lack of it, of our national team or local favourites. This prominence of sport has caused its own special problems on many occasions, and has led some dictatorial political figures to exploit its importance in the public mind for their own devious ends.

The marrying of many issues has led to a confusion for sports administrators and participants and has often given added pressure to their involvement. This, for example, can be seen in the relationship between sport and politics and the participation of women in sport. The purpose of this chapter is not to come up with definitive answers to any of the issues raised, but merely to identify relevant issues, put some differing views and indicate the possible implications for administrators. These are not matters where definitive answers can be easily provided, nor should they be, but administrators who see their operation in sport as an island, unaffected by other societal issues, are working in a false situation which will lead to ineffective action.

The range of issues to be considered includes the role of women in sport, the role of volunteers in sport (more of which later), professionalism versus amateurism, the use of drugs in sport, political influence in sport, and the role and importance of sport in our society.

Sport

One of the most interesting things about sport in the UK is its sheer diversity. While many bemoan, with some justification, the lack of a co-ordinated and common approach to sport, both across sports and within different governing authorities, the width of provision is beneficial for participants and probably allows a wider net to be cast, leading to most people getting caught in it at some time.

This causes sizeable problems in terms of the management and administration of sport, since it is delivered in so many different contexts. The agencies managing and delivering sport come primarily from three sectors – private, public and voluntary. There are, within each of these, enormous variations and each specific variation can lead to different provisions in a variety of situations.

Within the public sector – by far the largest provider – there are two main operators: national government and local government. The role of the national government is in setting a policy, determining thinking and implementation through the sports councils. There are other government agencies that have an impact on sports provision, particularly the newly titled Department of Culture, Media and Sport, and the Welsh, Scottish and Northern Ireland Offices. A considerable amount of money is spent in pursuing sport through these agencies and it is generally spent in encouraging others, laying down policy, and what one may call 'pump priming'.

While the home country sports councils claim to be executive bodies, in the sense that they have money to spend and the power to spend it, they are in fact enablers, empowerers and communicators. This must always be remembered by those involved, as it helps clarify lines of communication and action, and assists in reducing duplication or confusion on the part of the sports manager, or even the sports participants.

The roles of the national educational agencies can be significant, and sometimes are a little confusing. A year or two ago, the Sports Minister took a personal initiative to encourage the provision of team games (only four) within the school curriculum. While this may be welcomed by certain sports, it is discriminatory and is perhaps being done for ethical and moral reasons, rather than being a major beneficial sporting initiative *per se*. The effect, in any case, of a government dictum that certain sports must be part of national curriculum is not necessarily helpful in encouraging people to participate in sport. There may be much more suitable ways, such as the payment of teachers to undertake extra-curricular activities – in sport among other things – to ensure that there are many opportunities in a wide range of activities (both team and individual) for all those who desire to participate or can be encouraged to do so.

It is always worthwhile, however, for the sports manager and administrators to be quite clear as to what motivation government has in supporting sport and what specific emphasis is currently being applied. In recent years the pendulum of sport has regularly swung between participation and performance, although there is often a wider dynamic in the sense that politicians may espouse support for mass participation as the key purpose, while happily standing in a photograph with the current Olympic champion – perhaps to bask in the reflected glory and to give support to sport, but obviously not at a participation level.

The political impact on sport must not be underestimated, and the effects of decisions of politicians, even on the usual government cutbacks, can be quite significant in terms of sports participation. Equally, decisions can have a major positive impact: for example, the National Lottery is a substantial benefit to sport and should see an enormous return in terms of personnel employed in the provision of sport in the UK. It is all too easy, but very dangerous, to minimize the impact of national government and politicians on sporting activity.

Local politicians and local government can also have an enormous effect on sports provision and management. In practice, the money spent by local authorities in support of sport at all levels far outweighs the money directly spent out of central government funds. There is a common belief among some national agencies and politicians that they are the key players, when in fact the local authorities are the key providers for most sports participants in the UK. Their role is crucial and should never be underestimated.

Everyone involved in sport will have clear examples of positive, active authorities providing meaningful and sizeable opportunities for sport at all levels within their community. Other authorities, which have not seen their role in sports provision as being quite as large, will create more negative experiences, indicating how the withdrawal or the lack of local initiative and support can be significantly damaging and lead to under-provision in sport.

Local authorities, through relevant departments, can provide personnel and facilities to a variety of standards and levels. A trend in recent years, largely due to compulsory competitive tendering, has been for the amalgamation of generic direct services departments so that sport has often become part of an overall department along with environmental health and other such direct services. This is a further rationalization of the larger leisure departments formed around 1975 in the last reorganization of local government, but it is not necessarily helpful to take all specialist expertise out at middle management level. Obviously, the thinking is that economies of scale can be achieved. While this may seem beneficial to all concerned, there are possible disadvantages of a larger department, with a general manager, getting others to deliver the services.

One of the disadvantages is that sport may be fighting for funding and influence within a very large overall department, where it may be seen as quite a low priority compared to emptying dustbins or providing parks and open spaces. Equally, given that some significant amounts of finance can be obtained out of the general pot, there can be significant benefits to a large department in that the practitioner on the shop floor is allowed, with relatively little interference, to achieve their targets and plans. They are actually allowed to do things and make decisions without any bureaucracy above them interfering with progress. There can often be a bureaucratic limitation of work achieved in some local authorities because accountability is felt to be more important than action.

With the advent of unitary local authorities, the link of sport to education poses another possible threat to its status, but equally provides new opportunities that could see a wider range of activities made available on a more co-ordinated and widely organized community basis.

In the local, as in the national situation, the role of the politician is considerable in deciding what funds will be available to what specific facility or activity, and a good deal of convincing will often have to be done to get politicians to spend sizeable monies on sport, as opposed to related leisure items such as arts, parks and environmental projects.

The role and importance of sport in our society

One of the major difficulties facing sports administrators and participants in the UK is the apparent lack of importance given to sporting participation at most levels.

> Whoever said sport had nothing to do with politics made a very great mistake.
>
> Juan Antonio Samaranch, Past President,
> International Olympic Committee

Recently the government, and other political parties, have started to talk about how much money is going into sport through the National Lottery. This discussion is welcome and may be praised, but it prompts the question: If sport, facilities, excellence, development, and even a British Academy of Sport, are so important, why is such provision left to the whim of the lottery ticket purchaser? If politicians really value sport, surely some genuine commitment from the public purse should be made. While

Chancellor Gordon Brown has allowed some increased revenue funding to the Sports Council, it is still not a budget priority.

There must also be some justification for supporting sport on other grounds: economic impact, the health of the nation, international prestige, and the national 'feelgood' factor, to name but a few.

> The biggest problem today is that the Olympic Games have become so important that political people want to take control of them. Our only salvation is to keep free from politics
>
> *Avery Brundage in* Sports Illustrated, *1964*

Certainly for many of those who reach Olympic-medal level, fame and fortune can follow – though this tends to apply only to sports such as swimming and athletics and not to sports such as fencing, or even perhaps judo. For most people participation in sport is only for their own benefit in terms of health and enjoyment. Even the potential health links and benefits are often underplayed by the government and certain health agencies, and while this relationship is growing, a robust funding link has not been established.

The importance of sport and the need for funding of sport are beginning to be recognized by national government, and many now realize that the facilities available in the UK do not compare well with other countries, especially those in continental Europe and North America.

The support of John Major, then Prime Minister, for Manchester's failed bid for the 2000 Olympics was a significant move in the recognition of the importance of sport in the UK, and reflected the benefits that sport can bring in terms of economic return for an area looking to rediscover its soul as well as increasing the participation rate of the local inhabitants, with the improved facilities that such an event would bring.

The funding of sport in the UK has always been low when set against many other items of government expenditure. It has never enjoyed the widespread political support that the arts, for example, have had. The Sports Council has produced figures which indicate that a seat in Scottish Opera was subsidized by £30 every time someone sat on it, while each individual of Scotland was given 75p of government funding towards the provision of sport in total. These figures were calculated in the late 1980s, but the balance remains much the same up to the current time. Indeed, Scottish Opera has been 'baled out' with over £3 million of additional public funds. Would a similar rescue ever happen for a sports body?

The high status and position given to sports participants and coaches in the USA for example, has never been reflected in our society, and this may be seen as a significant weakness when activities seek publicity and resources. It is a considerable disincentive to participate if your achievements are not widely recognized. A former colleague – a Commonwealth athletics champion – reported how her status changed completely when she went to study at a university in the USA. Her success was widely acclaimed in local and national media, and, wherever she went to compete in the very competitive varsity matches, she became a media personality much sought after for interviews. Many sports media people in her native country would have struggled to know what event she took part in and the level at which she competed, but university-level success brought her fame in the USA.

The issue of high regard applies equally to the coach. In the USA a major college or league coach will be much sought after and very well rewarded in terms of status, standard of life and salary; whereas in the UK, only a very few can command payment outside professional sport, and generally the status is low, despite efforts by all the UK sports councils and Sports Coach UK to change thinking on this issue.

It has long been assumed in the UK that only past performers could possibly be sports coaches with any expertise, and no amount of training could substitute for this personal experience and playing ability. The notion that this past player would automatically become a coach or team manager and would not require any further substantial training has proved spectacularly unsuccessful in some of the major games in the UK. Coaching has never been seen as a profession that can be entered by serious professional people in order to improve the quality of sport. It has been seen as one aspect of voluntary support for many sports, therefore requiring substantial training or resources. Fortunately, this situation is beginning to change slowly as governing bodies, at all levels, increase their understanding of the requirement for coach education, and the National Coaching Foundation increases its work in educating coaches with generic coaching theory.

This lack of esteem and importance given to participation and coaching has spread to the area of administration, where the vast majority of sports administration, promotion and development has been left to volunteers on the assumption that they can, in their spare time, fit in all the necessary work and do the job required. Even the training of volunteers has only relatively recently started to be seriously considered by the Sports Councils, and, while training of coaches may have been limited, the coaching of administrators (whether paid or voluntary) was effectively non-existent until the 1990s.

The future will almost certainly see a growth in this area – indeed, it is hoped that this book may help towards that – but realistically sport can only progress if everyone involved in it has been trained and has sufficient funding and support from many sources, to service and support the performance on the pitch or the games-hall floor.

The benefits of sport

Chris Gratton and Peter Taylor, in particular, have written at length on the economic impact of sport and recreation, and their work is well worth reading for anyone who is advocating a case for sport (Gratton and Taylor, 2000).

In addition, sport can offer major psychological and physiological benefits through participation. There is some evidence to indicate that physical health and wellbeing can be improved through regular sports participation, although this participation does not need to be of a highly competitive, aggressive or 'sweaty' nature. A vigorous walk or a relaxed swim can benefit general health a great deal and the notion that only lung-bursting aerobics can produce the type of health benefits required is misguided.

People participate in sport for a wide variety of reasons, and the choice is theirs. It may be for competition, it may be for relaxation, it may be for enjoyment, it may be to get away from everything else, it may be for social reasons – the list is almost endless. The key for the administrator is to be realistic about why participants appear and to cater for them accordingly.

Certainly anyone involved in sport should be given a significant understanding of the benefits available and what they need to do to advance them or promote them to non-participants. There is also a need for all administrators involved in sport to work hard to promote the benefits and equally to be ready to counter any perceived disadvantages, many of which are quite mistaken. For example, it has become quite widely accepted that drug-taking is a major problem in British sport. This is not the case, and the few instances where it has been noted have revolved around a very small number of sports. Despite a major testing programme, very few of those tested have been found to take any performance-enhancing substances. The problem we face in our society with social drugs is much, much greater than the minimal problem that sport may have with drug-taking to enhance performance.

Equally, the anti-competition lobby should, perhaps, be opposed. There is a constant argument that competition is damaging and that sport promotes unhealthy competition, when in fact there is a strong argument that sport promotes the more positive aspects of competition rather than the potentially damaging ones which can appear in other aspects of our society.

It is an important role for those involved in sport to be quite clear about the benefits and strengths of sport and to advocate the case for participation in it.

Another societal advantage of sports involvement is that if people are actively participating in sport, at least they are not doing anything anti-social, e.g. vandalism or other forms of crime. This may appear negative, but it is a valid argument with a factual base – participation in sport, even highly competitive sport, is better than anti-social behaviour.

It was implied above that the economic benefits are better left to experts such as Gratton and Taylor (2000) to expound and examine, but one major factor has been the advent of the National Lottery. While a great deal of criticism has been expressed over the size of individual prizes, and the destination of certain funds (e.g. the Churchill Papers), or the perceived tendency to centralize funding in London, there is no doubt that the money being diverted into sport through the lottery has had a major economic impact not only for sport, but also for the construction and other industries. This will help with economic regeneration in a number of areas. It is somehow perceived that money from the lottery is taken from people's pockets and is then won by a few, who immediately save it. This is true of only a certain amount of the prize money; the rest partly goes to the Treasury but will also be a significant spend in sport and other areas. This will have a significant economic impact.

Additionally, now that the government allows some specified development programmes to be supplemented by the lottery rather than capital projects and individual excellence, occupational opportunities and development schemes in sport stand to benefit enormously. The impact this is having on employment in the sports area is considerable. The economic impact continues to increase, and will certainly soon be another potential study for Gratton and Taylor.

The aims and objectives of sport

There have been prolonged discussions about the aims and objectives of sport and its suitability to communities, especially in the educational setting. Many have felt that competition was damaging and should not be encouraged through sport or any other educational activity.

The relationship between education, sport, health and fitness has also been examined at length. While it is unclear what society's general view is, some members of the educational establishment (certainly during the late 1960s, 1970s and early 1980s) felt that sport, due to its competitive nature, was damaging and encouraged some of the worst aspects of human behaviour.

The evidence for this is patchy and many would argue that since much of our behaviour is developed before the age of seven, children, who do not have direct experience of competitive sport before that age, cannot be strongly influenced by it. Certainly there is an increasing amount of 'bad sport' in the media and that may be a factor, but it is likely that much of the influence occurs throughout childhood. Some, indeed, would argue that basic competition between human beings is an inherited trait, dating back to the time when humans had to hunt for food and compete with fellow humans in order to survive.

This argument may be equally flawed, but certainly sport by its very nature is competitive and therefore can produce the bad as well as the good elements of competition. If sport, like the rest of life, is seen as an individual challenge where one constantly tries to improve one's own performance, even in the team situation, then no damage will be noted, but if it becomes a competition against colleagues, then it is likely that societal and personal damage may occur. In essence, it is important to be aware of the personal challenge of sport rather than the challenge against other persons.

Sport has also suffered because of its poor image in relation to certain pursuits, through violent and deviant behaviour, as well as other issues such as gender inequality and a lack of recognition of different cultures and ethnic origins, as well as the issue of élitism.

It is undoubtedly true that sport carries a great deal of historical and cultural baggage and has a tendency (within the UK) to be massively dominated by white, largely upper-class, men. There have been noticeable exceptions to this, as football (especially in the professional ranks), rugby league and to some extent sports such as table tennis, gymnastics and swimming have developed through more working-class origins. None the less, many of what were seen as the major games and individual activities have been dominated by the higher echelons of society and indeed have been dragged round 'the Empire' (now the Commonwealth) by the Oxbridge 'mafia'.

The Commonwealth Games have until very recently been a haven for sports of a more traditional nature, largely in the Corinthian ethos – these were the sports taken round the world by the old colonial British. Lawn bowls, shooting, rowing, wrestling and weight-lifting, as well as athletics and swimming, have been the mainstay of this quite traditional event. It would appear now that this event is changing to reflect the sporting balance of the nations involved, and seeing the introduction of activities for teams and of a more modern nature for many of the participating Third-World countries.

The issue of female participation has also altered dramatically in relatively recent times. The last years of the 1980s and early 1990s saw the advent of new events such as the Women's Soccer World Cup and, most recently, the Women's Rugby Union World Cup, both of which no doubt, in time, will grow to be significant sporting events, as a number of other sports owned or now shared by women have become. The old idea of sport only being played by 'butch' women on hockey fields is outdated and does not reflect modern societal practices or beliefs.

The issue of race is much less clear, and has taken some time to develop. Part of the traditional imbalance of poor black boxers from the ghettos of the USA and other such stereotypes has gradually disappeared as black sportsmen and women have taken over many internationally recognized events and made them their own regardless of their country of origin. People such as Linford Christie, Tiger Woods and Martin Offiah have begun to break down any traditional barriers between cultures or ethnic origins as far as participation and strength of performance are concerned.

There are still, however, some big issues over the participation of Britain's Asian community in sport, even in football at professional league level.

Current issues

Women in sport

The role of women in sport, as in so many other societal situations, has been very mixed. There has been a marked increase in the number of participants in recent years, but the importance of the role of women as top-level coaches and administrators has not always effectively increased to the same degree. Much of sport's hierarchy is still a male domain.

There has undoubtedly been an increase in the number of female sports development officers, for example, though few of them have operated at the highest level within the home country sports councils, or the local authorities, or other key agencies in the sports field. There have been some notable exceptions such as Sue Campbell in the National Coaching Foundation and Youth Sports Trust, and now the DCMS (Department of Culture, Media and Sport), Dr Anita White in the English Sports Council, Sue Burgess in the Welsh Sports Council and Pam Scott in the Scottish Sports Council, but the role of women (as in so many other work situations) has not been balanced in terms of sports administration positions, relative even to (sometimes low) participation levels.

There is no doubt that women have not been fully represented in sport in a variety of ways – as participants, coaches or officials. Even in sports such as gymnastics, in which around 80 per cent of the participants are female, the top official positions have often been held by men.

Women have often felt discriminated against within the sporting sphere, and embarked on a long campaign through the 1970s and 1980s to increase their numbers in terms of participation. This has been successful, and figures indicate that the trend is significantly upwards. This increase is important and will very likely continue, though there are some sceptics who feel that the increase is somewhat contrived and involves only a limited number of sport and physical activity areas, such as aerobics. There has been, however, a definite increase in the number of women participating over the past 30 years, whatever the sport or the motivation, but there is still a great deal to be done to see an equality of action in many sporting areas. There are several major sports where women are still treated very much as second-class citizens, and in some cases they are almost not recognized at all.

Sports such as bowls and golf often still treat women in a very offhand manner, reminiscent of the way they were treated in every sphere in Britain in the nineteenth century. Women are not allowed to become full members of certain sports clubs, not allowed to play on certain days, not allowed to use certain facilities, etc. These situations are being fought against (in many cases by local authorities and sports councils in grant allocations) in order to ensure equality of treatment, but many are historically based and will only change in the face of continuing strong resistance.

Professionalism and commitment

> The only true amateurs in sport these days are those who are no good at it.
>
> *Christopher Brasher, past athlete and*
> *director of the London Marathon*

The issue of professionalism has caused, and for many sports is continuing to cause, significant embarrassment and heart-searching. The debate over whether performers, coaches or even administrators should be paid is ongoing. Many sports, such as athletics, have decided to go open and make all performers eligible for some form of payment (whether into a trust fund or whatever). Others, such as rugby, are still engaged in heated debate as to the activities which may be paid for. Many who, until recently, fundamentally rejected the concept of being paid for playing the game, increasingly accepted that financial rewards are acceptable for many other aspects related to success on the playing field. This debate also split the two hemispheres, with the south very much favouring open payment for participants. Now professionalism is here for players, and its effects have been dramatic. The long-term effects are not yet fully evident, but, as some had anticipated, the input of professional players appears to have made the rich stronger and the poor struggle. In Wales, the failure to face the 'who pays for this?' question has caused deep splits in the game's administration, while for Bristol in the English top league it has almost brought bankruptcy.

> The more that the historian looks for the halcyon days of 'pure' amateurism, the more they recede from view.
> Tom McNab, sports historian, author and consultant –
> Scottish Athletics Conference, September 1997

Increasingly, commercial pressures in many sports are such that money is a, if not **the**, major consideration, and it seems inevitable that performers will demand their share of this money increasingly as time goes on. The necessity to obtain sponsorship and commercial support to secure the very existence of sports events and organizations means that sport cannot continue to ignore the implications of that input. Some type of return and guarantee will be required by and from the performer, in terms of public appearances and marketing as well as good performances on the pitch or court; it means that he who pays the piper will be able to call the tune, and that the control of sport will move from the participants to the financer.

Another major consideration in professionalism is whether the coaches and administrators should be paid and professional. Many would argue that the age of successful sport based purely on voluntarism has passed. If the performers are to be highly paid, then surely all the people who support and enable their participation should be paid also?

Information technology

The advent of information technology and related technological advances will have a significant impact on sport, though perhaps not as much as it has in other forms of human operation such as the workplace and the home.

There have already been many changes, resulting in the ability to collate membership information on databases, to video and play back performances and to fax and email information around the world. Such developments for all concerned are rapid and are multiplying each year.

These changes will have a major impact on sport and in all its aspects throughout the UK and, indeed, throughout the world. Technological developments, and the global thinking accompanying them, will continue and will, in essence, benefit sport and sporting links within and between nations. The ease of talking to someone on the other side of the world, and making arrangements, can only make the sports administrator's life easier and the management of sport is potentially enhanced in the same way as other business areas.

There are additional implications in terms of the personnel involved and the skills they require to face up to the world we live in today. Rapid advances also place additional stresses on those of the older generation, to ensure that they keep up or catch up, at least to some degree.

The benefits of the technology are potentially enormous, but so too are the implications in terms of confidentiality of information, recording of facts, record-keeping, direct mailing and many other aspects of sports administration.

The arrival of the Internet and its ability to promote even easier world-wide communication has vast sporting potential. It could bring greater rewards for sports personnel with more international exposure, as well as easing the way for individuals world-wide to link together. Many individuals/stars now have their own website to publicize themselves and encourage their fanbase.

The potential for training individuals in sports administration and management over such an international computer network is significant and soon this aspect of training will match other initiatives in terms of creating training links and opportunities at home and abroad.

In essence, information technology and all technological advances should be grasped with both hands by sport for the benefits they could bring to the whole area, as they do to the rest of our society. If correctly handled and used to achieve agreed targets, these developments are hugely beneficial to sport and its administration.

The ethics of sport

A great deal is made by many different agencies, coming from different viewpoints, of the ethics of sport and the way in which it is abused by many people for a variety of reasons. Often the perceived negative aspects of sport are emphasized, and good and correct behaviour (which often appears in the practical situation) is forgotten.

As Sport England (1996) states, 'sport is governed by a set of rules and, often unwritten, principles of behaviour which usually come under the banner of fair play. Sadly, it is often these principles which are not strictly adhered to in a range of sports.' The Council of Europe has produced a code of sport ethics that covers a wide range of topics, defining fair play, suggesting who is responsible, suggesting what the governments can do to encourage it as well as, ultimately, the individuals involved in terms of personal behaviour and what to do when working with young people.

Key to the consideration of this text for the administration of sport are the duties identified for sports and sport-related organizations. These organizations are stated to have the following responsibilities.

- To establish a proper context for fair play.
- To publish clear guidelines on what is to be considered ethical or unethical behaviour and ensure that, at all levels of participation and involvement, consistent and appropriate incentives and/or sanction are applied.
- To ensure that all decisions are made in accordance with a code of ethics for the sport which reflects the European code.
- To raise awareness of fair play within their sphere of influence through use of campaigns, awards, education material and training opportunities. They must also monitor and evaluate the impact of such initiatives.
- To establish systems which reward fair play and personal levels of achievement in addition to competitive success.
- To provide help and support to the media to promote good behaviour.

A number of special additional points are identified relating to young people, and all of these can be found in the *Code of Sports Ethics* published by the Council of Europe (1992b).

Competition

There is also the issue, highlighted by Elvin (1993) and others, of competition. As we have seen, this is often used to criticize sport, and it is suggested that somehow competition is created by sport rather than created by the human race and is therefore an integral part of sport. While the very worst aspects of competition can be displayed through misplaced motives in sports participation, coaching and officiating, so, more often, can the very best qualities be demonstrated by competition in sport. Sport can bring out controlled competitive human displays of a quality seldom seen in other aspects of human existence. The genuine camaraderie witnessed even after the most intense rugby confrontation, or the shared joy over a team-mate's outstanding athletics triumph, are examples of the many situations where sport can control and build relationships, even from its base of competition.

Sport England (1999) suggests that sport can make a contribution to 'the new policy agenda' by:

- contributing to the reduction in youth crime
- improving health and fitness
- reducing truancy
- making a positive contribution to young people's attitude to learning
- assisting in community regeneration (especially by acting as a catalyst in multi-agency co-operation)
- improving the environment
- providing opportunities for 'active citizenship' via opportunities for volunteering.

Sport and society

Aggression v. team spirit

There have been prolonged debates, moralistic and practical, about the benefits of sport in modern society. Two diametrically opposed views exist – one is that sport can encourage competitive and aggressive behaviour in the individual and therefore should be discouraged; the second is that the social mixing and teamwork encouraged in sport are beneficial to the individual for their whole life – not just on the sports field.

Football hooliganism is probably one of the main manifestations of violence popularly associated with sport, though clearly this is not associated with participants but rather spectators. Sports such as rugby also allegedly encourage violent behaviour and discourage people from participating through violent conduct that, to some, seems to be acceptable even within the broad laws of the game. The rugby unions would argue that this is not the case and that their game is strictly governed and in fact encourages fair play, obedience to the referee and controlled physical contact.

A number of other sports rely on a degree of self-confidence and physical presence but avoid any aggression, at least within the rules, and the officials are charged to keep aggression to a minimum. Aggression on the soccer pitch has become a major issue since the police and local authorities began to take an interest, even on occasion prosecuting individuals for assault and other such misdemeanours even though they occurred in a football context. Such behaviour, it is argued, is illegal and unacceptable regardless of the fact it happens under the guise of sport.

While some would argue that the soccer authorities have been lukewarm about the action taken, this is not the case in most governing bodies, which have been quite strict about adhering to disciplinary standards and support their officials in doing so. Most sporting bodies give total support to officials and ban or suspend competitors who act in an aggressive or violent manner. Even boxing, an overtly violent sport, has very strict rules about behaviour which are rigorously enforced by the referees and overseen by the medical profession. Indeed, one of the strong arguments in favour of boxing is that the physical discipline in terms of training and the control of aggression – the rules that it brings – actually benefit the participants rather than supporting or encouraging illegal aggression.

The martial arts are increasingly popular with a range of ages. The argument for martial arts is that the primary aims are:

- to foster physical fitness and bodily control
- to encourage self-discipline and an ability to defend oneself, without showing aggression or leading aggression but only responding to it.

A strong argument for sport is that aggression can be controlled and beneficially handled in a way that is of long-term good for society rather than just an ego. Some psychologists argue that many people take part in sport to allow their aggression to be taken out, for example, on a squash court or the rugby field rather than in any anti-social or illegal way. Such an outlet for controlled aggression benefits society in preventing potentially major conflicts between individuals as well as encouraging a level of fitness and health which is obviously beneficial to them. It is argued that these benefits to society far outweigh any possible problems caused through aggression brought about through sport.

The issue of sport and its consequences for society with regard to violence is a sizeable one. Despite recent deaths in the boxing ring, shows of violence on the rugby field and civil prosecutions on the football field, the trend is still to believe that participation is a deterrent to violence rather than an encouragement of it.

Political context

One of the outstanding features of sport in the UK is that it has been an issue which is not highly politicized. It has never really become a political football, either at local or national level, and while politicians have clung to any success at the top level to claim some personal return in terms of publicity and image, it has never been given the same significance as it has in a number of other countries throughout the world. Nevertheless, the recent Cricket World Cup and England's refusal to play in Zimbabwe caused concern with politicians in the UK who didn't want them to go, and those in Africa who didn't want them to play. Sport is so important as media draw that it must have some political importance, since politicians want media coverage for their stance on sporting issues.

The commercial impact of sport in the USA is substantial. It is highly desirable for politicians to be seen to be supporting sport, e.g. to give the opening signal to the Super Bowl or to be a close supporter of the Chicago Bulls. This political public credibility through being attached to sport does not appear in the same way in the UK. John Major's interest in and, close link with, cricket did not necessarily make him a more popular leader or have a great effect on his rather grey image. No political party has ever claimed any significantly different attitude towards sport as a key issue in its manifesto when looking for public support at elections. This is not something that appears to be highly rated by politicians or, they believe, the voting public. It is equally true to say that sport has not been used in the UK at the other end of the political spectrum. At no time has any government – left-wing or otherwise – tried to use sport to ameliorate the population or force them to consider sport as a major instrument of governmental manipulation.

This is the type of system which did exist in the Soviet Union and in large parts of Eastern Europe for many years after the Second World War. Sport was seen as a means of keeping the population happy; keeping them fit so that they could be prepared to fight in the army as required; and to glorify the state through the success of particular sports performers. These highly structured sport systems were an integral part of the state's operation and were very heavily funded and encouraged by the government.

The position in the UK is quite different. Governments may make comments to indicate their joy about individual sporting successes and espouse support for sport and the benefits it can bring. However, they will not produce significant sums of money to back up their claimed support and, in real terms, the money given to sport is small.

The Labour Party has always said that it would give more money to sport than the Conservatives. Given the opportunity to prove this, it has, but only to a limited extent. All politicians make some positive noises, but in real terms they have made little significant improvement in the funding of sport in the UK.

The advent of the lottery has brought massive injections of money into sports facilities and talented athletes, although the overall percentage and the actual amount going to sport dropped significantly from 1999/2000 onwards. This is direct additional funding from individuals, not additional government funding support; indeed, the government grasps 12 per cent of all sales.

As an example of the impact of political policies, Table 2.1 gives (what turned out to be) government policy on sport.

Sport and health

Gratton and Tice (1989) came to the conclusion that 'the evidence seems consistent – sport participants seem to be healthier, lead healthier

Table 2.1 Executive summary of the Labour Party's election manifesto 1997

Labour will implement a national strategy for sport dedicated to providing excellence at all levels. This will increase sporting opportunities and improve national sporting performances.

- We will tackle the decline in school sport by ending the sale of playing fields and improving PE training for teachers.
- We will develop sporting opportunities for young people to help them foster a sense of their value to society and to help tackle the problems of youth crime. To achieve this we will set up a dedicated Youth Sports Unit within the Department.
- We will provide a more strategic approach to sports funding through existing government grants, the lottery and local authority services. By reducing bureaucracy and increasing effectiveness of delivery mechanisms more resources can be freed for sport.
- We will focus on play opportunities for children by setting up a new National Lottery good cause for children and children's play.
- We will develop a British Academy of Sport to meet the needs of élite athletes throughout Britain.
- We will set up a Taskforce for Football to tackle the problems of the game.
- We will make the Football Trust a recipient of lottery money so that it may continue its essential work for football at all levels throughout the UK.
- We will appoint an advisory body to oversee the listed sporting events on television.
  Its remit will be to ensure that top sporting events remain as accessible as possible for viewers across Britain.
- We will implement legislation to make the non-prescribed use of steroids in sport as well as the supply of steroids illegal.
- We will legislate against ticket touting.
- We will use all the power of government to help bring major international events such as the World Cup and the Olympic Games to Britain.
- Local authorities will be encouraged to develop and publish a leisure and sports strategy.
- Sport will continue to be a permanent good cause for the purpose of lottery funding.

lifestyles and have a more active attitude to other leisure pursuits than non-participants'.

The general conclusion of Gratton and Tice's study was that 'participation in sport not only makes the participant healthier, but also provides an enriched quality of life by stimulating participation in a whole range of non-sport leisure activities'. They felt that for government and other agencies the policy implication of this research was clear – 'greater emphasis should be placed on encouragement to take part in exercise as an important component of preventative healthcare'.

This research was based on a number of pieces of leisure research and data, in particular the General Household Survey. It indicates quite strongly that participation in sport, while not guaranteeing health in itself, can be a significant impetus to health or at least preventive healthcare.

It would appear that there is a real need to increase our sports participation, if only because it will improve our health. One would hope that one day politicians will match the two, and realize that one way to save money on the health service is to spend money on sport.

The importance of people just taking part in sport for enjoyment, fitness and health should not be underestimated. Their motivation will often be as strong as those with a desperate desire to win. While most people look for some sort of challenge in sport and/or satisfaction through a quality performance, at their own standard, it should be remembered that everybody is in there to be what might be more widely perceived as 'a winner'. The definition of winning is often a personal rather than a public perception – the feeling one gets if one has achieved the level of one's own best performance is often much more important and satisfying than any concern over beating others. Feelings of improved health and activity can also be a major incentive for sport.

The European dimension

In 1973 the UK became a member of the European Community (now the European Union) and, as a result, a party to the 1957 Treaty of Rome. This had significant implications in the short term and caused some major ongoing changes as the UK merged with past legislation and fell in line with new European directives (sometimes making considerable noise in, and about, the process). The changes that membership of the EU has brought about have been seen initially by some managers as necessary evils with which they have had to comply. Only in recent years have they really seen Europe as a commercial marketing opportunity, which everyone should be a part of and influence in a positive way. It may be fair to say that the public authorities, both national and local, were initially a little reluctant to change and have only recently begun to see the opportunities, while (as some would say is normal) the private sector has been quicker to try to seize opportunities and benefit from the integration of the sizeable markets.

At times, the many directives coming through Europe have added to significant internal change and brought about increased work through necessary additional legislation, its enforcement, and the need to comply. The areas of food hygiene, environmental concerns such as waste, water and noise pollution, and health and safety legislation inside and outside the workplace have grown enormously and have forced on some employers considerable additional staffing and organizational costs.

To balance this, the European Social Fund and European Development Fund have given out substantial amounts of money to various parts of the UK to help with a wide variety of projects which have had an impact in the sporting area as well as other aspects of social and cultural activity. There have been ongoing disputes with the British government regarding concepts such as regional regeneration (the areas in which EU funds have given an additional economic impact and produced many results) and the UK's government is sometimes reluctant to work in partnership with the community or add its share to projects. Nevertheless, a sizeable amount of money has come into the UK and continues to be available to a number of the regions of the UK – from 1979 to 1998 the UK received over £3 billion in aid from the funds, much of it through the ERDF (European Regional Development Fund).

The advent of the single market, which came into force in 1992, effectively removed many of the old trading barriers between the partners of the EU and made trade between countries a great deal more attractive for commercial interests. The impact has been slow in sport, but the Bosman Ruling (ensuring free movement of football players) has set a clear example of removing restrictions on trade.

Now Compulsory Competitive Tendering (CCT), introduced in the UK in 1998, is open to market contractors anywhere in the EU, and it may be that outside contractors are coming into the UK.

The single market has in some ways increased trade but in other ways it has caused a growth in competition for European aid, both inside the UK and with other competing countries such as Eire. Additionally, at present 65 per cent of the European funds are allocated to 'objective 1 areas', e.g. Northern Ireland and less-developed Mediterranean areas. Some areas of Scotland and other declining coalfield areas are being added, but the impact of such funding can be sizeable in attracting inward investment, which has a consequent effect on sport and all other activities.

The growth of the single market has also meant that public bodies, local authorities and others have been forced to form international, or European, bodies to represent their interests in the wider European scene. This has also been true of sport, where sporting bodies have had to begin to lobby in the European context to ensure that sport is indeed 'the inalienable right of every person'. This has still to be implemented in many places throughout the EU, but now it is at least an agreed statement of the European Parliament and, at least in theory, is an approved policy thanks to sport's lobbying of the European Parliament. It is increasingly important that sports bodies make their case for European influence and produce input at this level.

The European opportunities for sport have been growing through, for example, town twinning arrangements, which grew from 29 in 1973 to a peak of 90 in 1989 and continue to the present time. These are links between UK communities and those from other European countries and are seen to be healthy for social and cultural reasons. Many of them are spearheaded by joint sports participation in festivals, tournaments or competitions.

A number of other initiatives already exist across Europe. The European Network of Sports Sciences in Higher Education has been established to work towards the harmonization or convergence of qualifications in sport across Europe. A sub-group of the network, called the Sport Management Committee, has developed a European Masters degree in Sports Management.

Sports managers must also realize that their potential customer market now comes from outside the UK, and individuals should be better trained in terms of languages and provision for people from mainland Europe. In particular, facilities and services provided in the south of England, near the Channel Tunnel and the growing European leisure/tourism invasion, must be better geared to providing for this whole new band of customers.

The legislation governing the practice of sports management and administration must be seen in a European dimension, since Britain is now an active member (albeit reluctantly on the part of some) of the EU.

The European influence on sport at a variety of levels has been significant, especially due to factors such as the very strong sporting commitment of the former Eastern Bloc countries, and all the different approaches to sport provision and development in Western European countries, compared to the UK.

This pattern of difference is perhaps being eroded by the arrival of Eastern European coaches in Britain, especially for sports such as swimming, gymnastics and athletics, and by the consideration of certain Western European models of sports provision to promote excellence and increase participation, e.g. the multi-sport, one-site club. The differences, however, are still quite marked in the approach to sport at a political level in the UK as opposed to other parts of Europe.

There is considerable interest within Europe to develop links between various countries, and often this has been seen as an opportunity to encourage sporting links between (particularly young) people from different nations. Such initiatives have been assisted financially from European central funds, and there is a continuing desire to encourage these links in the sporting field. The European Social Fund has been used to promote the training of young people for sporting leadership and initiatives in this area, as well as providing training courses for young people getting involved in sports.

There have been a number of initiatives, e.g. one to produce 'a European sport and leisure management qualification'. This has been driven forward by Yorkshire Coast College and, while still relatively new, seems to provide a very worthwhile concept – linking sports students from different European countries.

The EU also has a budget which may be used to support sporting events. This is particularly aimed at events which will attract media attention and will involve participants from many countries throughout the EU. This initiative is normally implemented on a joint part-fund basis with substantial support coming, hopefully, from private sponsors and others in the locality of the event itself. It is still a worthwhile source of help. The UK Sports Council has an international branch which encourages such links in Europe and beyond, and can help clarify contacts and funding sources.

Where we practise our sport

One of the most challenging and interesting aspects of sports management and administration is the vast range of situations in which this takes place.

As mentioned above, it is important to note that we have a situation of sports management and organization within the private, public and voluntary sectors. Each of these has its own special problems and constraints from an ethical, as well as organizational operation point of view. There is an added dimension to much of sport due to the facility base, and the possible constraints placed upon organizers by the sports facilities available for the participant.

Many of the implications of management and administration are similar regardless of the facility, but equally a sizeable number of procedures and other factors will alter depending on the exact nature of the facility provision, and the demands that this puts on the skills of managers and other staff, as well as budgets.

Sports facilities

The enormous range of sports facilities makes them almost too many to mention – sport of some nature can take place in almost any indoor or outdoor facility. Many sports demand highly sophisticated facilities but others can take place, especially at the participation level, in the most rudimentary area with nothing but the bare essential equipment, or even adapted or invented equipment which approximates to the ideal.

Football, for example, can be played in the Olympic Stadium in Munich or in the back garden – it can be played by one person with one improvised ball of paper or by 22 highly paid professionals using a top-quality ball. Both of these situations are sport, and while one of them may require very little management and the other a great deal, there are levels between these, many of which require significant managerial, organizational and administrative input. The implications of the facilities must be recognized, however, and the desire of many sports people is to produce more sophisticated facilities. They hope for a level of participation and performance which will improve given suitable facilities. This is why so many sports groups are spending much of their time and resources in seeking lottery funding and other possible support, in order to try to take their sport's facilities to an appropriate level to enhance numbers and excellence.

Complex sports facilities can be very expensive in terms of capital construction costs, and often in terms of running costs as well. This causes problems for the organizations or agencies responsible for funding during the design and build stage, and on through to the service provision stage, on an ongoing basis.

The range of facilities includes the following:

- *Playing fields* – covering outdoor areas where sport and activity take place, such as school playing fields, private club playing fields and public playing areas.
- *Recreation areas* – these cover areas such as National Parks, outdoor education facilities, country parks, waterways and lakelands used by

many different groups for a variety of activities, from hill walking to canoeing, from rock climbing to orienteering and sailing.

- *Artificial surfaces* – this growing area includes surfaces provided for activities such as tennis, hockey and football on artificial turf. This facility is now used for an increasing number of sports, for example cricket. Considering British weather, it is likely that such use will continue to grow.
- *Ski slopes* – in a large part of the UK these are artificial areas managed by the voluntary and public sectors. There are a few ski slopes in the north of Scotland which are run commercially but have suffered greatly due to the vagaries of the weather and the lack of consistent snow over recent years.
- *Athletics tracks* – these are nowadays largely of a rubberized surface – running on an ash or grass track is no longer acceptable for anything beyond the most basic athletics.
- *Golf courses* – there has been a substantial growth over the past 20 years in the number of golf courses provided throughout the UK. This continues, perhaps most noticeably in the past few years in terms of the private sector looking to capitalize on the popularity of this sport, and farmers trying to maximize land use and profit. However, as for many sports in the UK, we are not willing to pay a high price and have a traditional view that golf is a game for everyone, played at a reasonable price, especially on local community courses. The number of people able to pay the high prices demanded by some of the exclusive clubs and the new private developments is limited, and this has led to a number of proposals for high-cost memberships and various shareholding schemes being unsuccessful.
- *Stadia* – in this area there is a significant range of provision by private, public and voluntary sectors, particularly for soccer and rugby, but there are a number for athletics and some other less well known sports, such as shinty in the north of Scotland or hockey at one or two specialist facilities. There can be little doubt that the UK has been very poorly provided for in terms of big sports stadia and still has nothing which would match the large range provided in a number of countries in Europe or further afield.
- *Specialist facilities* – a growing trend in a wide variety of sports is to require specialist facilities for top-level competition or training. For example, cyclists must have a velodrome, and such a requirement pushed the government into providing appropriate facilities for Manchester to back up its Olympic bid. To reach world-class level, gymnastics needs a high level of facility provision (pitted landing areas) for training. Tennis, as a sport in the UK, will only be successful if it has a continued significant growth in the number of indoor courts available.
- *Multi-purpose sports halls* – a vast range of these halls exists in the UK, but investigations by the Sports Council have shown that we are still

significantly short of such facilities. Also, because of their multi-purpose use they tend to be dominated by mass participation sports such as indoor football or badminton. Again, the specialist requirements for sports such as basketball and volleyball need to be recognized in the construction and management of such facilities.

- *Swimming pools* – swimming is undoubtedly the most popular specialist sport, and there is a wide community provision of pools. They tend to be leisure pools or too small for high-level events, though, and at that level Britain is poorly provided for. Swimming is far and away the UK's most popular (active) recreational 'sport' and obviously, with our inclement temperatures, it must be done indoors. The growth of swimming pools in recent years has tended away from the traditional rectangular pools which cater for competitive or fitness swimming, towards the leisure pool with flumes and water slides and chutes to attract all the family. It is increasingly recognized at this time that provision of both types of facilities will interest a wider range of the population, keep an active customer base longer and provide better for the health and fitness of the community. Now many leisure pool constructions attempt to include a 25-metre learning or fitness pool alongside, or even integrated into, the overall design.
- *Footpaths* – walking has many participants, but most do it more for exercise and fresh air than any specialist form of sports participation.
- *Ice rinks* – these facilities are very popular with a variety of client groups, being used by three main groups: curlers, ice skaters and ice hockey players. Programming can be difficult, as each of these groups feels that it is short of time or put off from certain times at the facility to allow for others. This natural dynamic causes significant problems on what is limited available, desirable ice time.

Natural resources are one of the strengths of the UK. While the weather can be somewhat inclement, it seldom prevents participation in one sport or another.

We also have a significant outdoor resource in the form of our extensive coastline and vast areas of grassland and hillside, which can be walked and enjoyed by the whole population. This is a major benefit which we must protect for many reasons, including the health, fitness and sports participation of the community.

This variety means that the sports manager has a responsibility for a very wide physical area in many situations. It is to be hoped that with the advent of the National Lottery, initially targeted at facility provision, many more developments will be seen in sports facilities in the UK, because we lag well behind many other countries – some cities in other parts of the world could put the whole of the UK to severe shame.

Self-assessment question

You are involved in and/or studying sport – which of the many contextual issues identified in chapter 2 are particularly important for you? Justify your choice by citing some examples of the points you have selected, and state why they are so important.

3 The voluntary sector

This chapter examines the cornerstone of sport in the United Kingdom – the voluntary sector. It considers the organizations involved and the structures and individuals involved, citing practical examples and the dynamics of the paid staff's relationship with the voluntary workers.

It also considers the management of voluntary sports organizations and the possibility of dominance by small groups or powerful individuals, the difficulty of delivering change in any such organizations and the increasing need to recruit, retain and reward more volunteers to keep sport functioning.

Hoggett and Bishop (1985) made the following statement about the voluntary sector in sport:

> This is a world inadequately studied and often insufficiently understood by those Local Authority officers who have to provide services alongside it and sometimes wish to use it to develop and spread the leisure activities it enfolds, or see a need to support it. What is needed in this relationship is a more widespread respect and mutual understanding that this is a world of self-determining groups which by inclination and constitution must be free to reject advice, support or the chance to work municipalities for a wider public good, if they so wish.

Voluntary organizations

The nature of sport in the UK is that it operates on the basis of voluntarism. This reliance on volunteers probably has many weaknesses, but it certainly has many strengths. The professionalization of sports administration and governing body and club organization in sport remains limited, despite their growth over recent years, and while some would argue that there is an ever-growing need to move towards a more professional attitude, most realize that it would be impossible to find the funds to pay the large number of people who work in sports administration in Britain.

A massive voluntary workforce drives sport forward in the UK, and it is important that everyone operating in the field, in a paid or unpaid capacity, understands the nature of voluntary organizations and the limitations which can be put on certain spheres of operation. For example, it is extremely difficult to be strictly businesslike and curtail individuals' right to speak at meetings if they are, at the same time, giving up a great deal of their own time to support the operation of sport. Such a sympathetic argument, however, is not a basis for supporting bad practice or for allowing people to talk forever on the same subject, going nowhere and benefiting no one. Individual volunteer officials can be seen as stakeholders in the business – the sports organization – through the input that they make, so they deserve to be heard and should always be considered. This never justifies not being businesslike about the manner in which organizations operate, but it does argue strongly against being ruthless in the operation of these principles – this may be justifiable (debatable!) in business situations, but it can never be seen as justifiable in the voluntary scene. While the principles in theory are the same, their implementation in practice should be softer.

The absolutely vital necessity for anyone working in a sports organization or a sports setting is to have a fundamental interest (not necessarily a technical knowledge, but an interest in the sport) and an empathy with all the other people involved. It is not necessary to be a fanatic, and sometimes it is a distinct disadvantage because fanatics can become blinkered to new ideas and different ways of doing things. It is, however, quite important that people understand the fanaticism and the love that people have for a sport so that they can relate to them on a meaningful level. There are many examples of people trying to come into the leisure scene, including sport, and telling others how to operate, while clearly not understanding where the sports volunteer organization or agency is coming from in terms of interest and commitment. This is a recipe for disaster, and has proved extremely unsuccessful in a number of situations and caused a good deal of antagonism and upset within organizations.

A classic example of this is for an organization to appoint an administrator who has no understanding of the sport. This can be fine, as long as they develop an interest and an empathy for the sport and the people involved, and they come to understand the old concept that the participant is king. What simply does not work is the situation where the administrator believes that the filing system is the most important issue, and where efficient administration does not recognize the unique situation of sport, as well as the quite remarkable commitment and interest of all the people involved in the body – paid or unpaid. There are many examples of this not working, and staff lasting only for a short period.

It also must be recognized that there are significant differences between sports organizations and other voluntary organizations – indeed, there can be noticeable differences between one sports body and another. It is always an error to assume that they are all the same and that they all have the same problems. This is simply not true. Many of the issues are shared, but they are never exactly the same and an open approach must always be taken – any attempt to approach such bodies with preconceived notions will be unsuccessful. There is no doubt that, as in many other situations, sports bodies and other voluntary bodies can learn from each other in many areas, but they should not automatically be regarded as the same.

The need for officials to understand the functioning of voluntary organizations generally, and sports organizations in particular, is vital, but it must be set in the context that each particular governing body and/or its situation is unique.

Charles Handy (1988), in one of his many excellent books, *Understanding Voluntary Organizations*, examines voluntary organizations generally and looks at the people involved in the organization and how they should be organized. This and other such texts are well worth reading because they show other examples which illuminate the sports situation. They should not be taken as the definitive type of text on sports organizations – probably such a text has not yet been written – but there is always much to learn from such general management books and, in particular, one which relates to voluntary organizations, which share many problems whether they come from sport, the arts, community care or charity situations.

An individual studying voluntary organizations needs to look at the organization, its culture, the people involved and its internal and external relationships, as well as learning from other bodies with similar characteristics.

Sport is a voluntary concept

It is estimated that in the UK between one in two and one in five of the population are volunteers on a regular basis – that is, they make a weekly voluntary contribution to some organization, individual or group. This volunteering capacity is increasing rather than declining. This growth is in response to increasing personal involvement in community life, and the potential such involvement gives for personal development.

The growth in voluntarism or the interest in volunteering reflects the change in our society in a number of ways:

- the removal of government or local authority intervention in a number of areas
- the reduction of funding available for certain activities
- the proliferation of new activities
- the changing policies of government, e.g. community care, lottery funding
- the increased number of retired (especially early retired) people
- the growing desire to be of service to the community outside the workplace
- the need to feel personal worth
- the desire to benefit others.

All these factors have caused a significant rise in the commitment of volunteers, but their role is always threatened as pressures build on them, and initiatives to support them are always required.

As mentioned elsewhere in the text, it is essential that volunteer support and training are given to maintain enthusiasm and interest where it exists or engender it anew in people who have not previously been involved in volunteering.

The voluntary ethic, although it is often decried, is important and will continue to be so for sport and other areas of our society in the foreseeable future. It should not be underestimated or in any way demeaned. Any effort in this text, or elsewhere, should be to streamline it, improve it and focus it, but never to discourage it because it has such a lot to offer and is irreplaceable. Sport in the UK is said to have over 1.5 million volunteers involved, who give an average of 2.5 hours per week to their chosen activity.

Case study 3.1: National governing body recruitment

A national governing body of sport employs an administrator, and is having difficulty in retaining him/her. It has taken different approaches in making appointments:

- recruiting someone from a sport background with relatively little administrative skill or background experience
- selecting an administrator with sports background, but an extensive administrative CV
- choosing someone, previously a volunteer, who now wanted to move into 'running the sport' on a full-time paid basis.

All had their own problems, not identified during interview and selection or addressed in inducting the person into the post. The problems exist in a number of areas, which often include:

- paid v. voluntary
- little technical knowledge v. lots of technical knowledge
- sport knowledge v. administrative knowledge
- fact v. perception
- commitment to sport v. commitment to job
- management v. leadership
- short-term knowledge v. years of experience in the sport.

Voluntary ethos

Voluntary organizations by their nature tend to be very jealous of their *raison d'être* and guard their voluntary role and their independence very closely. They tend to believe that they are involved as volunteers to further the voluntary cause almost as much as they are there as sports administrators to further the sporting cause. There tends to be a belief that organization, administration and management should be in the hands of the volunteer and should not require the same level of competence and organization as business situations. A sort of 'slapdash' amateur attitude is felt to be acceptable because there is no compulsion or salary attached. This ethos of the administrative support service being self-justifying or acceptable for its own sake is the traditional feeling in many sporting organizations. Such a belief is incorrect and unjustifiable because it does not produce quality support or delivery for the performer and the organization.

The voluntary commitment shown is enormous, and should be matched by a serious, professional attitude being adopted by such people to a level that does not embarrass or cause the performers any difficulties, and will deliver their requirements on a quality and consistent basis.

Proper management and administrative practices are vital to effective sports performance on the field of play, as are quality coaching and talented committed athletes. Ignoring the benefits of good business management may bring about a number of significant potential dangers to any sporting organization. In particular, there will be an almost inevitable lack of strategic direction or vision in the organization. This in turn will lead to poor direction which follows from indifferent or non-existent planning and goal-setting. Individuals will often see themselves as slaves to the organization and to the cause, giving their time to perform basic short-term tasks without any view to the future, when they may no longer be involved, or without any vision concerned with what the organization could achieve for its participants in the future. Service for service's sake and short-term performer excellence are sometimes seen as more important than real long-term achievement, or building lasting foundations.

For the future this complacent belief can lead to inadequate co-ordination and administrative activity, and means that the organization will not function as effectively as it could. It could imply a lack of leadership and everyone will tend to push their own point of view and stick to it doggedly, because they have a major role in the organization and a background of service, rather than speaking with a view to achievement.

A key factor in much of this lack of management and planning is often a lack of understanding by many of the participants at all levels of sporting organization as to what exactly the organization exists to do and what each individual's role within that organization is – whether as an administrator, coach, player, manager, official or member of the medical staff, each individual should have a clear idea of what they are there to do within the overall organizational structure. Both individual and organizational goals should be quite clear and explicitly stated for all to be aware of and understand.

Voluntary sports organizations

Amis *et al.* (1995) studied a number of sports organizations in the USA and Canada with a view to examining the role of and relationship between staff and committees, and the internal relationships in the organization and their function. A few notable conclusions were reached, the first being that 'analysis of the data does nothing to disprove the contention that conflict is endemic in VSOs'. It was also felt that 'the organization's design must be thought of as a major contributing factor to conflict in VSOs'. The many pressures facing such organizations were identified and it was suggested that they were causing stress and conflict within the organization. The various sub-groups and subcommittees working within the organization almost inevitably conflicted with each other. The authors suggested that this 'increased susceptibility to conflict must be addressed if the organization is to function productively'.

In addition, the findings indicated that

> the voluntary nature of these organizations adds considerably to the potential for conflict. While the combination of voluntary leadership and professional expertise is an appealing notion, it is also highly problematic. The differing values and expectations of each group . . . make the voluntary, professional relationship inherently conflictual.

The findings of the study were that this conflict degenerates into major issues. The very structure and informality of such organizations, especially as they face financial and other resource restrictions, exacerbates existing problems.

This study provides some very clear evidence that there are significant and difficult dynamics and conflict within voluntary organizations, but is unable to offer significant solutions because 'until the causes of conflict are understood the process of conflict management will remain unviable'. It does shed some light on the nature and scale of the conflict, but notes that further detailed research must be done to gain a deeper understanding of why such conflict exists and how it is caused. Such a study would substantially assist in identifying causes of, and hopefully in turn solutions to, the problems facing such organizations not just in North America, where this study took place, but in other areas such as the UK.

One final quotation from Amis *et al.* (1995) is very relevant for sports managers and administrators: 'it is worth reiterating that although the conflict may become manifest as a dispute between individuals, it is as a result of their membership in conflicting sub-units. The conflict remains, therefore, structural, not interpersonal.' This statement has major implications for sports managers in that they should perhaps be considering organizational structure and team operation more than personal or interpersonal skills. When considering the problems facing such voluntary sports organizations it is all too easy to rush off and blame various individual personalities, and strengths and weaknesses, without examining the structure of the organization and its inherent conflict-creating mechanisms.

Management of voluntary organizations

Thibault *et al.* (1994) drew on various research sources to establish that, in essence, there had been very little research into voluntary sports organizations and their use of strategic planning had been very limited. The study set out to look at this lack of evidence of strategic planning and tended in its conclusions to support the notion of contingency, i.e., that there should be a good fit between the environment and the strategy undertaken – that the strategy should match the specific situation and need, because there is 'no universal set of strategic choices optimal for all businesses'.

The conclusion of Thibault *et al.* was in fact that people will have 'a better opportunity to successfully implement a strategy when it is congruent with the environment'. This clearly implies that every voluntary sports organization must consider its own situation before developing a strategy and should not necessarily follow the strategy or direction of another.

Thibault *et al.*'s research is very interesting. It follows and strengthens the belief that each situation or voluntary organization in sport is different and should be assessed as such, and that the 'broad-brush approach' to sports organizations and any problems thrown up for administrators and managers is not appropriate.

This finding matches the belief that voluntary bodies in sport – clubs, governing bodies or other associations – have the right to go their own way and make their own policy, regardless of what others may wish them to do. The relationship with others in both the public and private sectors can be complex and often difficult for all partners to understand, but for volunteers autonomy is paramount.

Very often, the local authority or national sports council will wish the voluntary body to go in one direction – in line with a national or local 'political' policy – but that may not be what is perceived as being in the best interest by the volunteer. Ultimately, since much of sport operates in a voluntary sphere, the volunteers' decision is the vital one.

Sometimes the autonomy of voluntary organizations can be seen as a threat to politically motivated authorities or those with other perceptions as to the needs of the local community, who are, in short, coming at the provision of sport from quite a different angle to that of a self-motivated, sports-specific voluntary organization.

As far as the private sector is concerned, their relationship with voluntary organizations can be mutually beneficial in terms of generating business for them, through sponsorship and other such commercial relationships. They may be involved in a partnership which can lead them to supplying goods or services at a cost to the voluntary organization and its members. This is often a more clear-cut relationship than that which involves policy – there is an identifiable bottom line.

The scope, sphere of operation and diversity of the voluntary sector are almost inestimable. There are thousands of voluntary groups working in a variety of sectors in the UK, and in sport their numbers are enormous. It is very hard to estimate the number, but it is believed that around 10 per cent of the population give service to voluntary organizations and, in Birmingham alone, there are over 8,000 voluntary groups, of which three-quarters are concerned with sport, cultural or social welfare activities (Badmin, 1992, 1993).

Research by Sport England (1996) suggested that over 1.5 million people are involved in providing sports opportunities, for themselves and others, in the UK. The areas of interest covered by sport organizations include activities as diverse as wheelchair basketball, national dance, baton twirling, ice hockey and aerobics. Such organizations may have very different technical demands and requirements but, in essence, they have the same management requirements. Most draw on limited resources and finances, and they all put demands on a limited number of potential volunteers to keep them functioning.

This commitment of individuals within the organization, which is remarked upon several times in this text, must be understood by people dealing with voluntary organizations in the sporting sector. The motivations and motives of volunteers and voluntary organizations are perhaps the key issues that need to be clearly understood by all who have anything to do with them.

Sports organizations may also have some unique characteristics that separate them from other voluntary sector organizations in terms of their very clearly determined role, the disciplinary control over participants and officials, and their need to link and liaise with other organizations such as district leagues, national bodies or even international bodies. Such differences mean that it is often difficult for any sports voluntary group to remain totally autonomous and independent except for solely recreational organizations. As soon as a higher level of competition or performance is involved, the body must become very complex.

Another key area of knowledge for a sports organization is to recognize where volunteers come from. They will often come from past performers or the parents of current performers, while it is rare, if welcome, that someone enters as a willing volunteer just because of some desire to promote the good of others, or some innate interest in a particular sporting activity. One could argue that the scarcity of volunteers in the latter group has been a weakness: that there tend to be too many individual vested interests, and people only last in sports administration for 50 years because nobody else will do the job.

This view is perhaps a little negative when there are so many good people doing a high-quality job in a vast array of sports organizations, many of which have lasted for 100 years or more, totally dependent on quality voluntary effort.

The pressure on the organizations and the volunteers themselves appears to be growing significantly, and is perhaps best explained as follows.

1   The diminishing availability of finance from local authority, government or commercial support, set against the constant driving up of the cost of participation in sport, makes it more difficult for volunteers to have even their expenses met by the sporting organization. This creates costs for such voluntary administrators which many cannot bear for long.
2   The pressure in the workplace on many individuals has meant that they have very little spare time, and must consider using it in a paid way to help meet the growing cost of living.

In short, the lack of individual finance, the cost of sport and the cost of living are all threatening the commitment, interest and availability of volunteers in a variety of areas. A growing number of people are asking why, if their time is to be used in support of others, it should be at considerable additional cost to themselves, at a time when they could perhaps be earning money instead of paying out money for no return (apart from their own enjoyment).

The role of the voluntary sector, and its relationship with the public sector at national and local level, is another 'life-threatening' or, at least, enthusiasm-diminishing aspect of work in sports voluntary organizations. There tends to be a view among the volunteers that the paid officials and organizations should be doing more for them and their sporting organization, through grant aid or substantial administrative support. At the same time there is often an unreal expectation from paid full-time officials as to what volunteers can achieve in the limited time they have available to commit to their organization.

This divergence of positions and expectations can lead to strained relationships between organizations and individuals, in addition to the differences that the public and voluntary sector organizations may have, as outlined above.

The nature of voluntary organizations

Voluntary organizations can often be self-perpetuating, especially if they are not focused. They should be open organizations that seek out change and look for new members at all levels, all the time – people with potential to help the organization function should be actively targeted and brought on board at every possible stage.

There is a very common complaint of cliques and small introverted groups holding power within many sports organizations, and this can be off-putting for individuals that we should be looking to attract. It is in the nature of human beings that we do tend to socialize with people we know and are somewhat resistant to new people and their new ideas – we may feel threatened and often react in a negative fashion when someone tries to join in.

Again, it is crucial that the members of the organization know what the goals, individual and organizational, are and that everyone, new and old, is driving in the same direction. They must understand and allow for human quirks and differences, while not allowing these personal characteristics to destroy active achievement.

If the goal is always to seek organizational improvement, then good people will always seek the support and involvement of others to get the task achieved. The role of team-building is vital and all the participants in sports administration need to be team workers so that they can pull together towards common aims, and involve all other willing volunteers.

Appreciation of group dynamics, as well as individual personalities, will help sports administrators recognize that each group needs different personalities to play different roles both formally and informally, and while they have their individual roles they also help the group function together – helping push forward a decision or showing the leadership what is required to achieve progress. It is always best that people are sympathetic and understanding to such processes and roles, especially informal ones, rather than resistant to them. An understanding that people have their views, desires and targets, individually as well as within the group, and that they have a role to play in the cohesion of the group, will help everybody work together for the benefit of the organization.

Organizational structures and personalities

Within the sports world there are a variety of structures – both formal and informal – and there can be conflict between them and the official structures or the structure recognized by outside agencies. Many informal structures are stronger, and in some ways more important, than the formal structure. Often one individual can dominate the sports setting: where this person is the club coach or the national governing body president, they can be the dominant figure leading the organization forward or holding it back. This strong individual can be a major benefit to an organization where he or she is working for its betterment, but there is a danger of some type of personality cult forming and one individual becoming too dominant. A good co-operative leader is extremely valuable, but an authoritarian or dictatorial individual could cause major problems for the organization, internally and externally.

Inevitably an organization will be associated with the personalities in it and, while they can be a major strength, no one personality should dominate or exclude all others. Regardless of their abilities, such domination will be limiting in some way and will detrimentally affect the organization's reputation.

Sport, by its very nature, is personality-dominated and strength of character is one of the qualities it produces in people. Inevitably sports management and administration will be no different from performance on the squash court or hockey field in this respect. Equally, to continue the on-field analogy, individuals need to be part of a team to be most effective, regardless of their talents and abilities, because the sum achievement of many will always outweigh the efforts of one.

As mentioned, the key concept for all individuals involved in the organization, at whatever level, is for them to understand what tasks have to be performed for the most effective operation of the agency to the benefit of the sport and those involved in it. In essence, it is always much better for any organization to be focused on the tasks to be performed and to take account of personalities and feelings than to be focused only on personalities themselves. It is important that individuals and structures are aimed towards achievement of the task in the most efficient and effective way.

To adopt a task-focused approach will be most effective, as long as such an approach allows individuals to show their true talents and allows others to realize their individual aims within the organizational structure. If we focus on the task then solving problems and making decisions becomes a great deal easier, and can, usually beneficially, be de-personalized.

Many sports organizations have what might be referred to as the club – often social club – ethos. This is where a small group dominates the operation and involves others only when it sees fit. It could be seen as a series of concentric circles with fairly strict boundaries between them which are difficult to penetrate (Figure 3.1). There is often a real difficulty for individual members in penetrating the inner sanctum and having real effect on the operation of the organization.

While a central, small, active management group may be effective in getting things done, it always needs to be aware of what is happening around it and should be keen to draw other individuals into the organization and its activities, rather than fight hard, as many social groups do, to exclude others and their expertise. By keeping to a small clique you will inevitably restrict the activity of the organization to the aims of a few, which will be to its major detriment in the short or long term.

Such a clique can often build up round the club coach, manager or similar type of person, with a strong personality, views and commitment. Such people have a capacity to destroy rather than create small interest groups.

It is essential for a sports organization to have a clearly identified structure – probably hierarchical, where each individual has a clearly identified role to play in achieving progress for the organization. This type of structure is

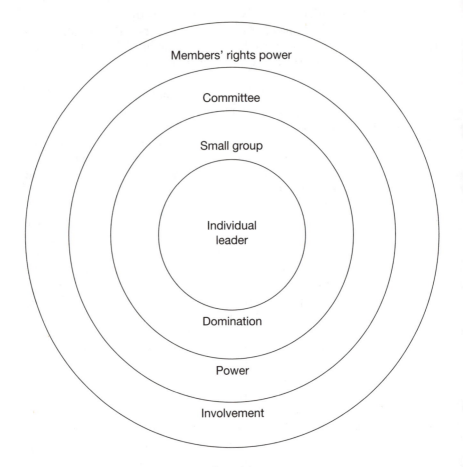

Figure 3.1 'Social club' organizational model

perhaps a little dated because it relies on clearly defined levels of management, but it gets things done and means that people are quite clear as to what they are in the organization to do. It can be especially useful in 'spare-time amateur' organizations. In essence a highly structured organization can be quite helpful in that it helps clarify and delineate individual roles, and allows people to achieve their tasks within the clear structure.

It is vitally important that sports organizations have an open approach to involving everyone who has something to offer to the sport and its participants. An attitude which excludes individuals is most inefficient, ineffective, divisive and damaging, and can create strife within the organization.

The ethos of any sports organization is key in the sense that the morals, attitudes and standards it portrays will be carried right into the games hall or sports field, through its organizational structures. There is a moral side to sports administration and this must be understood and appreciated by all those involved, so that it can underpin everything that is undertaken.

A dated 'public school' type of organizational belief and behaviour may be quite inappropriate to sports organizations in the twenty-first century, but still the principles of morality and fairness they brought to administrative and management roles as well as performance are essential to retain the very nature of sport.

Governing bodies

In terms of sport in the UK undoubtedly one of the most significant influences is that of the national governing bodies. These organizations represent the clubs, districts and interested individuals who constitute sports participants at different levels in the UK – in other words, the very sizeable voluntary sector.

These governing bodies can range in size from only a few people, in cases such as a minor martial art or hang gliding, up to thousands of members with a substantial professional organizational base in sports such as association football and rugby union. There can be many problems with the operation of these organizations since, as they act as the representative voice of a specific sport at all levels, the demands on the organization are substantial. Responses to initiatives and developments such as coach education, government policy and sports council initiatives are many and varied and impose strains on often low-key, small-scale operations, largely made up of volunteers who sometimes are expected by larger professional organizations, such as the sports council, to respond very quickly.

This situation, where the organization is operating on a largely voluntary basis but is constantly dealing with many professional organizations, causes problems. Demands for immediate response can be damaging to function and operation as well as personal relationships. Many frustrations are created for paid staff involved in sport or local authority personnel, private sector or national agencies because they cannot get a prompt answer from the national governing body, owing to the need to wait until the next committee cycle decides on governing body policy on any specific issue.

By definition the voluntary sector must be voluntary and largely depends on people giving up their spare time, but it must aim to take a professional attitude and, wherever possible, appoint professional people to implement the policies of the organization, as laid down by the volunteers involved. The more professionalized the organization, the more likely it is to be really effective and have the ear of the major players of the sports council (who have an enormous influence on the resources available to governing bodies and the sports they represent). There must always be a link between effectiveness and efficiency in terms of the costs imposed on the sport by any type of central administration, but in essence professionalism is the aim and is largely beneficial, provided it is done in an efficient, cost-effective manner.

Another issue for governing bodies to consider is the relative age of the committee personnel and the participants. It appears inappropriate, as happens in so many places, for young performers to be 'governed' by much older people; performers at the age of ten may not benefit greatly from chief officials who are 50 or 60 years older than them – it can be very difficult for people to relate to performers where there is such a significant age gap, and indeed it is difficult for the performers to relate to them. Certainly mechanisms for participant input to administrative systems need to be devised.

There have been instances in the past where there has been a total lack of communication, and indeed understanding, between the individual participants and the sports organization. In some cases this is aggravated by an age gap and by a gap in time between the governing body personnel's actual participation in the sport and their attaining some official post. Very often comments such as 'things were not like this when I was performing' will be made – a statement which displays astonishing naïvety and ignorance. It implies that sports participation remains the same despite the fact that everything round it is changing with time. Society in general moves on; so too must the requirements and provision for participation in sport.

For example, to compare the commitment required from a rugby player to play first division or premiership rugby to that required to play in the top flight of rugby some 20 years ago is impossible. There are light years of difference in terms of the fitness levels and commitment required today, and with the professional game the gap is growing.

This tendency for ageing officials to try to relive their youth through others, or advise players how to cope with modern pressures which they themselves never faced, can cause rifts within sports organizations. Sensible sports administrators realize that they exist to support and help the performer but should not be reliving past performances or applying dated criteria as to how performers should behave in the modern era. Administrators should try to be sympathetic to the enormous pressures facing modern-day sports performers – it is difficult for an ageing amateur player to realize the major challenges faced by a young, highly paid professional, who is subject to enormous media and commercial demands. Administrators should try to have a feeling of sympathy, or empathy, for the performer facing such pressures, and try to keep up to speed with sporting developments in the fast-changing modern world.

Volunteerism and change

It has been often and wisely stated that the only thing that is constant is change. This statement needs to be reiterated all the time to allow people to understand that the status quo is not an option, that things do not stand still, time passes, hair grows, human beings age and society changes.

Sport has to face up to almost constant change in our early twenty-first-century society – among the many factors that affect sport dramatically are political changes, the ageing of our population, the advent of the National Lottery, the changing business climate, technological advances, creeping professionalism, international competition, the funding of sport, sponsorship implications, media changes and pressures. With all these quite radical alterations surrounding us, sport cannot stand still. Certainly there is a desire to keep some of the more potentially damaging changes from affecting sport, e.g. the extraordinarily high commercial pressures and the fast-developing production of drugs. But the change must be faced up to and coped with in a positive way by sports organizations as for any other individual and organization in our society. There is no point in burying one's head in the sand and believing that things will not or cannot change.

Change is constant but we must try to anticipate and lead it, not just follow it. Structures should be put in place to allow change to be acted on promptly, and indeed anticipated wherever possible. A good example of this is the sports governing bodies that were ready to be first in line with lottery bids. Even before the legislation was through Parliament, some groups had already detailed the outline of their bid. Consequently they were successful and now have the concrete benefits drawn from their anticipation of a major initiative and how they could react to it, and exploit it to the benefit of their sport.

This is perhaps the key to change – to be positive and take any changes which will inevitably happen and turn them to your favour. Every threat can become an opportunity. To do this you require structures which are responsive to change and individuals who will see a clear way ahead, reacting positively as required and leading forward into the future, looking for change and its positive effects rather than fearing it.

Voluntary commitment–paid staff dynamic

It is by no means essential to have been an excellent performer to be an excellent administrator; sometimes, in fact, it can be a disadvantage because such a view of sport may be limited. It is vitally important to understand what sport is all about, why people get involved, and why they get so keen and fanatical about it. For many people involved, sport is the major consideration of their life outside work, and sometimes even ranks as a higher priority than their work. It is extremely important to them, and it is essential that administrators understand such a viewpoint and have an empathy for the commitment and interest that everyone involved in the activity shows.

Sometimes 'lack of commitment' or perceived 'lack of understanding' of full-time paid staff can cause a major clash with voluntary officials who feel that the whole of their life and interest is committed to this activity, and cannot understand when a paid official wants to leave a meeting before

11 o'clock at night, or not give the '110 per cent' commitment that they sense they themselves give to their sport. They often forget that they probably do not give that same '110 per cent' commitment to their work or their full-time paid employment, but they expect it of their employee, just because they happen to be involved in sport. More than once such a paradox has caused significant problems in sports organizations due to the lack of understanding of respective viewpoints, roles and commitments.

Sport is demanding and demands enormous commitment from all those involved in it – failure to understand the commitment and interest shown by the volunteer on the part of the paid worker will cause difficulties for all concerned. Equally respect for paid staff must be shown by volunteers, by understanding that their love (sport) can be 'only a job'. Sports and sports interest is almost unique in terms of the passion it can engender and the all-consuming commitment it can produce, hence the legendary tale of the 'golf widow' where golf is put above all else. It is important to understand that the 4th XV rugby players are just as committed to their sport and interested in it and will go to almost the same trouble as the top-level performer who may be playing in the modern day for hundreds of thousands of pounds – even millions in some sports. Commitment and interest in sport cannot be measured in purely financial terms.

The nature of sport is such that it engenders enormous passions and enthusiasms, and it is constantly helpful for individuals to empathize with such emotions because they have a major impact on management practices and procedures. The passion and commitment must be present within managers and administrators as well as within participants at all levels.

The commitment of sports performers to take part in sport at all levels, through the coldest or the hottest of weather and at extreme personal inconvenience and expense, has to be matched by the understanding of the organizers – paid or voluntary. Perhaps this requirement for an understanding of the enormous commitment of the participants is the most important point in the whole of this book. If such an understanding, empathy and shared interest does not exist then the whole relationship between the performers and the administration will be based on misapprehension, confusion and misunderstanding.

Many people in sports administration have shared the commitment of the participants and given their life, just as enthusiastically, to the organization and support of sport, in much the same way as participants give it to the playing on the field. Commitment is not the only thing required; it must be marked by professionalism and professional attitudes. However, the sheer joy of participation must be understood and beneficially experienced.

In a wider field of operation, the author has been involved in passing on management and operational advice to people in the sport and leisure field, and has thrived on the basis of understanding the whole business and field of operation. Frequently business has been obtained because other management trainers and consultants do not have the specialist background, but more particularly, the understanding of the ethos, atmosphere and commitment of sport and leisure. Staff, paid and voluntary, enjoy the company of others who share that enormous capacity for work and commitment to customer enjoyment.

After all, if you are going to be involved in an event or promotion, perhaps into the early hours of the morning, several days a week, or even over a period of weeks, then it is absolutely vital that the necessary understanding and commitment are there to drive you forward to produce the best quality of organization. As in any organization, the mission statement, aims and objectives must be clearly understood by everyone concerned, so that everyone is pulling in the same direction and knows where they are going and why they are there. Only in such a situation can you achieve and maintain the necessary levels of motivation to ensure successful professional operation by everyone involved.

How to retain volunteers

When asked to identify what they wanted from their involvement in sport, a small group of voluntary sports officials suggested the following:[1]

- reward
- involvement
- encouragement
- empowerment
- value
- information
- training
- interest
- clear and agreed objectives
- praise
- debriefing
- appropriate post
- responsibility
- acknowledgement
- progress
- feedback
- opportunity to socialize.

[1] Relayed to the author during a 'running sport' training session in 1997.

Self-assessment question

Think of a situation in which you have taken part in sport where a key volunteer administrator was involved. (Perhaps they collected the fees, arranged the travel or arranged the matches.)

- What exactly was their role?
- Why do you think they did it?
- Were they properly rewarded?

Suggest at least six ways of keeping them involved and rewarded better in the future.

4 Sports development

This chapter begins with a definition of sports development, then cites the basic principles and values expounded by various organizations and individuals. It analyses the meaning of the concept and examines some of the practical delivery situations in which sports development is implemented.

Thereafter, the consideration of sports development identifies all its constituent parts and also looks at the role of the sports development officer. It examines the various skills and job role required of such workers.

The chapter closes by remarking that sports development, as it is seen now, is a relatively new concept and still has little history or background research to base its performance on.

Sometimes colleagues in the leisure department will not understand the true role of the sports development officer, but for the purposes of this text the following definition of sports development is seen as appropriate:

> Sports development is a process whereby effective opportunities, process, systems and structures are set up to enable and encourage people in all or particular groups and areas to take part in sport and recreation or to improve their performance to whatever level they desire.
>
> *Dr Ian Thomson, University of Stirling, FIPRE/ILAM*
> *Scotland seminar, Glenrothes, October 1992*

To define sports development is inevitably difficult, and it means different things to different people. Basically, sports development is about providing and improving opportunities for people to participate in sport at whatever level to the best of their ability and in fulfilment of their interest.

The basic principle is that sports development should give opportunities for people to participate in sport as well as supporting the development of new facilities and activity sessions.

The sports development process requires some underpinning values. These have been agreed by the Institute of Leisure and Amenity Management (ILAM) Specialist Panel to include, for example, the following.

1   Participants must be at the centre of the process; opportunities provided by the organization which supports, co-ordinates and then manages participants should always start with the participants' needs and be sufficiently flexible to meet these.
2   Sports development work should offer participants an opportunity to achieve and exercise self-determination and self-reliance in the activity of their choice.
3   Prejudice against people with disabilities or who suffer from social and economic disadvantage, racism, sexism and ageism have no place in sports development.
4   Every participant has a right to an environment which provides for their physical and personal safety, in which they feel physically and personally safe.

This list of values has been developed by the Sport and Recreation Industry Training Organization (SPRITO) and now has been fully adopted by ILAM and others working in the field.

Sport, by its very nature, is all about development. In particular it is about the development of the individual and the group. It can also be helpful in the development of the organization and its structure. In some cases sport is the whole reason for the existence of a group and its development. In other instances it can develop team spirit or group coherence in more general-purpose groups.

The added value that sport can give to life is recognized by even the most reluctant politician and features perhaps, most noticeably in the UK, in the old public-school structure of team spirit and personal development, with the belief that moral fibre, team playing and other desirable social skills and beliefs can be inculcated by sport into people for the benefit of society.

The argument about the beliefs of sports participation continues, but there is some justification in the belief that it can act as a social agent in terms of developing individuals in society towards some desirable goals, such as working together and interpersonal reliance. There is an equally strong argument (from what might be described as the anti-sport lobby) that there are some bad aspects to sport, which should, perhaps, be discouraged, such as competition and the belief that the strong, fit and healthy will prevail.

Such philosophical debates about sport can be treacherous and diversionary, but the aspect of human and personal development, as well as societal development and the development of sports organizations themselves, should be considered when the subject of sports development is on the agenda. It is all too easy to ignore these important aspects.

Sports development is about developing not just sport but also the individual within sport, the sports organization to better provide for the sport, sport within the community and sport for its own sake – in terms of the sheer enjoyment that well-structured and organized sport can bring to the individuals involved. All too easily the wider philosophical considerations are forgotten, and while there are occasions when they should be, the benefits of the work of the administrator can be underestimated and the commitment undermined if the deep-rooted philosophy is absent or constantly ignored. The individual and societal progress achieved through effective sports development can be an enormously beneficial motivation for sports administrators.

The massive positive impact which can be achieved is seen in many countries in the world, perhaps most notably South Africa. There the active development of sport was (and is) a major influence in cultural integration.

Eady (1993) defines sports development as 'the process which enhances opportunities for people of all ages, degrees of interest and levels of ability to take part, get better and excel in their chosen sporting activities'. This definition coincidentally hits on the very essence of sports administration, which is also about catering for all levels of interest, ability and desire. It can be argued justifiably that sports administration is an integral part of sports development and that while it might need somebody with the specific title of development officer to push things forward, and achieve the innovation necessary to get new schemes up and running, it is often the 'more mundane' manager or administrator who actually delivers the sport to the participant in the practical organizing of sessions.

Perhaps the concept of sports development has been about driving forward new initiatives and giving different emphases to various considerations within the sporting fraternity, but much of the work is involved with the administration and organization of sporting opportunities. The key difference with the development officer is that they are often much more active. Indeed, they exist to plot the way forward and to look at innovative ideas. The sports development officer tends to be much more proactive, while in many cases the manager and administrator, because of the burdens of these two tasks, are much more reactive. Good managers would of course hope to be proactive as well, but this is not always possible due to constraints of time as well as perceptions.

Sports development tends to focus very strongly on target groups such as women, people with disabilities, or ethnic minority groups, and there is a constant emphasis on creating new opportunities for participation and marketing sporting opportunities to people who do not already take part.

Increasingly in recent years we have moved, in the UK, from the position where most sports development officers were employed in general posts, and dealt with a number of areas and sports, to a position where many are either theme-based, i.e. directed towards, for example, women's sports or sport for people with disabilities; or sports-specific development officers, focused on one sport, such as soccer, netball or cricket. This change in emphasis has been to stop 'the broad-brush approach' where an attempt is made to dabble in a variety of areas, rather than spending a sizeable (arguably more effective) amount of time in one specific area where real achievement can be made and seen.

Sports development has been considerably affected by compulsory competitive tendering (CCT) – initially adversely. In drawing up the initial contract specifications in the first round of CCT, many opportunities were missed to detail what developmental responsibilities would be laid upon any contractor. This resulted in a tendency to concentrate on numbers through the door and financial returns, without considering the important factors of expansion of client base and the involvement of the whole community in sport – the developmental factors. This neglect and emphasis on finance became almost epidemic, to the point where many development officers found it difficult to gain access to sporting facilities within their own authority.

This situation has been remedied as authorities, companies and facility managers, operating under CCT and now Best Value, have begun to see that they too need to develop or to work with the sports development officer in developing new customer bases, programmes and activities for specific groups, such as older people or women. It seems likely, from this experience, that when contracts are drawn up in future, sports development will be much more a part of the contract specification and more prominent in the minds of managers, on both the client and contractor sides of provision. The need to have sports development officers developing new initiatives is no less (arguably it is even greater) within a Best Value context. The provision for the community of new opportunities must continue whoever is managing the contract; after all, new customers bring new money.

A major current consideration as many local authorities move towards leisure trusts is whether to leave the development section with the council or take it into the trust. Opinions vary and different councils have taken different approaches – City of Edinburgh choosing, for example, to leave development services within the local authority control. Many have chosen to encompass sports development in their trust from the beginning, as South Lanarkshire do.

Issues of finance, structure, control and liaison all need to be considered, but from a sports point of view the key test is 'where will sports services most effectively be delivered?' The worry for sport could be that trusts become more interested in cost efficiency than in quality or range of service provision. There are arguments on both sides, but lengthy research, consultation and discussion are certainly necessary before any decision is taken.

Sports development is very much about community and individual development through sport. It has close links and parallels in community education and community recreation fields. There is a danger, however, that individuals will become embroiled in the political and academic arguments and discussions that can bedevil community education, rather than continuing to be involved on the shop floor with provision and delivery of sporting opportunities for participants of all levels.

Sports development is not an academic subject. It is a practical ability, a set of skills and a role that is about quality delivery of opportunity. Sports development is about the promotion and provision of sporting possibilities

Figure 4.1 The sports development process

to the population. It is not, and never should be, about talking about it. There is always a danger for sports development officers that talk and meetings will become their daily bread, rather than really being out there supporting coaches, clubs and other organizations, to give people of all ages and abilities the chance to do sport.

The key, then, to sports development, as to other sports provision, will be efficient administration and organization (Figure 4.1). Many aspects of this text will be of benefit to sports development officers, and while it is recognized that their role may be slightly more innovative, proactive and developmental in general terms, they need to deliver the organizational goods in a quality way.

A sports development officer has a very significant number of roles to cover.

The many roles of the sports development officer

The sports development officer's roles will have to include the following:

- achiever
- administrator
- adviser
- communicator

- contractor
- co-ordinator
- customer
- deliverer
- diplomat
- educator
- emissary
- employee adviser
- employer
- evaluator
- implementer
- influencer
- innovator
- leader
- liaison officer
- manager
- marketer
- mediator
- mentor
- monitor
- motivator
- negotiator
- organizer
- partner
- pawn
- persuader
- planner
- provider
- representative
- researcher
- strategist
- student
- subordinate
- supervisor.

Even this list probably does not cover all the specific roles that the sports development officer can be called upon to perform in some radically different situations, varying according to venue, age group, economic, sport and social settings, among others.

This wide range of roles is one of the main motivators towards reducing the generalist role of the sports development officer – no one human being can be all of these at any one time or will have strengths in all of these areas. By limiting the requirements on technical knowledge to one specific sport, and indeed to the politics of one particular sport, the chances of success in delivery are probably greatly improved.

In order to perform these many roles, sports development officers will require a wide range of professional skills. They need to be competent in:

- organizing
- leading
- communicating
- evaluating
- politicing
- being patient
- persevering
- thinking
- planning
- researching
- sourcing
- selling
- understanding
- dealing with people.

Again a sizeable list, but arguably not yet comprehensive – there still appear to be gaps. Like any list of skills, all that the active, ambitious and driven sports development officer can do is try to match up as much as possible, and work to enhance and develop their skills at every opportunity.

The sports development officer, with all these roles to fulfil and these skills to demonstrate, will get involved in the 'sports development process'. This is fundamentally about providing sporting opportunities for people of all ages, sizes, sexes, colours and creeds in a proactive way. It is about seizing the initiative and looking for opportunities to make the appropriate provision.

Sports development is certainly about facing up to change and getting voluntary groups to react positively to it and seize opportunities that arise. It is about being very focused and targeted on each specific project, whether or not the overall plan is specific-sport or target-group focused.

It involves working with partners and the (almost hackneyed) concept of partnership. To be effective, sports development officers must cultivate the skills to work with other people and be realistic in what they can provide. There needs to a dynamic, innovative approach to provision to influence and interest the experienced, almost embittered, sports participants and administrators. The job of enthusing them comes by providing genuine new ideas and approaches to which they can see some benefits.

Certainly, the concept of being able to use governing body or other organizational support to promote and publicize the activities of sport is openly seen as beneficial, even by the older 'blazer brigade' because they are always keen to see their sport getting the limelight (even if it is only so they can have some reflected glory themselves). They do see that everybody should be aware of and interested in their sport and, in the vast majority of cases, they warmly welcome significant amounts of publicity.

The ability of sports development officers to build local, regional and national networks of contacts and support for sport is enormously important, and is one of the key strengths of what is still a relatively small profession. Sports development officers should also lead the way in creating opportunities for all levels and abilities in sport – they must take the wider view and be interested in everyone, while some specific sporting bodies tend to be very much focused on élite performance and excellence groups.

The ability to be adaptable and flexible in approach to people and to projects is fundamental to sports development. Rigidity and pre-set notions of how everything must be done will be almost as damaging as the dreadful negativity which may come to some sports development officers as they face frustrations from their employers or their customers. This negativity and pessimism can totally overwhelm their work and influence their customers to the point of inactivity or indeed damage of existing activities.

It should always be recognized that sports development has a number of special problems and difficulties which make it a challenging profession and an area in which it is sometimes not easy to see achievement on some occasions. It must always be undertaken, though, in a proactive, positive manner.

Basically, sports development is still a new concept to many people involved in sport. The traditionalists have tended to see sport as just existing rather than needing to be promoted, developed and enhanced in any active way, but today this is necessary and this is a difficult concept for some to grasp. People's experience of sport is limited, and any desire to expand and bring innovation can sometimes be resisted.

Individuals working in sports development can really struggle if they do not receive support and direction from their superiors or their organization, as well as some sort of strategic planning support, leadership to keep them focused and time actually to achieve what is to be done. Sports development cannot be an overnight panacea; to be effective it will take time.

There is little doubt that in the whole area of sports development there is a dramatic shortage of knowledge for the practitioner, politician and senior official. There is a need for this issue to be addressed by all the UK sports councils, and indeed by the educational institutions, which should be looking to provide more courses, up to and even beyond degree level, to support this developing area of activity in the UK (and indeed other areas of the world).

To be effective as a sports development officer, individuals have to be self-motivated and controlled; they need to be able to keep focus on a direction; work with enormous commitment; relate well to all different types of people; and, while opposing it, know how to deal with bureaucracy to get things done.

In essence it would be wrong to discriminate strictly or to differentiate too heavily between sports development and sports management and administration, because sound administration and management are vital to effective sports development.

Case study 4.1: Leisure and sport strategy in Dumfries & Galloway

The following information is taken from the summary of the council's strategy (published in 2001) and gives an idea of the type of strategic document which sports development needs in order to focus its direction, purpose and action. It is vital that all such strategies fit within other organizational framework documents, such as community plans or departmental service plans. The Dumfries & Galloway strategy sets out a vision of Dumfries & Galloway as a place where individuals are:

- encouraged to be active and to take part in sport
- supported to recognize and achieve their full potential.

It further sets out a number of aims and actions under the following headings.

Health

'Our aim is to promote opportunities for all sections of the community to lead a healthy, active lifestyle through taking part in and enjoying leisure, sport and play.'

Action will include:

- Win the ILAM Healthy Leisure Award status for all Dumfries & Galloway Council-built leisure facilities.
- Work with Dumfries & Galloway Health Board on projects to address health inequalities.

Education

'Our aim is to develop sport in schools – both inside and outside the curriculum – to give young people the chance to take part at all levels from Foundation to Excellence.'

Action will include:

- Partnership working with education in order to develop the TOP Play/TOP Sport programme in Dumfries & Galloway.
- Work in partnership with education department to complete the Merrick Pool Phase 2 Leisure Development at the Douglas Ewart High School, Newton Stewart.

Partnerships

'Our aim is to develop strong partnerships with a wide range of community and national organizations to provide the highest achievable standard and range of leisure facilities.'

Facilities

'Our aim is to ensure that existing and new leisure and sport facilities are developed to make best use of sporting and recreational opportunities.'

Action will include:

- The relaunch of the Ryan centre pool.
- Developing plans for a new swimming pool and other leisure facilities in Dumfries.
- Major upgrading of the running tracks at athletic facilities in Annan (in partnership with Annandale & Eskdale Sports & Leisure Trust), Dumfries (David Keswick Athletic Centre), Sanquhar (Lorimer Park) and Stranraer (Academy Athletic Facility).

Sport-specific development

'Our aim is to make the most of opportunities which will help as many members of the local community as possible to become involved in and enjoy specific sports, and to develop their sporting potential to the highest level possible.'

Target groups

'Our aim is to promote sport opportunities for a number of target groups, encouraging them to be involved in sport and to develop active and healthy lifestyles.'

Outdoor amenities

'Our aim is to provide a network of quality parks and open space development throughout Dumfries & Galloway. These will be well-kept, safe and accessible, and will cater for the needs of the local community. They will include adequate provision for children's play, both informal and structured.'

Children's play

'Our aim is to ensure that all children have the chance to play in safe surroundings, with access to services which encourage their social, physical, intellectual and emotional development.'

Action will include:

*   Working with partner agencies and the local community to develop a play strategy for Dumfries & Galloway.

Conclusion

The summary concludes by emphasizing the 'active' nature of the document.

'The process will be a continuous one, where we will:

*   seek views
*   put policy into action
*   review how it is all working.

The leisure and sport strategy will provide the framework to make it more and more possible for people to take part in sport.'

Self-assessment question

Identify a situation where you have seen someone delivering sports development. What would be a suitable definition of sports development in this situation? Which of the sports development roles identified in this chapter did this person perform in this situation?

5 Leadership

This chapter analyses the meaning of leadership and considers various styles: the concepts of transactional ('managing the status quo') leadership and transformational ('moving individuals and organizations by carrying them beyond basic performance levels') leadership. It goes on to consider the leadership qualities needed in the sports situation. The specific leadership qualities needed for working in sports administration are noted, and the skills which need to be demonstrated are identified.

> Reason and judgement are the qualities of a leader.
>
> *Tacitus*

One of the key features of sports operations on the field of play, and also the key to successful management of sports practice off the field, is leadership. Leadership must be provided in any industry to give direction and pull everyone together towards a common goal. If planning is to be effective, someone has to take everyone along with them towards the agreed target. Someone has to do the pulling together and forward, as well as the motivation of others to keep them going towards the same goal.

This is not the place to get into a long debate over the theories of leadership. In practical management terms it is academic whether managers are born, are made or just appear as the need arises. The key point for the organization is that leadership is shown and that it is encouraged rather than squashed at any point. Again, training will be key to produce a quality of leadership and to draw it out at all the points of the organization. It is important that leadership is encouraged and is trained, where it already exists, to be better.

The style of leadership can vary from laid-back to authoritarian, depending on the organization and the situation. However, is an overly dictatorial presence is usually inappropriate in the voluntary situation, where we are trying to build a team. The leadership style has to match the requirement of any particular organizational situation, and the best approach is the one appropriate at that point in time.

One of the difficulties with many sports industry situations, especially that of the voluntary sector, is that there is a need for democratic operation, and democracy does not always produce clear policy or unity of purpose, or even the best situation for leadership potential to be demonstrated. Sports bodies must work hard to allow true leaders to come through despite any traditions or overarching democratic desires.

Heading up any organization in the twenty-first century involves leadership skill. It is quite different from the traditional style of leadership as understood in the past. Today's leaders are required to focus and inspire a leaner, more demanding workforce. The structure of organizations has become flatter and most leaders' span of control has greatly increased. Leaders have to develop followers, increase their motivation, and activate and promote positive changes in both individuals and organizations.

This can be particularly difficult in any sports situation, where many of the leaders are part-time, voluntary people. The dynamics of leadership are still very important and, while sport itself can be a great producer of leadership and leadership skills in individuals, this should not be taken for granted. Like any other skill required in the sports management and administration area, it should be trained.

A good deal of the leadership that can be achieved, and exploited, in a sports situation is down to personality and charisma. Many people involved in sport are well endowed with appropriate personality traits and are well used to getting people to follow a leader. The ability to support, cajole, motivate and inspire people is part of this process, but this inborn characteristic is crucially important where change and vision are required.

Charisma, like beauty, has been said to be in the eye of the beholder, rather than something that can be worked on. It is, to some extent, the traditional 'charmer' linked to the almost manipulative individual who can 'convince' people that the chosen direction is the right one and make them follow this charismatic lead.

In the area of sports management and administration, a great deal of effort is required to lead what is often a committed and determined band of people towards a common identifiable goal. The whole concept of leadership has been investigated by many intellectuals and put into action by many practitioners over a long period of time. The military influence in leadership is noted and scholars in the UK, such as Adair (1988), have elucidated militaristic applications of sound practice derived from theories of human behaviour.

Transactional or transformational?

One American guru of leadership has identified what he calls transactional and transformational leadership (Bass, 1990). He sees transactional leadership as based merely on 'managing the status quo – the situation as it exists and competently organizing round about that'. He has suggested in various

books that it is necessary for a good leader to go beyond the basic transactional level and move to transform individuals and organizations by
carrying them beyond basic performance levels.

Very few situations today remain static – certainly not sports organization – so it would seem that the transformational approach is the way to
approach sports administration and management.

Bass (1990) has identified four 'i's for such transformational leadership:

- intellectual stimulation
- individual consideration
- inspirational leadership
- idealized influence.

He identifies each of these as being vitally important, and it is suggested
that sport and recreation managers will benefit by putting such beliefs into
practice, and that this will help them carry out their role in what is a very
challenging atmosphere. Sport involves enthusiastic, dynamic people who
need to have some significant inspirational leadership to get the best out
of them, and this is best for the organization as well.

Sport, like other businesses, requires improved leadership so that innovation can be heightened, change managed and entrepreneurship increased
to make sporting organizations more effective. As with leaders in any
situation, training and personal development are required to ensure that
individuals can lead their organizations with creativity and into risk-taking
situations, which is necessary in order to see progress achieved in the future.

The sports fraternity sometimes believes that it has 'instant' leaders, and
that they will come to the top naturally and make all the right decisions
and take the right initiatives because of their sports participation. This is
obviously not always accurate, and support must be given to potential leaders
to produce quality in the organization's operation. The training of individuals from a sports background must be linked to sound theory and
knowledge if the organization is to progress in a time of change. The UK
at the start of the twenty-first century is a place full of change and uncertainty, and many organizations face this situation with some trepidation.
To go forward they need leaders who must be highly educated, trained and
developed individuals – in sports organizations as elsewhere. The changes
faced will not suddenly become easier but look likely to be set in a more
confused cultural and global context calling for more innovative, creative
and entrepreneurial leadership applications.

It is important that leadership, rather than supervision or control, is seen
as the job of the manager. He or she should try to lead the staff forward,
encouraging all team members to get involved and to get to a point where
they are clear about the objectives of the organization.

To use an old maxim: 'tell me and I may remember, show me and I may
see, involve me and I will understand'. This type of approach is certainly

the most effective leadership approach for sport, as for so many other situations. Staff, particularly volunteers, cannot just be ordered about and must be involved in the decision-making and in agreeing a course of action.

Leadership qualities in the sports situation

There is a great deal of debate among both practising executives and academics as to what exactly constitutes good leadership. There is, however, some agreement that some technical expertise or ability in the area in which leadership is being practised will help gain respect and get people to follow the example given. This does not mean that they need to know it all, but they must show some understanding of the work that has to be undertaken and some knowledge of what is required to work in sport. If, after all, the leader knew everything then perhaps he or she would do everything themselves.

Certainly the importance of recognizing and empathizing with the commitment required for effective operation in sports administration (so often mentioned in this book) is a crucial leadership skill. In addition, many different qualities are sought in a leader by different people. There is, however, some agreement that good leaders tend to be extrovert, enthusiastic and have an 'attractive' personality and character which is appealing to others.

In sports management and administration, the leadership qualities required are a bit like beauty – in the eye of the beholder. But here is a list of some of the qualities the author considers important:

- technical knowledge (or at least credibility)
- integrity
- honesty
- inspiration
- commitment
- enthusiasm
- 'thick skin'
- willingness to work hard
- love of sport
- administrative ability
- people skills
- sense of humour.

A leader in any situation must be aware of individual needs, task needs and group-maintenance needs if the dynamics of the individuals and groups are going to be combined successfully to get the necessary tasks completed.

This is a step beyond the basic concept of the hierarchy of individual needs espoused by Maslow (1954), which included:

- physiological – the need to eat, drink and rest
- safety – to be safe from danger and feel secure

- social – have a feeling of ease with other people in friendship and belonging
- esteem – self-respect and recognition by others
- self-actualization – a feeling of achievement and personal development.

These are all valid, but need to be set in the group and task setting to see real achievement. Leadership must not be seen as dictatorship; it is a necessity to draw everyone together to get them pulling in the same direction rather than having them working in a disjointed way or towards the wrong objective. The leader's job is to bring cohesion and involve everyone from the beginning in the big decisions to be made. To be leader does not mean making all the decisions – group decision-making is preferable and promotes group responsibility and involvement. There may be some occasions when the leader has to take the final decision or make a decision on their own, but, particularly in the sporting sphere, the involvement of others will be vital to gain their support – as it is most likely that strong personalities will be involved.

It is vital to remember that while leaders are often thought to have some innate qualities, they will also need to develop and add to these qualities. Adair (1988) has identified a number of skills which are relevant to the sports situation:

- defining the task
- having the ability to identify exactly what is required to be done
- planning – making the necessary plans for the task to be carried out
- briefing – telling everyone what their involvement is (in a shared discussion)
- controlling – monitoring through the work to ensure that everything is proceeding according to plan
- evaluating – having a realistic assessment of what is happening in the process and how close the successful completion of the task is
- motivating – keeping everyone involved, enthusiastic and committed to fulfilling the task
- organizing – ensuring that everyone is working in a planned co-ordinated way towards the end goal
- setting an example – showing a commitment and enthusiasm which will encourage others to follow and so ease the functioning of the operation towards the end goal.

One area where sport is often sadly lacking is that of establishing a training programme for its managers and administrators. It has tended to expect a high level of commitment and innate ability coming off the sports field into the organization, and so has tended to believe that sport has people with the natural leadership ability and does not need to train or support them in any significant way.

This may be a major error, since the skills required for leading a team on the park are not necessarily the same, and most certainly not **all** the same, as those needed to head up a governing body or to be a manager of a sports organization. It is important that all sports bodies seek to develop leaders and encourage personal and professional development for those individuals, whether they are involved in a voluntary or paid capacity. The growth of the Running Sport programme by the sports councils for volunteers, and vocational qualifications implementation in sports administration for paid personnel, will both have a significant impact on the development of administrators and managers in the area of sports administration.

The importance of such initiatives cannot be overemphasized, as sport must not expect people automatically to possess leadership skills; they have to be nurtured and supported.

Following from this training and effective leadership development, it is hoped that everybody involved in the organization will work better as a team and work towards the common objective. This will benefit everyone involved in terms of personal satisfaction and will also produce the results the organization is looking for.

Good leadership is the key to developing good teams, but the existence of a good leader does not automatically mean that the team will be effective. Other issues have to be considered and developed to produce a good effective team operation. These are considered in the next chapter.

Self-assessment question

Sports organizations need appropriate and effective leadership to perform in the twenty-first century. Consider some sports leaders you know (on, and more particularly off, the pitch), and suggest what made them successful. Examine too the degree to which your chosen leaders reflected the transactional or transformational model of leadership.

6 Working together

This chapter considers the various agencies involved in administering and controlling sport in the United Kingdom and argues that they need to work closely together to be effective. A clear set of shared objectives, leading to strong partnerships, which benefit everyone involved and could lead to the involvement of other agencies in support of sport, is specified.

The UK and national sport centres, national governing bodies, the Central Council of Physical Recreation, Sportscoach UK, Sports Aid Foundation, the Foundation for Sport and the Arts and the professional bodies (ILAM, ISRM, NASD and BISA) are described. The role of each is specified, along with its positioning and a short statement of its history and work in the UK sporting scene.

Partnerships and liaisons

While much sports provision in the UK, especially at grass-roots level, is by the voluntary sector, a significant amount of support is given by a number of agencies, in particular local authorities. The private sector provides a significant range of opportunities, and since the advent of compulsory competitive tendering (CCT) and Best Value the relationship between the private sector and the local authority sector has become blurred in many situations.

Much private sector provision is very limited and very specialized, focusing on activities that are specifically mass participation or have the potential to make significant returns. Examples of sports traditionally based in the private sector or which have developed under its auspices are snooker, professional football, rugby league, aerobics and fitness training. This list is not exclusive and is constantly growing as the commercial return for previously smaller sports increases, due to the potential for further publicity and television coverage caused by the vast growth in the media coverage – especially satellite and cable television.

The key issue about sports provision is not who provides it, but the increasing necessity for liaison between all parties due to the limited resources available, or, in the case of the private sector, the need to target customers and focus on efficient practice. There is a great deal of talk at present of networking partnership and liaison mechanisms – all of these are vitally important to successful projects run by any aspect of the industry. There needs to be a clear demarcation within these partnerships of who is doing what for whom, and what costs, in terms of time and finance, are attached to each partner in such an arrangement. Glib talk of networks and partnerships is all very well, but there need to be clear guidelines and specific means of operating within any such partnerships and networks if they are to be effective.

Some of the guiding principles required to make partnerships work are:

- clear project objectives
- shared desire and commitment to achieve these objectives
- honesty and trust
- clearly allocated work roles
- strong interpersonal relationships
- dedicated hard work and effort.

The future of sport is founded in partnerships between various agencies within and across industry sectors. It is beneficial to voluntary clubs to link into possible public sector (e.g. health authority) or private sector (e.g. bingo club) initiatives in order to benefit their sporting activities.

As funding becomes more difficult and yet more and more essential for successful sport at all levels, partnerships will become more and more crucial, and every opportunity to establish them must be pursued. Potentially there can be partners in many initiatives from unlikely sources, and viewing sport in its widest community-benefit sense can often assist. The more traditional view of sport as an élite performance activity is limiting and inappropriate.

The implied public health benefits of sport will suit certain people, including the media, local health boards and the social services. They would be much more interested in becoming involved and forming a partnership than they would where success for one or two individuals was the aim.

The agencies that might want to become involved include:

- enterprise companies/councils
- tourist boards
- private companies
- health boards
- local authorities
- voluntary clubs
- national governing bodies
- educational institutes.

Partnerships can bring together different organizations with their own aims to achieve agreed common goals. Through partnership everyone involved can be a winner.

Increasingly networks – previously colloquially known as the jungle telegraph – have a role to play in sports administration. Primarily these are just about keeping in touch and learning from others active in the field of sports administration and management. This can be informal – through a telephone conversation or a chance meeting – or promoted formally at conferences or training seminars. Often these are encouraged or established by a national or regional sports council.

Agencies involved in sport in the UK

The sports councils

The sports councils for the four home countries and the newly formed UK Sports Council (branded as UK Sport) are the key national government agencies for implementing sports policy and spending government money on sport in the UK.

The idea behind forming the UK Sports Council is to have a co-ordinated approach to certain overarching concerns such as international policy, doping control, strategic development and education of coaches and others.

The individual sports councils have overall responsibility for the development and promotion of sports within their area and increasing public awareness of sport, focusing on increasing participation levels and raising standards; in addition to providing facilities and increased opportunities for people at all levels of sport.

These councils have a sizeable influence on the activities, while it must be recognized that some other agencies have a more direct input to sport – actually delivering sport on the playing field or in the gymnasium. The national sports council's role is largely that of an enabler, facilitator, funder, supporter and promoter of sport; only in recent years have the individual sports councils started to make more direct provision of support for individuals who actually deliver sport through coaching individuals. Such initiatives as Active Sports and Team Sport Scotland have been successful in encouraging increased participation at a variety of levels.

The home country sports council's job is to implement the policies adopted by the government in its country – it is charged with developing specific plans to meet general government policy. It has, however, the potentially conflicting roles of representing the views and feelings of sport to the government and representing the view of government to sport. It also has control over the distribution of central funds, which in itself is a major task that can cause some potentially difficult relationships with governing bodies of sport and other agencies to be funded through such grants.

The role of the sports councils in the UK is to adopt strategic plans and policies for the coherent and cohesive development of sport in the whole country, working with whatever other agency is appropriate in specific situations and projects. Many initiatives of the various national sports councils are implemented in partnership with local authorities and can develop in many different ways depending on the specific facilities, personnel and resources available.

The Department of Culture, Media and Sport, including the Minister of Sport, decides on policy in the UK setting and in England, and takes decisions on how monies will be directed through the appropriate sports council. At the time of writing there is an definite indication that government policy will move away from a focus on élite sports development towards mass participation – as if they were mutually exclusive! The long slow climb to excellence may be halted, although gradually enlightened people, including politicians, are beginning to see that there is no real conflict between excellence and participation, one very much encouraging and developing the other.

However, it is always worth remembering that sports councils, officials and members are appointed by and directly funded by the government; they act as the government's principal advisers on sporting matters and work with the government in implementing its sports policies. The national sports councils give substantial support for the development of facilities, as well as the development of sporting initiatives.

It is worth remembering that other public bodies such as the Countryside Commission and the Forestry Authority also have roles to play in ensuring that there are suitable recreational amenities and facilities under their jurisdiction, as indeed in some cases have river and inland water control authorities. The tentacles of central government can stretch quite far into the heart of sports provision and will be able to exert influence through a number of organizations as well as the sports councils.

Basically, the home country sports councils exist to:

- promote the general understanding of the social importance and value of sport and physical recreation
- increase the provision of new facilities and stimulate fuller use of existing facilities
- encourage wider participation in sport and physical recreation as a means of enjoying leisure
- raise the standards of performance.

Their role in allocating funds is significant, as is the amount of monies now being made available to governing bodies, especially with the addition of lottery funding for projects and individual athletes. Several UK governing bodies now receive over £1 million per annum, and even at the lower level significant amounts of money can be dispersed by national sports councils.

These national agencies (Quangos – quasi-autonomous non-governmental organizations) are immensely powerful in terms of sports delivery, and their actions and policies have a considerable influence in UK sports development.

National governing bodies

Perhaps the key organizations involved in the provision of sport in the UK are the national governing bodies (NGBs). These are the autonomous gathering together of the various sports clubs, individuals and organizations in specific sports. They represent the sports people with an interest in a particular sport and are the main agency that represents the views of those sports participants. Governing bodies vary widely in nature and enormously in size, from small ones such as lacrosse or fencing to huge ones such as swimming, gymnastics or football.

Ultimately, regardless of all other agencies, these NGBs as amalgamations of sports participants are the key agencies in the co-ordination and provision of sport in the UK. They do not always possess large amounts of money and may sometimes be lacking in direction, but they are the voice of each particular sport. As such, they are consulted by other relevant partners such as the Foundation of Sports and the Arts, the various sports councils and local authorities.

Their role is enormously important – indeed it can be argued that without such an association representing the interests of any particular sport, the future existence of that sport may be jeopardized. This can be supported from the point of view of the body's role in the determination of rules and disciplinary procedures, or the interpretation of international rulings, or the co-ordination of international activities.

In essence NGBs are made up of the individual participants (at whatever level of activity), officials and administrators, most of whom will also have a role in a local club or association, sometimes in a district or regional association as well as the national body. The officials of governing bodies are almost always voluntary and are under tremendous pressure, with work coming from a wide variety of sources, while being subject to the pressures of any democratic organization which has political (with a small 'p') moves and issues to resolve on an ongoing basis.

Most governing bodies of any size in the UK will also have a number of paid staff – including administrators, chief executives and clerical staff, as well as technical staff, national coaches and development officers. Only the latter staff will necessarily have deep technical knowledge about the performance and the rules and regulations of the sport. For the former, it is more important that they have the ability to organize on a businesslike and professional basis.

National governing bodies of sport may be seen as autonomous gatherings of sports clubs and/or associations or individuals joining together to promote and represent a particular sport. While these bodies vary significantly, e.g. from a large wealthy organization such as the Football Association to a relatively small and resource-short organization such as the Lacrosse Association, a number of distinct similarities and characteristics can be identified.

They are **grant-aided** – at least most receive money through the relevant sports council to support their activities. Only the larger, more affluent ones, e.g football and rugby union, do not receive a substantial portion of their running costs.

They are **autonomous** – ultimately they are self-controlling and, while the sports council may fund them, and others may have views on what they should do, ultimately they decide internally for themselves.

They are **voluntary** – most governing bodies of sport run largely on the basis of voluntary support in terms of staffing and assisting with organizational duties at events and promotions or even on a routine basis. A number now have significant numbers of staff on a paid full-time basis, but even they rely significantly on voluntary help from officials and administrators.

Pressure group/lobby – one key role for any governing body is to operate as the public voice, speaking for that sport and requesting, from all appropriate sources, support for and interest in that sport and its participants.

Financed by members – while support will be drawn from a wide variety of areas and commercial activities may be sizeable, the vast majority of governing bodies rely substantially on member contributions to ensure they have money available in order to function in their various roles.

Amateur (amateur in this sense means unpaid and spare-time – it should not be construed as 'amateurish'!) – most governing bodies rely on committees, structures and functions undertaken by people in their spare time away from their normal form of employment. While, as mentioned above, many have employees, most are heavily dependent on this spare-time commitment.

Strong public sector links – at both local and national level governing bodies of sport rely substantially on their links with public sector bodies such as their local and national sports councils, and on sports development officers and others from these organizations to assist with projects and events.

Club members – most governing bodies have individual membership but many, in addition, have club members, and some even have regional or district associations in membership. The club structure is a key part of most governing bodies, as it is for sport in the UK.

Individual members – ultimately many of the payments and much of the activity in support come from the individual members of governing bodies, whether through clubs, regional associations, or just by direct individual membership. The support of a mass of these members will be necessary for any successful governing body project.

Sport council links – whatever the location of the national governing body, it will have to link with the Sports Council or one of the home countries' sports councils. This relationship is vital in terms of governing bodies relating the patterns of national development laid down by government through the sports councils and then working with sports council officials and programmes to achieve the aims of any such initiatives.

Democratic – in most cases governing bodies are truly democratic in allowing one member one vote on major constitutional issues, and ultimately in sanctioning development planning or direction changes. However, it is all too common for governing bodies to be dominated by limited 'cliques' which represent the views of only a small number of people. This may be because such a small group is influential, because they do all the work, or because there is apathy on the part of others. The principle of democracy certainly normally pertains and facing the annual general meeting is often the biggest problem of such dominant small groups.

Committees – Like many voluntary organizations, governing bodies tend to be dominated by committees and committee structures. This is often a very slow and inefficient way of making decisions, but allows for the democratic process to be implemented.

The types of roles or duties that a governing body may undertake include:

- administration of the sport
- marketing award schemes
- staffing
- servicing committees
- producing publications
- various membership services
- producing teaching aids
- organizing a coach education scheme
- developing new initiatives
- providing publicity
- representation at national and local level
- international representation
- providing a drug-control programme
- event organization and management
- providing and educating officials
- framing, altering and applying the rules of the sport
- administering disciplinary procedures
- organizing national squads or teams.

Increasingly, as society and sport change, national governing bodies of sport have a wide range of new challenges and future duties. These include:

- the preparing, delivering and monitoring of a corporate strategy
- attracting more people into the sport, in the face of growing competition from home-based leisure activities and even other sports
- developing more effective partnership networks
- improving media relationships and the image of the sport
- sourcing and servicing sponsorship arrangements and other commercial partnerships on an ongoing basis
- enhancing self-reliance, particularly through training of administrators, officials and coaches
- pressurizing policy-makers to support sport in general as well as a particular sport.

Whatever the future brings, it seems likely that the role of the governing bodies of sport will continue to grow, and if they are proactive and organized then they will flourish. The future is a land of opportunities, and for those organizations properly prepared to meet them some progress and benefit will accrue. Certainly sporting bodies at all levels will have to get their form of planning right – they will have to be professional about their strategic planning to meet the challenges of tomorrow. Reviewing existing processes, focusing on direction and deciding on the methods of achievement are key issues for any governing body.

Such a plan can vary in its requirements, but for most governing bodies it will probably involve the following steps to a greater or lesser degree.

1 A current situation audit assessing the present situation for the organization and the items which directly affect it – what is happening within and outside the governing body itself which impacts on its current and future operation. Such issues as the number of members, facilities available, government policies, national sports council policies, available finance, technological development, internal and external demands and needs will need to be considered.
2 Devising a corporate strategy – arising from an accurate professional assessment of the current situation, steps forward can be identified by bodies to see where they move to in the future. Key to this will be the identification of a mission statement – an overall reason for existing now and in the future.

Following on from this mission, a number of specific objectives can be identified – they will need to be:

- specific
- measurable
- agreed
- realistic
- timed.

They will be structural or individual in nature.

Arising out of these objectives a number of specific targets will need to be identified along with who is going to achieve them, how and when. The list of considerations for governing bodies will be long, but will include:

- finance
- target groups
- marketing
- coach education
- government policy
- staffing

- sponsorship
- event organization
- media liaison
- external relations
- competition
- facilities
- local authority relationships
- national sports council relationships
- sports competition programme
- society and demographic changes
- the role of volunteers and professionals
- performance indicators
- interim review stages.

These are just some of the topics that will be vital to producing a corporate plan which is useful and appropriate. As ever, sport should study the procedures developed in other industries and where appropriate apply them to the sports business – even if it is largely voluntary.

Central Council of Physical Recreation (CCPR)

The CCPR is an independent voluntary body made up of around 240 governing bodies of sport and other representatives in the area of physical recreation (largely in England and Wales). It aims to represent these governing bodies in a variety of forums and support their work. A key role is representing their views to the sports councils (particularly UK Sport and Sport England) and other public bodies in the field.

It is widely regarded in government circles as a strong, independent voice for sport and is consulted by government and others, including the media, when seeking a view of the voluntary sector. Additionally, the services offered by the CCPR, which include annual conferences, sports sponsorship advice and community sports leader award provision, are valued by a number of governing bodies and other agencies involved in the field of sport and recreation.

There is, however, some doubt as to how representative the CCPR is. Certainly in Scotland, for example, it is not considered the representative organization for governing bodies in sport – that place north of the border is taken by the Scottish Sports Association, which provides, on a smaller scale, similar services to the CCPR and speaks as the voice of Scottish sport on behalf of the governing bodies.

National Playing Fields Association (NPFA)

This is a major charitable organization whose voice is heard principally in the area of providing playing fields and playing space for people of all ages

– in particular children and young people. It is keen to support all playing activities which take place on outdoor playing areas, has a role in supporting activity in the general sense, as well as games in the more formal sense such as rugby, hockey and football.

One of the main battles it is currently fighting is to avoid the selling-off of playing fields by schools and local authorities in pursuit of the sizeable amounts of cash available for land for housing and retail developments. The growth of the grant-maintained sector and developed school management through government policy are also seen as possible threats to the playing fields in schools, which form a large sector of sports facilities in the UK.

The NPFA also offers some financial support to organizations in the form of grant aid to protect or improve playing field provision.

Sportscoach UK

Formerly known as the National Coaching Foundation, this is the major provider of centralized core coach education in the UK. It was formed in 1983 with support from a variety of agencies including the Sports Council, British Olympic Association and British Association of National Coaches.

In 1987 it was designated the coaching arm of the Sports Council, responsible for the co-ordination of coaching and coach education. It now works on the UK remit and in partnership with the four national sports councils. It encourages governing bodies to look at their coach education plans, provides core knowledge relevant to all governing bodies and coaches in all sports, and runs courses and seminars as part of an education programme operating throughout the country focused on a series of national coaching centres in various parts of the UK. It also produces coaching publications, magazines, and provides support and up-to-date information on developments in coaching in the UK and beyond.

Sportscoach UK has also been very active in the development of vocational qualifications in coach education and has pushed ahead, with support funding from the sports councils, to encourage governing bodies to update their awards in line with vocational qualification standards.

This impetus has been significant and has seen a rewriting of new coach education standards in many governing bodies over recent years.

Sports Aid Foundation (SAF)

The Sports Aid Foundation is an independent organization managed by a board of governors who award grants to amateurs for expenses incurred in preparation and training for top-level sports participation. Such awards are given with the consent, approval and support of the appropriate governing body of sport.

The SAF has a Scottish branch and a number of regional branches throughout the UK, which allocate monies in support of this programme.

It is a charitable enterprise and money is raised through a variety of fundraising efforts including dinners, sponsored events and donations from major commercial firms.

This area of individual support for top-level sports people is of increasing importance since the costs facing such talented individuals grow all the time, and even the National Lottery will not produce all the finance required.

Foundation for Sport and the Arts (FSA)

The Foundation for Sport and the Arts was founded by the football pools companies with the agreement of the government in order to set aside some of the income from the pools to direct into a variety of sports.

In recent years it has given away over £5 million to facilities and other projects to help with the development of sport. In addition, it has given substantial grants to the SAF in order to assist in its grants-support programme for top-level sports people.

The money given by the foundation has greatly increased the money available to sport in Britain, and perhaps emphasizes the rather miserly amount given from official public funding directly by the government.

Professional bodies

There are a number of professional bodies involved in sport in the UK, as well as a number which represent specific interest groups.

The British Institute of Sports Coaches

This institute (formerly the National Association of Sports Coaches) is a body set up to represent coaches. It has very close links with Spors Coach UK.

Institute of Leisure and Amenity Management (ILAM)

The Institute was formed in 1983 as a result of an amalgamation between various bodies operating in the sport, leisure and recreation fields. Its membership is over 7,000 and is drawn from all aspects of the leisure field.

While ILAM represents the wider view of the leisure profession, the sports influence within it is considerable. There is an active sports service, in addition to a panel which looks at contracting issues across the wide field of leisure, including sport provision.

In essence ILAM's purpose is to represent and support the leisure professional in all aspects and to provide a lobbying voice for the needs of the profession and the whole sphere of leisure, including sport. The Institute also has a role in identifying educational and training needs and providing appropriate qualifications and courses to answer these specific requirements.

In addition, the Institute offers advice on careers and leisure policy locally and nationally, while working in partnership with a wide variety of other agencies to ensure that the sport and leisure profession is recognized and listened to.

Organizations such as the CCPR and the Sports Council wishing to ascertain the views of the profession will contact ILAM and also, where appropriate, the ISRM (see below).

The work and strength of ILAM has grown significantly over recent years as the profession has increased in size. The role of sport and sports development within the leisure profession has also grown, and it seems likely that this trend will continue with the presence of the National Lottery, the continuation (if on a smaller scale) of the Foundation for Sport and the Arts, and rather grudging and slow governmental recognition of the importance of sport. All of these developments mean there will be a continued place for and growth in terms of the leisure and sports professional working through organizations such as ILAM.

The Institute of Sport and Recreation Management (ISRM)

Formerly known as the Institute of Baths and Recreation Management, the name was changed in 1993 in order to recognize the overall role this organization has in sport and recreation, not just in swimming pool management.

The focus is still very much on the technical issues and mechanical level course provision, but the ISRM's influence grows even though it tends to operate more at the operational than the managerial level – more with supervisors than directors of leisure. This pattern was historical – it arose from the older style of technical knowledge ('pool plant') bath managers who are now being overtaken by more managerial and less technical operators, as swimming pools become more sophisticated.

British Institute of Sports Administration (BISA)

BISA was formed in December 1993 in succession to the British Association of National Sports Administrators (BANSA), which was founded in 1977 by full-time administrators in national governing bodies of sport. They saw the need to set up an organization to enable them to meet regularly, exchange information and expertise, and generate a corporate viewpoint on behalf of professional sports administrators. The formation of an institute has widened the objectives and membership to encompass the needs and wants of both professional and honorary sports administrators from the full range of backgrounds and organizations, including national governing bodies, national and regional sports organizations, and sports clubs and associations.

BISA has established itself as a responsible body which recognizes that sports administration is a very specialized and demanding profession. By organizing conferences, seminars and in-service training, BISA assists sports administrators to attain the very high standards required for British sport to flourish at all levels. BISA gives sports administrators a chance to share solutions to common problems and to use their combined experience for the overall benefit of British sport.

Although other forums exist which give opportunities for sports administrators to meet, these invariably involve the administrators attending as representatives of their governing body or sporting organization. Only through BISA do these administrators get the opportunity to attend in their own right, to represent themselves, and gain from each other the skills that are of particular relevance to their work.

Membership of BISA is open to all administrators of sport and recreation, and currently includes people working for a wide variety of sporting organizations. BISA members include senior professional officers of national governing bodies, senior honorary administrators of national sports organizations, and members of staff of national, regional and local sports organizations and clubs.

BISA has adopted a higher profile recently, so as to play a leading role on behalf of sports administrators at all levels. It is expanding its services in a number of essential areas of work, and intends to:

- seek to increase its membership
- continue to play a full part in the development and promotion of the Running Sport training programme for all professional and voluntary sports administrators, at both national and local level, so as to improve the overall quality of sports administration
- continue to organize in-service training workshops for professional and leading voluntary sports administrators and provide the specialist high-level training part of the Running Sport programme for senior sports administrators
- continue to provide a forum for discussion of matters of mutual interest to sports administrators, including an annual conference focusing on matters of national significance in the field of sports administration
- perform the role of a professional institute and represent the views and needs of sports administrators on appropriate bodies, including the SPRITO National Council and Education and Training Committee
- provide an advisory service for sports administrators (professional and voluntary) on matters of personal interest and concern, including personal employment issues
- promote the category of associate membership for voluntary sports administrators working at regional and local level
- consider operating as an assessment centre of S/NVQs in sports administration
- continue to draw on the knowledge, experience and expertise of the membership to benefit British sport at all levels

- provide information to members regarding employment possibilities in sports administration
- seek recognition by appropriate bodies as the consultative body to represent the interests of sports administrators
- improve the status and recognition of the profession of sports administration by awarding honorary fellowships and granting fellowships and memberships on application, based on the known and proven knowledge and experience of candidates and by providing the quality control and regulation of standards for these awards
- establish courses leading to academic qualifications in sports administration, in co-operation with suitable educational institutions.

The National Association of Sports Development (NASD)

Formed only in 1998, this organization has begun to grow in importance due to its very specific nature and its direct communication channel to government. It has formed a strategic partnership with ISRM to try to service its members. It has, for many years (even before being formalized), held a two-day conference in Nottingham each year.

Self-assessment question

In your sporting situation, identify some of the key players in sports delivery and administration (from those noted in this chapter). Suggest some of the ways in which they have worked together and how this partnership approach has benefited sport more than a single-agency approach might have.

7 People

This chapter looks at a wide range of people management issues and applies them to the sports situation. It starts with the assertion that people are the most important asset of any organization and need to be nurtured and developed. It considers a range of relevant issues including performance appraisal, managing people (including motivation), the skills and qualities of a manager, staff appraisal and motivation, delegation, communication, recruitment, team building (including achieving unity of purpose), team development and personnel management. All these concepts are discussed in the context of the sports industry and examined as they apply to practical administration situations.

As mentioned earlier, change and challenge face everyone employed or occupied in the sports industry, in whatever sector. In facing change the personnel and their response to challenge will be the key factor.

The Audit Commission (1988) has stated that: 'the single most powerful reason why some organizations are consistently more successful than others is that their employees are better trained and more highly motivated than those of their competitors. They must feel that their contribution is valued by the organization in which they work.'

Performance appraisal

Effective managers within any situation, especially one in which a tremendous commitment is required, should spend considerable time on developing their staff, recognizing their needs (both personal and in terms of job skill requirements), and do everything possible to support and train them to improve performance.

The process of review in itself will lead to increased performance and, in turn, can improve staff morale. Through such appreciation, staff will feel that they are being taken seriously and that people are endeavouring to assess their training needs.

The attempt to produce motivated and trained staff implies that a number of steps are taken by managers at senior level and implemented at a lower level, by middle management and supervisory staff.

A performance review system can be seen as threatening, but rather should be seen as supportive – the aim is to examine an individual's progress in a particular post, assessing achievements or failures, strengths or weaknesses. It is not a job-threatening but rather a job-strengthening intent.

This performance review can take place in many situations and in a variety of ways, but, whatever the mechanism, it should be carried out by the direct line manager. Both should be clear of the details of the process and what it is aiming to achieve. Staff appraisal would certainly be a part of any performance review system. It would include a review of the individual's past performance in the post, over a pre-set period (e.g. a year, six months, or three months), and would judge performance against previously identified objectives that both staff and employer would hope to have achieved within the post.

Such a direct appraisal system is often wrongly seen as a potentially threatening or disciplinary situation, possibly even a conflict situation. This incorrect impression often grows because neither the person appraising nor the appraisee is trained or briefed as to how to handle the situation and what to expect. Staff appraisal sessions should:

1 be set in the context of the aims of the organization overall
2 be limited to the specific job role and feelings of both parties
3 be undertaken by people who clearly understand the purpose of the appraisal sessions
4 emphasize the positive rather than the negative and look to the future rather than the past
5 identify achievement of past objectives and set future ones for a specific person in the post
6 be a two-way process so that there is some feedback from the person being appraised to their immediate line manager
7 leave both parties feeling they are part of a team operation and working towards the same ends
8 result in a confidential written record of the meeting, agreed by both parties, which should be retained by both as well as kept on file for future reference.

The appraisal system is intended to lead to more positive performance and beneficial team moulding. Any attempt by either party to focus on confrontation should be resisted, and the positive possibilities must be emphasized.

Managing people

In the sport setting the coach or team captain must be able to manage people if effective results are to be achieved. This is equally true of the manager or administrator within the sports industry.

To achieve improved human performance it is necessary to create, initiate, maintain or coach individual and/or group motivation. The 'desire to perform', either as an individual or as a group, is key to performance. Managers must know where all the employees, workers, volunteers are coming from, and they must know where they are all meant to be going. They must recognize individual and team goals and help everyone to play their part in them. Individual goals may not always be exactly in tune with the organization, and that is another task managers must undertake – to try to get them both to head in the same direction.

The original thinker on motivation was Abraham Maslow. In the late 1930s he identified the levels of need shown in Figure 7.1. This is the

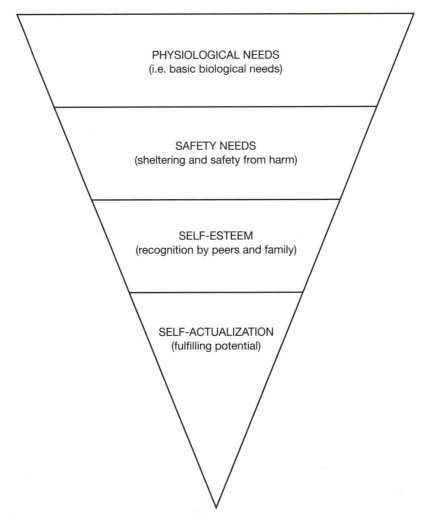

Figure 7.1 Maslow's hierarchy of needs

classic structure of Maslow's hierarchy of needs: human wants must be recognized at all these levels and individuals' desires must be realized (Maslow, 1954). Not everyone will get to self-actualization, but it is something that many strive for, especially in the field of management and, indeed, that of sports performance.

There are many other theories of motivation; for example:

- McClelland (1985) who talks about achievement, affiliation and power
- Herzberg *et al.* (1993) talk of maintenance factors and motivational factors, their thinking being that people must be maintained in a relatively cosy environment in terms of safety, security and status, while they would be developed through achievement, recognition and advancement.

Such theories are merely a context into which to set identification of what individuals are striving for. If this can be achieved, then more effective organization will be produced. Managers must understand that individuals look for fair treatment and equal opportunities to advance; they must recognize that money is not necessarily a key motivator. It may be an incentive, but is not the crucial motivation that many people are driven by – self-esteem and recognition are as important as finance.

It is important to recognize that individuals working in various sectors of the industry may be motivated in different ways; for example, the motivation of someone working in public sports provision may be different from someone working in a governing body or in a private snooker club.

What makes a manager?

A group of staff working in the sport and leisure business were asked what they identify as important for their manager. The results are interesting, and produce a worthwhile checklist for managers to gauge themselves against.

A random list of items identified by staff as what they would want to see in their manager includes a range of skills and personal qualities such as:

- being organized
- always getting results
- patient
- approachable
- decisive
- interested
- enthusiastic
- assertive
- communicative

- listens and acts
- firm but fair
- punctual
- confident
- good motivator.

While this list is not, and probably could never be, comprehensive in all sport situations, it is a useful checklist and managers should consider whether they are able to match up to what staff are looking for.

Characteristics that staff would not like to see in their manager included:

- self-centred
- moody
- gossiping
- dictatorial
- intimidating
- not understanding
- looks down on people
- poor attention to detail
- lack of feedback
- shy and nervous
- fixed views
- fails to value staff.

This is another interesting list for managers to try to make a honest assessment of themselves against. These lists are just indicative, but might well be something that managers would consider in a quiet moment – how do they really measure up to what practising staff identify as the positive and negative aspects of their job performance?

Staff appraisal

Oh wad some Pow'r the giftie gie us/To see oursels as others see us!
Robert Burns

Part of any good staff management and development programme is an individualized appraisal system, either with the line manager or 360° (with subordinates, colleagues and superiors). There should be an opportunity for staff reviews and appraisals on a regular basis through direct contact of each staff member – whether voluntary or paid – with their relevant superiors to review their input into the organization and its functioning. The review is a two-way process where staff are encouraged to comment on the functioning of the organization and even their immediate superior's performance, as well as reviewing their own personal performance within the organization.

Such an individualized appraisal process should be seen as supportive and beneficial, not threatening. If properly undertaken it should see people building on strengths and moving forward into the future, not being threatened over poor performance – such situations, should they arise, need to be dealt with through disciplinary procedures and should not be the basis for a staff appraisal interview.

If properly handled, staff appraisal will produce staff who are clear about their duty and the perceived perception of their performance and are well motivated to undertake their role because they feel their opinion is valued. If it is handled badly it can have the opposite effect, which can be detrimental to an organization. It is vital that all staff who undertake appraisal interviews should be trained in how to approach the whole issue in a positive manner. It is equally important that all staff understand that appraisal is a positive approach, and that this message is loudly and clearly communicated to everyone involved.

There is also an issue of organizational appraisal – a measure of the effectiveness of the organization overall, as well as specific projects, but this is a distinctly different issue from that of individualized appraisal, which can also be used to form the basis of an individualized training needs analysis and progressive personal development.

Staff motivation

Motivation may be defined as:

> getting people to want what we want, while manipulation is getting people to do what we want
>
> *Anon*

People in sport are very highly motivated – from performer through to the Chairman of the British Olympic Association. People are motivated by many different factors to take part in sports administration, and these can include status, recognition, personal achievement, personal interest and even, to a very limited extent, financial gain. It is possible, however, as in many other work situations, to demotivate people and not be aware that we are doing so.

Certainly it is important to ensure that some careful guidelines are followed in order to keep people involved and interested so that they are not lost to sport, particularly scarce volunteer staff. People are much more likely to remain involved if they have:

- a clear sense of the purpose of the organization
- a clear sense of their role in the body
- the ability to manage their own input
- a set of predetermined guidelines

- a degree of authority, power and responsibility
- the opportunity to be challenged and to measure themselves against high standards.

It is important that the organization shows that it favours shared responsibility and co-operative working, ensuring that the power is jointly held so that everyone feels involved in achieving success for the organization. This is established through getting everybody working as a team member and co-ordinating the efforts of all and focusing them on established and agreed objectives.

In terms of personal skills, any leader who is making any effort to motivate people must be careful to:

- be an active listener
- thank and compliment
- provide rewards where possible
- look for positive achievement

It is important to take account of what people say and give thoughtful, considered answers rather than rash, rushed responses which can be demotivating. It is equally important to be aware of what individuals want in return for their input and to give them enough responsibility and authority to make the post challenging and interesting, with a feeling that they are doing a worthwhile job.

It is now realized that in order to obtain better performance, workers need to be motivated by more than fear or economic reward. The concern for quality consciousness, together with a greater market orientation, may be seen as the dominant concern for the private sector management in Britain since the 1980s. But the problem of motivation and commitment which it addresses is not new.

It has been clearly identified that people will be happier in their work, and their commitment and effort will be increased, if they:

- obtain a sense of achievement from what they are doing
- have some responsibility for what they are doing
- are recognized for their efforts and abilities
- have a feeling of personal and career development
- face some type of challenge
- perceive their work as interesting or worthwhile.

Equally, people can be put off their job role and find work frustrating, less enjoyable and their motivation diminished due to factors such as:

- overly bureaucratic structure
- difficult superiors

- poor physical surroundings
- low wages and salaries
- uncooperative colleagues
- perceived incompetence of superiors and/or colleagues
- their views not being listened to
- lack of direction
- dictatorial management
- lack of involvement in the decision-making process
- not knowing what the organization's aims are
- being excluded by personal cliques
- being overwhelmed by work
- not being respected as part of the business.

An important issue in considering management and motivation of sports organizations is the degree to which voluntarism plays a part, and volunteers' ability as individuals to express their **own** views and play their **own** part. They are not compelled to do anything, even within the management structure, but do it on a voluntary basis and have the ultimate control over whether they contribute. This is a key aspect of the voluntary participation of individuals and groups in sports administration. It is a significant difference between sport and business organizations and must always be recognized. It is not necessarily a weakness, and tends to lead to high degrees of motivation of the individual within a sporting structure – there is no control or compulsion, but there is enthusiasm.

For the sports person the desire to excel – to achieve their personal best and attain the highest standards of performance – is what drives them forward. This aim for achievement and personal and societal recognition is no bad thing: as an example, it can be copied by a quality administrator in the sports field, driving with the same ambition to be the best they can be in their role of supporting this dedicated sports person. They do not have to be high-level sports people themselves, but their motivation should be to be the best administrator they can.

It is very beneficial for the administrator constantly to remember where they are coming from and what they are there to do – to provide sporting opportunity so that everyone who wishes to can perform to the best of their abilities. This common bond of purpose, motivation and standards with the performers and all the participants is the ideal partnership all round.

For the sports performer it is quite likely that their sport will be the number-one thing in their life, and for many administrators it is the same. This is perhaps why people who go into sports administration for the payment, rather than the environment, often flounder: because their commitment falls short of that of the performer. It is fairly obvious that the more committed athletes are the more successful; this is generally the case for the sports organizer as well.

Delegation

Delegation is often done badly or not at all, because human beings have a tendency to believe that they can do things better themselves and it is simpler to do them that way rather than involve other people. This really is short-term thinking, and although in the short term things may be done better, eventually the system will break down. This is a recipe not for success but for frustration, both personal and organizational.

Delegating tasks means that the individuals who are receiving the tasks to perform require specific training. There will initially be a need for additional planning to ensure that there is a report-back system as well as clear parameters as to what has to be delegated. In the first instance delegation will take longer and tasks must be monitored on a regular basis, but in the longer term delegation will enormously aid organizational efficiency. Basically, delegation requires a clear statement of what has been delegated and why, and how the supervisory or report-back relationship will continue.

It is also important to make more time available for key personnel by allowing others to take on tasks. This will help the others' personal development and sense of achievement: given some sort of responsibility, most people are much more highly motivated. Particularly in the voluntary sports situation, if you can get 1 per cent out of 100 people it is going to create a great deal more than trying to get 100% out of one person. Delegation encourages people to feel responsible and be part of the organization or team, and will enhance their job satisfaction and enthusiasm for the tasks they are required to perform. Sport has a strong history of enthusiasm, commitment and dedication, but this commitment can only be effective if a strong organizational structure is established and tasks are performed at the appropriate level. Teamwork will be important, but this is often a clear and happy relationship for sports people. The clear identification of working roles, tasks and structures to be used helps achieve effective and efficient organization. Governing bodies of sport can lose effectiveness through unclear or dated organizational structures and poor delegation – an old belief 'that everything is done better by myself'.

Delegation, if it fails, very often does so because the delegator does not have faith in the individual they are giving the work to and gives them the wrong tasks for the wrong reasons. It is important to delegate tasks for the right reasons and to the right person. It must be clear that they have the right skills (or at least are going to be trained in the right skills) and are given the necessary knowledge and confidence to undertake the tasks set.

A lack of clarity, direction and leadership leads to poor organization and in turn a lack of effective and efficient operation. If any of these problems are apparent then the sport and its participants will be damaged. As in any other business, good planning and thought combined with appropriate monitoring and leadership will ensure maximum achievement.

Communication

Communication may be defined as 'The giving, receiving or exchanging of information so that the material communicated is clearly understood by everyone concerned'. As far as organizations and managers are concerned, communication must be clear, frequent and involve everyone necessary. If the organization is to function smoothly then there must be clear lines of communication, in various forms, and everyone must know what these lines of communication are.

Today we have the most advanced communications technology ever seen, and this brings about possibilities and potential benefits to many situations, not least the management of sport in all its forms. The massive growth of electronic communications, including the electronic mail system, fax machines, mobile phones and computer communication, still must be set alongside the traditional (and essential) verbal and non-verbal communication which takes place between human beings for progress to be achieved harmoniously. In addition, in a sporting situation where we are trying to get in touch with our clients and potential customers, written and visual communication can be important.

If communication is to be effective then it must be:

* clear
* concise
* courteous
* correct
* complete
* correctly directed.

Any blockage in the lines of communication will cause unnecessary delays in getting things achieved and will significantly damage customer relations, which for everyone involved must be the number-one priority.

It should be emphasized that within many sports management and administration settings communication may be quite a complex process; it will not go solely from A to B, but may go from A to B to C, directly back to A and shoot off to D, at something of a tangent. This is caused by the informal 'jungle telegraph' which exists in so many places within sport. Many people know others well because of the variety of contexts, different subject meetings, playing abilities, past contacts and informal networks, all of which are major factors in the industry.

Communication can be vertical, horizontal, diagonal or, as mentioned above, it might be quite complex – almost like a spider's web or jigsaw network. In many cases this can be a benefit as long as managers are aware of the potential problems and/or benefits that exist in such an informal system and which, at times, may seem to work behind their back.

Getting the right people

In sports administration, as in all other aspects of industry, it is important to get the right people in the right post. All too often in the past in voluntary sports organizations, for example, the treasurer has been an automatic appointment because they have been a local accountant or the secretary has been the least unwilling of the assembled AGM members, and the committee has been elected by those who were too slow to take their hands down from a previous vote. This sort of *ad hoc* appointment needs to be discouraged if progress is to be made in the planning and development of sport at club, local and national level.

The future must lie in recruiting, through appropriate processes, the best people available for such posts, then training, appraising and supporting them through the process – as would be the approach in any other dynamic, progressive work situation.

Adopting such an approach means that a job remit needs to be drawn up for every post, which should be drafted into an advertisement which is then placed in appropriate outlets ranging from the club noticeboard to the national association mailing or even the press. Only by doing this will it be possible to attract and select appropriate people to apply for the vacant post.

There will need to be application forms, CVs, references, interviews and all the other procedures normal in industry if this process is to be followed through. It is unrealistic to believe that every single step will be adhered to every time, but certainly in the case of national governing bodies and large sporting bodies such procedures should be adopted as opposed to *ad hoc* elections at poorly attended, geographically remote annual general meetings. Poor methodology militates in favour of domination of sport by small groups, often out of touch with mainstream progressive developments, or people not always motivated by the best interests of the sport. While this rigid 'quasi-industrial' regime may seem a little harsh, it has to be used for real progress.

The more positive side of posts should also be advertised, e.g. high-ranking national governing body officials may benefit from several international trips and the possibility of being selected for management posts at major international games such as the Olympics, as well as being listened to by government ministers, sports councils, etc. For any post there are some positive opportunities – these should be stressed so that it is not always the least unwilling who are attracted, because everything is painted black. Sports administration, like all other sports links or involvement, can offer some very enjoyable and positive times. The emphasis must always be on the positive to help attract the best people, because many quality people are available.

Performance appraisal and support once the post has been filled are essential, mechanisms should be set in place to support and encourage staff (whether voluntary or paid), and management lines of communication should be clear. The establishment of an appraisal system which allows people to have their progress in the post assessed and commented on is essential and allows them to make comments on the organizational setting where a paid official is often employed and managed by spare-time volunteers. This appraisal system in normal industrial situations may be on a monthly or six-monthly basis, but in a sports situation it is desirable that it happens at least monthly so that individuals are not left to feel isolated or under pressure.

The purpose of appraisal is to improve job performance and look at individuals' potential, based on objective standards or targets previously set. It is important that both the person being appraised and the appraiser are prepared for the session, preferably with a written and previously circulated agenda. Any criticism should be analytical, not personal and be aimed at supporting, helping and improving individual (and organizational) performance.

Work appraisals should be measured against a detailed plan previously agreed between the two parties and should match performance against previously set objectives. The issue of salary should not be negotiated during appraisal sessions, nor should they be set up as potentially threatening for either party. The aim is to see the individual and the organization develop harmoniously because the development of both will be beneficial to both.

An appraisal system should not be seen as separate from ongoing day-to-day support for employees, since that too is essential to ensure that both develop well. Such systems are vitally important in sport, where gossip and allegations can become the basis for widespread misperceptions.

There is a massive informal network in sport and it must not be allowed to pressurize individuals or the organization excessively or unfairly. Only by adopting appropriate, businesslike mechanisms will such gossip be squashed. All appointment mechanisms and staffing procedures should be open and fair (in line with equal opportunities) and be widely recognized as appropriate for the organization.

Team building

It is very helpful for leaders (and indeed all members of a working team) to understand how groups and individuals function, and to beware the group dynamics within any group and their organization. This does not need to be a theoretical understanding but rather an awareness of how other people and groups function, when people are brought together.

> Every individual on the team is focused on the objective, which involves co-operating with others while carrying out your own particular set of duties.
>
> *Hammer (1997)*

It is important that groups have a common goal and can see how they all, as a group and as individuals, are working towards this end.

There can be a conflict in sport of individual and group interests and understanding, as well as a lack of understanding of the concepts of inter-dependence and group consciousness – everybody must be working towards the same goals, in the same way, if team spirit is to be obtained consistently.

Individuals need to see their role within the group but also to have a leader to involve them in the group and towards the fulfilment of the group objectives. The role of leadership, as discussed in Chapter 5, is the key in achieving a successful creative group. One member of the group will have to show considerable leadership skills to put together a group of sports-minded people – often strong-willed and self-opinionated people – to achieve a set of agreed objectives to the benefit of the sport involved.

It is beneficial to give some consideration to concepts such as group creativeness, team development, structure and organization if there is to be any growth in the development of the group towards its common purpose.

Individual members must be aware of their roles, functions and respon-sibilities, and these must be clearly defined and written down to avoid any confusion. Individuals must see their role clearly themselves, with their own personal duties as well as their duties to help make the group function and achieve the task. It is also very important that the group, and the leader, recognize the abilities and the potential as well as the natural personalities of the individuals involved.

An awareness of how groups operate will be of benefit in the sports situation, especially because much of the administrative action is taken by groups and teams. Group practice in terms of how it normally operates and sets its programme, how it decides to go forward and how individuals use the strength of the group and recognize achievements and performance within it, is very important and should not be underestimated.

The ways that individuals within a group respond to authority and inter-relate are very important. In order to get group cohesion and everyone working together it is important to consider how individuals react within groups and see their respective roles. Sporting bodies are often made up of committees and subcommittees and therefore an understanding of group processes is very important for efficient functioning of the organization overall. The action of smaller groups and possible conflict, between indi-viduals or even between sub-groups, are factors that must be considered.

There are a host of important matters to consider when looking at group processes, but cohesiveness, individual perceptions, conformity, competition, co-ordination, atmosphere, and structure are among the key issues to be aware of.

Perhaps the most crucial overarching concept in terms of group processes and even team building is that of communication, as we have seen earlier in this chapter. The necessity of letting everyone find their role, being aware of others and ensuring that everyone knows quite clearly what is going on in the whole group is vitally important. Communication, in all its forms, is the key issue and a great deal of attention should be paid to getting the form of communication right, as this will ease many of the problems that can exist in group, and indeed organizational, functioning. This is even more true in the context of a voluntary body, where communication can be complex since individuals see each other spasmodically, as opposed to a normal work situation where they may meet on a more regular basis.

The other problem with groups is people – the human being is a complex animal and in its own way very difficult to legislate for. It reacts and functions in a complex manner and can cause many problems for itself and others. If we can promote strong interpersonal relationships and encourage skills in dealing with others then there is little doubt that we will be better able to withstand organizational problems that may arise, and difficult people who may cause problems. The balance between people is the key to getting things right – if individuals can co-operate then they will have a more effective organization. It cannot, however, be expected that individuals will automatically come together easily, because often there is a conflict between people and groups or sub-groups. The pulling of such people and groups closer together and the removing of cohesion difficulties is a crucial role for the competent leader and can bring major benefits. In addition, increasing the skills of individuals will help them greatly in ensuring that they can contribute to group and organizational success by being able to relate well to others with high-level interpersonal skills in areas such as communication, listening and motivation.

It is vital to make this effort to build teams rather than just assume they exist, to give people the skills which they can use to work together and to work at group process and cohesion in order to get this co-operative effort.

The key issue in building any team is to get a unity of purpose where there is a total commitment by all concerned to achieve the task or organizational efficiency. Any lack of understanding about objectives or lack of clarity about the aims of the organization will cause problems for the organization. Pulling towards a common aim helps with team building, as long as it is an agreed aim, and everyone is quite clear what it is.

Managers and administrators are trying to produce quality organization and administration for the performer in sport. The cohesion of the group can add significantly to this common aim and development can be aided because we all have the same goals at heart. Within sport there is likely to be a common objective and desire – whether it be for a specific rugby club to be successful or for more people to take part in lacrosse, it is likely that a number of people gathered together in a committee or subcommittee will share that purpose. This is most helpful in getting some cohesion into our operation and getting a unified drive towards achieving the set target.

We have already considered exactly what the leader has to do to achieve this, and their role is crucial in getting things going for all concerned. They must lead the way and concentrate group thinking on building a successful team, but they cannot be expected to achieve everything on their own. Good leadership will be beneficial not just for the leaders themselves but for everyone involved, and will help to achieve the objectives.

In terms of getting the team correct, the selection of team members is a crucial step. There have been suggestions that selection in a democratic process such as an annual general meeting does not necessarily lead to the correct people being chosen. This, however, is the traditional method for most sports bodies, especially those of a large membership, and the consequences can sometimes be that people who are 'willing rather than able' are chosen. This can mean that they may not necessarily work together, although in some voluntary situations individuals are chosen (or unofficially pre-selected) by the existing committee because they can see that it may be possible to work with them. In a commercial situation selection would normally be very much on the basis of how individuals would fit into the team, and if it is perceived that they would not be helpful in achieving a task then they will not be selected, through interview or other processes.

Selecting team members may seem an easy task but, depending on the situation, a great number of skills may be required for the team member; there will be a necessity for some type of technical knowledge and other attributes which will be beneficial to the sport and its performers. Unquestionably, the key considerations for any selection should be the ability of individuals to work as team members, and their personal attributes and skills which will help build a team towards the successful accomplishment of the task in hand.

It is vital that the team is able to react well to problems or crises, and handle them – it should be able to identify what is wrong and do something concrete about it fast.

In addition, it will be necessary to maintain the team morale once it is established and keep everyone focused on the end purpose, working at maintaining standards through supporting each other in a variety of situations that the group faces.

The continual definition or re-evaluation of roles within teams will also be beneficial to successful functioning and will cause individuals to be happier about their duties and responsibilities. If they have a clearly defined role, individuals will feel happier and more secure. This role may change from time to time in response to what the group actually needs or all the performers need. It is very important that the roles should not be static, but rather be seen as an ongoing requirement, with the possibility of changing or fine tuning as required to help the team achieve the identified tasks. Remember, teamwork is about:

- motivation
- achievement
- confidence

- challenge
- goals
- trust
- openness
- relationships
- effectiveness.

Team development

Six stages of team development have been identified (Chaudhry-Lawton *et al.*, 1993):

- getting together
- getting on
- getting going
- getting things done
- getting stuck
- getting out.

These points are all fairly self-explanatory, but we must be continually looking to develop our team strength and have everyone working together and understanding this process. Everything may not go easily immediately, but everyone working together must go through necessary processes to get things achieved.

Research has indicated that team members have identified a sizeable list of ideas and comments as to why the teams they were in worked. These include:

- 'we got on well together – and socialize together'
- 'the leader was very clear about what he wanted, but was never bossy'
- 'loyalty'
- 'clear about what I had to do'
- 'it was enjoyable'
- 'I felt I counted and was valued'
- 'I knew what was going on'
- 'it was something we wanted to do'.

Chaudhry-Lawton *et al.* (1993) have taken such points and divided them into four main thrusts – clarity, commitment, communication and celebration.

Clarity. In terms of clarity, sports organizations are often found lacking, but if we analyse successful operations then we will always see complete clarity of organizational and individual aims.

Commitment. In terms of commitment, sport is very fortunate and probably second to none, since few on-field participants or behind-the-scenes administrators lack commitment and most have notable determination to achieve.

Communication. This is an area in which there can be significant problems, especially within voluntary organizations, but even in full-time staff relationships. Because of the nature of sport many of the people involved will be heading off in different directions on a regular basis, so getting the message through to individuals and various organizational committees and structures can be very difficult. This is a major problem for sports organizations and methods must be constantly examined to see if practices can be improved and updated to ensure that as much information as possible is passed on to all team members to ensure their clarity of objectives and understanding of current issues and tasks.

Celebration. Celebration, or one could say recognition and reward, is often ignored for people operating behind the scenes in sport in the UK. Recent years have seen enormous changes for the on-field performers; the rewards now can be enormous and set individuals up for life totally due to their physical abilities. For workers in sport behind the scenes the opposite is true – very often they have to put their own personal effort, commitment and time in for no reward whatsoever; indeed, it may cost them money. This makes it more difficult to enthuse such people and guarantee their commitment. Every effort must be made in an organization to recognize the supreme efforts of the volunteers and to give them whatever little rewards may be available in terms of merit awards, service to sport awards, international trips, etc.

Looking at team development in this way will assist in efficient management practice supporting participants in an effective drive towards success.

Personnel management

The management, training and development of personnel is the key quality of the sports industry and perhaps what marks it out from many others. All aspects of human resource development should be applied in the sports business as they are in others in terms of training people to bring out the best in them and to understand procedures and practices.

In addition, all processes of personnel management in terms of consideration for staff, legal obligations to staff, health and safety, and employment regulations must always be adhered to and clearly understood. It is essential to ensure a happy staff in order to make it an effective staff.

The key difference in terms of personnel in the sports industry as opposed to others is commitment. The commitment will be driven by a host of agencies and will come from a variety of sources, but it will exist to a level not seen in the vast majority of other work situations (although it is also seen in some other employees who work for relatively small financial remuneration, sometimes not in great conditions, merely because of their considerable love of the activity). This commitment has a number of real benefits, but equally has a number of difficulties and dangers. Extreme commitment should be built on, while its tendency towards fanaticism or blinkered thinking should be discouraged as much as possible. Staff training will help here, as will appraisal and counselling.

The management of people is basically what sports management and administration is all about. The human factor is a common thread to all aspects and situations – it is the essential ingredient to quality provision and operation. In every situation the manager, or leader, will need to recognize the role of the people in the organization and encourage and support their positive input at all times. Concepts such as customer care come from quality staff operation at the delivery level every bit as much as, if not more than, they come from the thinking and action of the person at the top of the organization. The quality manager will recognize the role of individuals and groups of staff within any organization and will capitalize on their abilities, working with them to try to improve the provision given to all client groups.

The manager in the human resource dimension will have many roles to fill, including those of:

- leader
- motivator
- disciplinarian
- role model
- team builder
- trainer
- organizer.

Each of these roles has its own implications and means that managers must be multi-skilled and need to be trained, supported and encouraged by their superiors (even if these are a committee) if they are to perform their personnel functions well.

Admiral Nelson is often quoted as saying: 'a happy ship is an efficient ship and an efficient ship is a happy one'. This is particularly appropriate in the sports industry, which is a service-based community provider that survives on delivery experiences in the physical activity arena for people. It relies on interpersonal relationships, personal commitment, enjoyment and participation. If the sports organization facility is not organized on the basis of sport for participation and the enthusiasm of staff to provide for this, then it will fall short of the target for quality provision. The involvement of everyone in a co-ordinated dynamic effort to cater for customers is what the provision is all about, whether it be for a governing body or for a local sports centre.

The role of any individual charged with personnel support and development is to work with people to produce what the customer actually wants, while paying attention to the demands of staff in terms of motivation and satisfaction within their job.

Often in the sports situation the demands of the customer can be extreme through their commitment to the sport, and this can put unrealistic pressures on staff to respond seven days a week, 24 hours a day, because there will always be people wanting to take part in sport at any time of the day and they will to some extent expect staff, especially paid ones, to be present at that time. A good manager will recognize the conflicting demands of the voluntary participant and the paid staff, or even the committed volunteer, who will sometimes want to turn off from the sport and just go home – a view not often understood by the fanatical participant.

Such a relationship can lead to extreme stress on individuals, whether voluntary or paid, and be a disincentive to increasing their commitment and performance. The answer is to follow proper personnel procedures in all instances and ensure that from recruitment onwards appropriate 'industrial' procedures are followed. In particular in terms of staff, it is essential that an appraisal system is maintained so that there is an ongoing two-way review of job performance – this can often be useful in the voluntary sector. In order to retain staff we have to look at all the ways they are treated by all the agencies with whom they have contact, and what sort of reward and remuneration package they are given in return for the inevitable hassle they will face.

Well-thought-through personnel policies are essential for any sports organization as they are for any other successful business; they are perhaps just a bit more necessary because of the inevitable dynamic of conflict that can exist between customer and staff (voluntary or paid). A strong policy in this area will pay dividends in terms of the returns obtained from staff performance as well as staff retention.

Self-assessment question

People are the foundation of sport – Assess the validity of this statement in the practical areas of sports delivery with which you are familiar. Then examine some of the people management issues identified in this chapter and suggest the ways they are seen (or not) in the specific sport situation you are assessing.

8   Organizational management

This chapter looks at organizational management from the point of view of the sports manager. It starts by identifying the role of the sports manager and the skills they require.

It goes on to look at general management technique, and then considers quality management and its focus on customers and delivering their requirements efficiently and effectively. This approach is seen as relevant to the sports administrator as it centres on planning, objective setting and delivery mechanisms for management practice. It is not about concepts, but practice – sports management, like sport, should be practical.

Strategic management of the organization is then considered, as well as the processes involved and some of the settings in which it is necessary. The possible contents of a strategic plan, ranging from a mission statement to a marketing plan, are listed. The need to assess performance and the complexity of sports management are mentioned, as well as the issues of SMART objectives, control, organizational change and its management – set in the context of 'moving goalposts' in which sport operates.

The chapter closes with a brief consideration of the concept of decision-making.

> Management is the art of getting other people to do all the work.
>
> *Anon*

The role of the sports manager

The sports manager's role can vary enormously depending upon the setting, but the specific task of the manager will be to take general management functions and perform them in a sports setting. All management functions can apply in different situations at different times – the really skilful manager will know when each applies and will use that process appropriately. It is essential for sports managers to realize that they are managing in a sports situation, and that they should be applying the correct business principles and practices as appropriate and relevant to that situation, as colleagues will be doing in other industrial situations. There has been some delay in service industries generally in recognizing that they have to apply management principles, as do product-based industries. There has been a further gap in sport realizing that it is actually a service industry, but now it is hoped these thought processes and then good practices will begin to be applied.

Skills of a sports manager

Sports managers will require a background knowledge in the process of management, but they will more particularly require a knowledge of sport and the people involved in it. To be genuinely effective they will have to a have a feeling for the business of sport, as well as management skills. In essence, sports management is all about managing:

- the workplace
- the people
- day-to-day operations
- the facility
- the activity
- the development process
- partnership working.

Sports management may be seen as a limited or short-term career for most in the UK at present. While realistic careers and salaries are few and far between in the UK at present, in North America it is quite possible to see sports management as a significant career. If, as in other areas, this American pattern is followed in the UK then there is no doubt that sports management will become a genuine career opportunity in the UK very soon. Indeed, some would argue that this trend has already started.

General management approaches

It has been recognized in a number of settings that there are five general approaches to management.

1 The **classical** approach deals with the content, suggesting that there is core knowledge that each manager should possess. This includes the functions of planning, organizing and controlling.
2 The **behavioural** approach considers the role of the individual within the management process and identifies that each individual has needs, wants and desires. It considers that individuals are different and need to be appropriately treated.
3 **Management science** sets out to use mathematical approaches in management to get better efficiency; it relates to operational problems and methods of solving these.

4   The **systems** approach is based on designing a precise system of management made up of a variety of parts which must be brought together to function as a whole to meet the organization's objectives.
5   The **contingency** approach works on the assumption that there is no single best way to manage. The manager must be able to manage in different situations and recognize that organizations can vary in the best way.

There are always a variety of theories and ideas when managing in any given situation, and they should be applied at the appropriate time and in the appropriate manner.

Quality management

The race for quality has no finish time.

Anon

The secret of success is constancy to purpose.

Benjamin Disraeli

Total Quality Management is a concept originating in Japan which has been extensively used by businesses throughout the Western world, particularly the USA and the UK. It is designed to produce increased performance through more efficient operation.

There have been many definitions of the concept. In 1989 the British Quality Association stated that 'Total Quality Management (TQM) is a corporate business management philosophy which recognizes customer needs and business goals as inseparable. It is applicable within industry and commerce.' This generalist definition will suffice for purposes of sport, management and administration, and allow a degree of interpretation by individuals in their own specific setting.

The concept of Total Quality Management has been enshrined in the management standards BS5750, ISO9000 and ISO9001. Many companies have striven to achieve these standards in a wide variety of industrial situations, and the general consensus has been that those who have made the effort to go through this process have found it to be worthwhile whether or not a certificate was achieved at the end.

In essence, the search for certification focuses the mind on company operational practices, and this in itself is beneficial. Quality management systems, however, should always be focused on the customer and the key issue is the satisfaction of customer needs in an efficient and consistently effective manner.

In the search for quality management the manager should be looking for excellence in planning, control and implementation, focused on delivering at the end of the process what the customer wants.

To ensure quality planning a number of steps can be outlined:

- determining who the customers are in general and specific terms
- determining the needs of each sub-group of customers, in general and very specific terms
- developing services and schemes which meet the identified needs
- developing efficient processes to deliver these services on an ongoing and consistent basis
- ensuring that all provision is delivered in an attractive and community-relevant way
- ensuring that all relevant practicalities, such as health and safety, and other organizational policies are adhered to throughout the process.

Beyond the planning it is essential to carry such quality intent into high-quality delivery of service. This is fundamentally about taking the aims set down during quality planning to a set of specific measurable objectives and carrying this right through into practice. Operational procedures must always be set against these aims and objectives, and constantly monitored to judge their effectiveness and efficiency. A good manager will identify weaknesses quickly and take action to ensure immediate improvement in the service being delivered.

Several times in this text, the issue of competition has been considered and it has been pointed out that it is a growing challenge to sports managers and administrators in a variety of situations. If any sports manager is to remain competitive then they must look to delivering the services required by properly identified customers in a quality manner. Quality, like beauty, is in the eye of the beholder, and only by monitoring the progress in terms of returns (both cash and attendance), as well as financial efficiency and sporting success (in terms of participation or excellence) of the organization, will the manager be able to see if true quality is being delivered.

Successful organizations can only achieve quality programmes and consistently improve on them if there is careful attention to detail and planning, and practice. This must involve all the staff, and particularly middle management, targeting certain areas of action for quick results and having an effective communication system throughout the organization to ensure that everybody is involved in the process. Sports organizations are often accused of having poor internal communication, and in an audit for quality achievement it will be identified that poor communication makes the achievement of policy absolutely impossible. For many, introducing appropriate internal and external communication is the first step on the ladder to achieving quality operation.

Organizations, in sport as elsewhere, accepting Total Quality Management have as an important ingredient to their proper operation the identification of a number of key issues in this procedure:

- the establishment of clear aims and objectives
- involvement and agreement of all the relevant people with these aims and objectives to ensure unity of organizational purpose
- clearly established policies and, indeed, charters for customers and staff
- identification of critical points in the achievement of successful operations – both general and specific
- aiming to become an organization which in its very culture believes in quality
- clear identification of the supremacy of clients or customers in the drive for quality
- clear identification of the role of individual members of staff or specific groups within the quality process.

The overall aims of installing quality management systems or practices are:

- an increase in customer satisfaction
- a reduction in costs
- an increase in market presence
- a reduction in accidents and staff absence
- increased efficiency, productivity and profit
- improved service delivery at all levels of the organization
- increased participation and/or success at all levels
- long-term stability and successful operation of the sporting organization.

In practical implementation terms the formation of a quality circle – internal or external – can be extremely useful in aiding the implementation of quality management systems. Such circles are made up of key staff within an organization or series of organizations who are working towards the implementation of quality procedures. Such groups give a real focus to the work to be undertaken and become a forum for ideas from inside and outside the organization to aid the process.

The key function such groups can fulfil is staff involvement, because without all of the individuals within the organization being involved, true quality will never be achieved. It must be felt to be a staff (paid or voluntary) initiative and potential benefit. Without a real commitment on the part of all the staff and a unity of purpose in the organization towards achieving quality, the whole venture is doomed to failure. For the sports organization, facility or service, the key is to devise a working action plan towards achieving the desired quality policy processes and practices. The desire to pass on the commitment of sports involvement and participation is not hard to find in such staff, but the realization that a lot of hard work and action are required makes this goal harder to achieve. Sports participants and sports staff like to see action rather than talk, and a working action plan can produce this.

This action plan should be enacted by all the staff and implemented on a controlled and ongoing basis with constant monitoring as appropriate. As mentioned above, a sound communication system in individual and organizational terms will be necessary to inform everyone what is going on at present, what is going to happen and what the results of all their efforts are.

This process should be characterized by seven 'p's:

- positive commitment
- planning
- participation
- process control
- problem identification
- problem elimination
- performance.

If these 'p's are put into practice, you will have a practical working performance quality management system which will be beneficial to customers, to staff and to the whole sports organization. Everybody will feel happier, more content and better pleased with their efforts and their treatment.

Total Quality Management will be achieved with the managers, then all of the staff can give a total positive commitment, do the planning, operate the process, and be open to change and amendment throughout. Of necessity, this process can involve a lot of paperwork and logging of procedures that have to be followed and may be seen as a little tedious, but if everyone is clear as to what the end is, then they will become sufficiently committed to attend to the details required. This exercise can sometimes be slow and a little painful, but it will ultimately produce a result for everyone and will be of benefit to the organization or facility.

Fundamentally, it is essential, especially in the lower-key voluntary organization, that the concept of Total Quality Management be examined and some time spent examining potential benefits. The process can be time-consuming, but in practice efficient processes will be extremely helpful to the organization and its customers. Most of those who have been involved in the past have found it very demanding but in the end a useful tool for efficient organization and function. This will be as true in sports organizations as it is in many other industries. The exercise of examining management procedures and practices in itself is very worthwhile – self-examination is always useful and should be a constant process in any case. The examination of working procedures and practices should also be an ongoing process, not just a periodic review. The key aim is to ensure consistent and constant good management practice which must be the target for sports administrators and managers as it is for key staff in other organizations.

Providing quality in leisure services is about meeting customer needs, putting the customer first and delivering the service the customer wants. The exceeding of customer expectations is true quality customer service.

The Sports Council (1984) considered four key areas of customer orientation:

- finding out what the customer wants through effective communication
- quality standards – specifying exactly what the customer might expect
- quality of staffing systems – well trained and motivated staff providing a service through a good management system
- quality process service provided through clear procedures clearly understood by all concerned.

This specifies very clear and simple models for those working in the field of sport and recreation, and again emphasizes the importance of putting the customer first, clear communication between customers and staff, and clear procedures enabling quality processes to be carried out. In the field of quality there is much talk of customer charters (following on the Government's Citizen's Charter), but there are dangers that these can be seen as 'in vogue' at present and token gestures not really put into beneficial practice. It is essential that steps taken should be towards quality customer service, not merely a gesture in that direction.

Quality management has a number of fundamental principles.

- There needs to a clear definition of quality agreed and understood by everyone in the organization.
- There needs to be a clear organizational structure which allows for the management and delivery of quality standards.
- The aim of quality organization and management is to remove all errors from the organization's performance.
- There needs to be some measurement of quality, including the comparative cost of not producing quality.
- There needs to be a total understanding that the concept is ultimately about competitive edge and quality delivery to customers.
- Managers must understand that significant staff training and involvement will be essential to ensure that there is effective understanding and delivery of quality principles and systems.

Additionally, quality has to do with a lot of principles and issues for everyone involved in the organization, and it requires individual and organizational commitment to ensure that the customer ultimately benefits. It is wrong to believe that quality can only come through the stamp of quality such as ISO9000 or following an Investors in People programme – these are structured methods but the certification or the public recognition should be secondary to the need for the organization to run effectively for the benefit of its customers. How this is actually achieved is a matter for everyone involved to have a view on and hopefully ultimately agree. In sport and recreation, for example, a number of organizations have chosen to follow rigorously the vocational occupational standards route (collecting further employee vocational qualifications on the way) as a way to ensure that everything done by the individuals and the organization is done on a basis of competence in the workplace – this system, if totally understood and enjoying staff commitment, is another way to ensure quality for customers.

Whatever the implementation method for producing quality, a number of significant items have to be considered. Some of the following concepts will have to be addressed before the programme is implemented or becomes effective:

- commitment
- cost-effectiveness
- systems and structures
- training
- objective setting
- performance indicators
- overseeing
- groups
- quality circles
- error elimination
- recording mechanisms
- external advice.

Quality systems are sometimes perceived as being only about statistics, performance indicators and measurement mechanisms. This is very wrong, because while these measures are important, sport and recreation is a people business about experiences, and sometimes a quality experience is required as much as an appropriate performance indicator. In essence, however, quality in many sports situations can be measured through the return of participants or other customer groups – a lack of quality in a sport and recreation situation will certainly see the customers voting with their feet and not returning.

Sport and leisure facilities rely a great deal on return business, and steps must be taken to ensure that quality is always provided for customers so that they will return. Customers must be left in no doubt what is available to them, what is provided for them and who can help them through any participation programme they wish. Information will be a key aspect to quality in the sport and recreation field, staff should be well informed, and customer care must be a key part of the business.

To know whether it is effective, any sports organization must have some type of performance indicators, as must individual administrators within the business. This does not mean setting unrealistic or overly demanding targets which simply cannot be reached or which are set by external agencies that lack specific knowledge. Nevertheless, if efficiency and effectiveness are to be fully emphasized and put into operation genuinely, then some type of quality check will be required.

Quality should always be seen as something which pervades the whole organization and relates to everything involved in it – not only systems and procedures but also staff training and effective resourcing. The cost of quality should be seen as a positive rather than a negative influence, in that not having quality operation is going to cost more than adhering to quality, despite the fact that it takes time to establish the appropriate systems and organizational ethos in the early days.

Ultimately, everyone involved, no matter their place in the organization, must have the customer in focus and see that their role of satisfying customer needs, wants and desires in an efficient and effective manner is going to be crucial to delivering quality. Whether a member of staff is answering the telephone or putting across some complex customer information system, it doesn't really matter; the principle is the same – quality of effort and delivery will be vital to success.

It is somewhat ironic that sport, which in many cases is measured by figures and times (statistics), is not always managed in the same way. Perhaps more measurable sets of targets in term of administration, as well as performance on the track or playing field, would assist in producing improved administration and management. Sports administrators should use the many statistics they assemble on a regular basis to help give some indications of performance. It is common for statistics on membership, participation levels, new members, international performance records, championship records, etc. to be recorded in sport, and they can be the basis of some form of measurement of organizational achievement in administrative as well as technical terms. This would mean that performance indicators as judges of quality would not form an onerous task but would in fact be part of standard operational practice.

Other issues such as staff training or staff performance appraisal are worthwhile in themselves and should be implemented by an efficient modern organization for effective and efficient operation; they will improve the quality of the organization's functioning. It is crucial that staff appraisal, training and evaluation should be ongoing and not occasional or spasmodic. A fundamental principle of quality management is that there is consistency to the practice and it is not limited by time or commitment.

Other initiatives, such as Investors in People (an initiative by the Department of Education and Employment), stress the input of personnel to quality organization and make great play of the motivation and training of staff to get them to achieve business goals. Adopting such a system can also be the impetus (or part of it) towards quality.

Practical quality considerations

Based on a now superseded standard, BS5750, some of the issues in practical terms that a sports manager/administrator would have to consider in order to go down the traditional quality management route and develop quality standards to the point of certification would be:

- the scope and field of application
- quality system requirements
- management responsibilities
- quality systems
- contract review
- document control
- purchasing
- purchaser supplied product
- product identification and traceability
- process control
- inspecting and testing
- inspection, measuring and test equipment
- inspection, test and status
- control of non-conforming product
- corrective action
- handling, storage, packaging and delivery
- quality records
- internal quality audits
- training
- statistical techniques.

All of these may not seem appropriate initially, but when it is considered that the words may change slightly and the focus may move to services rather than products in the traditional sense, one begins to get the feel of the items to be covered in a formalized quality appraisal against national standards.

The system might not always be appropriate, even in its new and revised editions, but the benefits of considering the headings are sizeable and can be translated well into the sports organization operation.

Strategic management

Even the best plan degenerates into work.

Anon

In any sporting situation, public, private or voluntary, there is a need to establish a strategy for ongoing management and future development of the organization and the individuals within it. Sadly, the lack of strategic direction is often the downfall of the organization and, while mission statements and visions may be seen as fancy management jargon, they are beneficial to the function of a successful organization.

If we do not know where we are going, how are we going to get there, and how will we know if we have got there? This is essential in facing up to change, which seems constant in the sporting situation. It is also essential if good customer service is going to be achieved, income targets met and facilities or services provided in an efficient and effective manner (Figure 8.1).

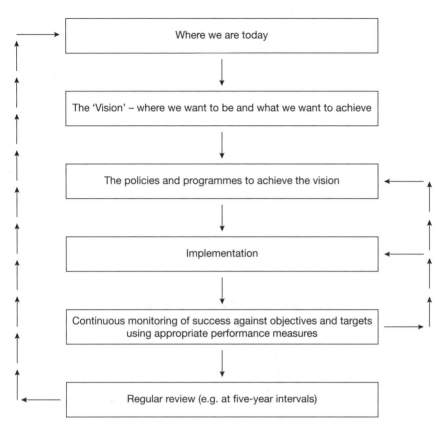

Figure 8.1 The strategy process

Any strategy development will look at:

- establishing clear organizational aims and objectives
- developing policies and communicating these to relevant parties
- preparing appropriate documentation
- establishing a system for a regular review of implementation of these plans.

Establishing a strategy should be a shared undertaking by all the staff members, voluntary or paid, and should be used as a tool to improve team-work towards these jointly agreed objectives – ideally all employees should be involved in developing these objectives. A strategy which is not based on shared ownership involving all the participants will be much less effec-tive – the imposition of such a strategy is certainly not the best way for successful organizational operation.

While there is a need for an overall plan, focusing on strategy and policy development, planning should be a concept which is taken into the practical situation and not just perceived as a theory. One of these applications is that of business planning, in particular preparing a business plan for relevant new initiatives, facility development, seeking finance or diversifying into new areas of operation.

The key areas of any business plan are the aims and objectives, the methodology of achievement and the obtaining of resources, and the overall time-scale for the project.

It is essential that sports managers, as with other industrial sectors, take business planning seriously for new initiatives and do not embark on new projects or schemes without having clear business plans laid out which can later be used as a measure of success or failure, as well as an ongoing performance guide and check. A key issue in relation to business planning is to be sure that finance can be found to make the proposition viable, whether this is from income, sponsorship or local authority subsidy. Any business plan should bring forward detailed evidence that monies can be found in the short, medium and long terms to make the project viable and worthwhile from the commercial point of view – everyone can have great ideas, but only the proper planning will put them into practice effectively. If, when considering a business plan, things don't come together then in essence we should look for a new and different project.

To quote from the Sports Council (1995–5): 'the development of a business plan is an invaluable discipline for managers and once developed and agreed, it becomes the implementation framework for the development operation of the project'. Such sound professional thinking should underpin all other operations within the sport and recreation field. Only by such good practice will progress be made and easily monitored and measured.

Strategic planning

The Sports Council (1994–5) goes on to say that a sport and recreation strategy enables a local authority to:

- ask itself some fundamental questions, i.e. undertake a service review
- identify future needs and demands
- assess performance.

In addition, the development sport and recreation strategy will:

- enable authorities to review policies and redefine them as necessary
- modify and set clear objectives
- identify distinct roles for each area of the service
- form the basis of the facility management specification

- indicate how provision in the authority can be integrated and co-ordinated
- identify who can best provide the different aspects of the service – voluntary, private or public sector
- give authorities regular appraisals and updates on current sport and recreation provision
- provide local authorities with a clear rational strategy for provision of a recreation service to the community (Sports Council 1994–5).

Sports development will be an integral part of this strategy but it will follow rather than lead. Strategic planning, facility planning and departmental organization will be key factors in ensuring that this sport and recreation strategy can be implemented and if practical this will enable effective sports development as well as improved facility management.

Strategic planning can be a difficult exercise for any organization, especially when it faces somewhat unpredictable change from external factors, as well as internal personalities and, in sporting situations, concepts such as volunteerism. This has a major effect on the planning process and implementation of operational business plans.

It is interesting to note that Peter Woods (of Direct Line Insurance fame) does not have a long-term business plan, but rather a rolling business plan which is reviewed annually and altered in light of changes and developments arising from the past twelve months and the likely future over the next twelve months – the longest term that he believes is likely to be predictable. His feeling is that a 'set in tablets of stone' business plan for three or five years, which does not respond to changes during that period, and is not reviewed annually, is more of a millstone than an effective business tool for a dynamic organization.

Mission statements

Organizations benefit from having a mission statement which is clear and distinguishes their operation from others in the sector. The statement should change periodically to reflect change in the organization and the society in which it operates. A great deal of cynicism exists about business statements, but this should not be taken too seriously since in essence it is a good idea for everyone to know what the organization as a whole is up to.

The mission statement for any organization can be set at a variety of levels and in fact it is very often better for the shopfloor worker to produce it than the managing director. It is certainly essential that the staff agree and understand it and that everyone pull towards this vision.

Depending on exactly what sector of the sports business you are operating in, the mission statement may well vary considerably, e.g. is your motivation for public service, private profit or voluntary satisfaction? A possible mission statement could be to:

- 'establish hockey as the number-one family team game in Scotland'
- 'provide sporting entertainment for potential business clients at a realistic price'
- 'encourage the involvement of parents in supporting their young person's sport'.

Every organization needs to know what, in overall general terms, it is trying to do, and a mission is designed to specify this quite clearly so that everyone knows it and agrees it.

Organization

Organization is about establishing and maintaining practices and processes to maximize the performance of your sporting body by clearly identifying what each person within it has to do and ensuring that there is joint working – effective teamwork – as well as clearly defined roles within the prescribed structure. An appropriate organizational style will help clarify responsibilities and ensure clear lines of communication between individuals and sections within that organization. Such organization, in sports situations as with a number of other bodies, needs to be spelt out with power and authority within structures being definitively specified. The recognition of the potential need for change should exist in any vibrant organization, and this change should be pursued at any point where the structure is felt to be inappropriate, or where internal and external relationships are not clear.

Fundamentally, good organizational structure is about a clear chain of command and identification of specific responsibilities – such structures make organizations very much more effective than agencies in which everybody wanders about wondering what exactly their specific roles and tasks are. Clarity of roles and responsibilities makes it easier to delegate specific tasks. This should be done along with the delegation of the relevant power, authority and finance to allow the tasks to be undertaken in an appropriate manner – as we have seen, delegation is arguably the most important role of any good manager. This does not mean that the manager delegating tasks does not hold the ultimate responsibility; it means, rather, that the superior can spend time on work which may be even more vital to the organization. No effective top-level manager will be involved in dealing with trivia, or indeed any item which other members of staff have the time and ability (present or potential) to deal with.

Business planning for sports bodies

Business planning is essential for sports bodies, as for any other organization wishing to achieve progress. The process involves examining, clarifying and documenting the current and future operation of the sports body. It doesn't need to be a lengthy or complex exercise – its extent depends on the size and nature of the organization.

The process will need to be co-ordinated by an individual or small groups; through this they must consult widely before finalizing any report to ensure that it is truly reflective of the association's view. The compiler(s) will need to drive it forward very hard to avoid any unnecessary delays.

It is impossible to list every factor that will have to be examined, but the following are some that should be considered.

MISSION STATEMENT	The overall *raison d'être* of the association, e.g. to give everyone in Jersey the opportunity to play . . .
AIMS	The general purposes of the organization, e.g. 'to increase public awareness', 'to increase participation levels' or 'to support élite performers'.
OBJECTIVES	Here specifying trends for the association's activities for a forthcoming period, e.g. 'to emphasize activities for young players' or 'to introduce more squad training' (these will be quantified into specific targets in the action plan).
REVIEW OF RECENT ACTIVITIES	
EXPLANATION OF STRUCTURES AND METHODS OF ORGANIZATION	
FACTS AND FIGURES	of participation, young people, number of coaches, past against present, etc.
FUTURE PLANS	Facility, personnel, coaching and development plans.
FINANCIAL STATEMENT OF BUDGET PROJECTION	
PARTNERSHIP/RELATIONSHIPS/NETWORKS	
MARKETING	Especially promotion.

The immediate steps to be taken in an action plan will be laid out, giving:

1   a list of exact targets
2   a detailed list of actions to be taken
3   a timetable or schedule for action.

Measuring performance

Regardless of the type of operation that we are running, or the nature of the structures we have put in place to achieve our objectives, it is going to be important to measure how much we actually achieve. 'Performance indicators' is a term which has fallen into disrepute and causes some immediate antagonism because of a historical perspective related to the compulsion involved in competitive tendering in the sports business for local authorities. The principle, however, of having some clear indication of achievement and measures against which this achievement can be gauged is very sensible – it is certainly essential for an effective business, and it really is the measure of the efficiency of the business.

The problem with performance indicators is who dictates them and what is their nature. If sports administrators decide on and select their own performance indicators, then that seems to be quite acceptable and they can set them down realistically for six-month, twelve-month, 18-month or 36-month periods, or whatever seems appropriate, and they can judge performance against a set of clearly established guidelines.

The first measure of success is always against the objectives of the specific organization or project, bearing in mind that they will have had SMART (specific, measurable, agreed, realistic and timed) objectives set against them. Each of the quantities set down in the objectives will be measurable, e.g. an increase in membership of the organization by 10 per cent.

Going beyond this it can be more difficult to measure achievement, but it is none the less important and failure to do so will certainly have an adverse effect on the performance of the administrator and staff involved.

It is always important to remember the principle that no measurement equals no management. Or, expressed another way: if you can't measure it, don't do it. While such statements may be extreme, they are accurate and reflect the need for competent managers and administrators to measure their individual and organizational performance.

Quality, for example, can be measured through questionnaires on both efficiency and service quality – testing the economic use of resources and whether it is consistent provision in line with customer expectations.

The complexity of sports management

The settings for sports management and administration are many and varied. They occur across a variety of sectors of the industry and are sometimes enacted in the most unlikely situations.

In the private sector there is a vast range of areas where sport and recreation are managed, e.g. health clubs, tourism attractions, corporate fitness situations, professional sports, as well as the related sporting goods manufacturing situations, the sports marketing and PR sectors, sports event management and sports management agencies.

The public sector has many of its own settings at local authority and national level. These range from local sports councils to major international sports complexes and can include dual-use school facilities and local village halls.

The voluntary sector is enormous throughout the UK (1.5 million people in 1996) and its settings range from national and international governing bodies right down to local sports councils and clubs, in some cases very small clubs. The management role in the voluntary sector is often of the organization, but these organizations can sometimes run their own facilities on a small, or even fairly large, scale.

The range of facilities, which cuts across all the sectors, is enormous – they range from motor-car racing facilities to horse-racing tracks, from athletics tracks to swimming pools, from mountain faces to indoor climbing walls, from village greens to Lords, from croquet lawns to golf courses; the list is endless.

In every setting, from international sporting arena to village bowling green, these facilities require a degree of expertise to be run efficiently and effectively. The functioning of all of them will benefit from a professional attitude to their management, even if the person doing the management is not a paid professional.

Planning

The best laid schemes o' mice an' men/Gang aft a-gley

Robert Burns

Any good manager in any situation will have to plan – sport is no exception. There is a need to prepare for the future and to make the organization as efficient and conflict-free as possible. Good planning will effectively achieve both these aims and prepare the organization for change – a state which almost constantly faces everyone involved in sport.

Planning is the aspect of managing which establishes aims, targets, goals and objectives, and identifies the methods by which these targets can be achieved. Plans should be detailed and comprehensive, but should always be responsive and designed in adapted stages to cover both short-term and long-term operation. Planning should be based on detailed research and be specific and realistic to the organization being managed. While it is very easy to have business plans and to set the latest generic business standards, one of the key aspects of sports management is to remember that sport, while it should be organized in a professional and businesslike manner, has this extra quality and element of commitment, desire, enjoyment and voluntary input which can never totally relate to purely business operation.

Objectives

In order to plan properly and to manage at various stages, a set of clear organizational objectives is vital, and a set of smaller objectives (or targets) for each individual and sub-group involved would be helpful to organizational process.

Wherever objectives are used they need to be SMART: specific, measurable, agreed, realistic and timed. A number of other terms could be applied to objectives in a sports management situation, such as understood, clear, simple, financially accurate, manageable and unambiguous; all of them must be set into an achievement timetable identifying critical points along the way.

Time spent on devising these objectives and careful planning related to them is time well spent; it is time which will be repaid later because it will help eliminate wasteful and misdirected effort.

Good planning in a sports situation should produce a strategic plan for the overall organization, as well as specific plans for any separate parts of the organization, and the necessary administrative procedures should be clearly laid down for the achievement of previously set, and agreed, objectives.

Control

Any effective organization must have controls of some sort which will ensure that what is desired is what is delivered. The structures must be in place to ensure that the objectives are achievable, and the mechanisms in place to ensure that achievement can be undertaken, but there will have to be a degree of monitoring and control to ensure on an ongoing basis that implementation is going as planned.

Control may be looked upon in three aspects: recent past performance, current performance, and feedback from previous experience. Controlled techniques can help monitor capital, resource, personnel selection, procedures and practices as well as the budgeting process. For some organizations employee selection could be seen as the most important primary control technique. Care taken in designing accurate job descriptions and using appropriate advertising outlets, as well as efficient and effective interview techniques, will help put the right people in the right posts – a vital control step for any organization driving for efficiency and effectiveness.

Additionally, reporting systems for staff involved through incident reports and other routine procedures can help monitor employees on a daily basis, and again such practical control techniques are part of any sound agency operation.

Obviously, the checking of financial data and its careful analysis, coupled with any other information returns, will help in controlling the organization's operation. Too often, figures are received and not checked on a regular basis to assess performance against objectives. For sports organizations, participation, attendance and income figures can be extremely important and are gauges, at the very least, of trends in organizational performance.

Quality procedures (discussed earlier in this chapter), appraisal of employees and management audits are other tools which can help ensure organizational effectiveness on a prolonged basis. Many other initiatives are examined and implemented but they tend to be spasmodic and not necessarily helpful or enduring. Employee appraisals are essential and can be extremely effective in controlling performance of individuals and organizations if the individuals involved are well briefed, and properly trained in how to make appraisals objective and ensure that appraisals are a genuine two-way process.

Practical finance control is essential for any organization, and monitoring of income and expenditure on a daily, weekly and monthly basis is essential to ensure cost-effective operation as well as to avoid any such major difficulties as liquidation problems and cash flow difficulties. This financial control starts at the very early stages of any organizational review or establishment in the setting up of accurate and appropriate budgeting techniques, with built-in monthly reviews of financial performance.

Organizational change

In terms of change, structure always remains an important element but the values held by key people within organizations have a distinct effect on how organizations change.

Change involves much more than just introducing or suggesting changes; it means that old beliefs and values have to be broken down and that new directions have to be charted. Individuals in sports organizations can have a major input to this, both positively and negatively.

The structures have to be in place which allow this change to take place, but individuals, personalities and attitudes are just as fundamentally important in achieving any real change.

The management of change

A bend in the road, is not the end of the road – unless you fail to make the turn.

Anon

'The only thing that is constant is change.' This is an oft-quoted maxim, and it is true that things seem to change constantly throughout industry and, indeed, life in general. It is no less true in the sports business. In a new millennium people live in a turbulent world, and with the changes in technology; demography; the single European market; the disappearance of the Eastern Bloc; Best Value; political change and a vast array of other developments, there seems to be constant change facing the sports manager.

There is no single answer to all these challenges, but if we are to be competitive and face up to potential threats then we must look to management procedures and practices – we must consider quality management and look for a Total Quality Management approach.

The recent past has seen enormous change in management circumstances and style, in both the public and private sectors. Some authors suggest that the 1970s was the last decade of the traditional order in management terms in the western world.

> In today's world there are two kinds of companies – the quick and the dead.

Anon

Sports organizations in the private, public and voluntary sectors have to operate in a totally different situation to that which faced them previously. The political changes have been enormous and have resulted in sport having to face the pressure of justifying itself in the face of spending cuts, rather than survive on the traditional ethos that sport is worthwhile for its own sake.

The advent of compulsory competitive tendering for the management of the vast majority of public sports facilities put different pressures on sports managers, and caused local authorities to look at the financial, rather than the service, priority in many situations. This was not always of benefit to sport, and caused significant problems for the participants and organizers of sport at a wide variety of levels, in relation to rising costs and reduced availability.

This has now been replaced by the Best Value policy – making it legally binding on local authorities to ensure they are delivering the most cost-effective provision on services. This presents new challenges and competitive and financial pressures on the sports managers involved.

The changing structures of local authorities themselves, and fundamentally different philosophies, have caused problems for everyone in management in the local area. The various changes to management practices and structures have also caused significant challenge.

The sports manager must be able to foresee change developing in order to react appropriately, efficiently and effectively. Most changes, large or small, throw up opportunities as well as threats. It can be argued that the successful manager is the one who ignores or avoids the potential threats and seizes the opportunities unreservedly. This tends to be true in the wider commercial scene, but applies in sport as well.

The implementation of vocational qualifications is a good example of how sporting bodies could have seized the opportunity to push the standard of training of their staff and volunteers to a higher level, but many still ignore the opportunity and tend to regard such developments as threatening and too complex for them to undertake.

It is often suggested in sports situations that 'we are very bad at marketing ourselves'. This can be seen as a result of the same intransigence – being set in our ways and failing to identify the potential opportunities and align sport with them.

The marketing concept is not one which fits in easily to many sports situations as there is often no professional expertise, nor any appropriate enthusiasm to produce the increased participation or awareness that is desired. Reaction to change is the measure of the health of an organization, no matter how strong.

Everyone has to be involved in the team effort to face the current challenges. Changes affecting sports in recent years have been many and their implications have often been very complex for the facilities, the staff, and the service offered. These changes can be internal, coming through the organization from the staff or customers, or external, coming from politicians (local or national) and other influential sources, such as the national sports agencies.

Changes which have had a significant impact on sports managers and providers include:

- the formation of the Foundation for Sport and the Arts
- the reorganization of local government
- the advent of the National Lottery
- the restructuring of the sports councils in the UK
- consideration of the national curriculum and its impact in sport
- the need for drug-testing facilities at all major sporting events
- the abolition of minimum rates of pay
- the move towards more part-time and fewer full-time staff
- the increased demand for sports and leisure facilities
- the changing trend of sports demands (e.g. the growth of basketball due to massive television coverage).

Any change can be perceived as threatening by the personnel involved, but can also throw up opportunities which should be portrayed positively and taken advantage of as appropriate. A good manager will involve staff fully in facing up to changes affecting their operation. It is not adequate to tell staff that certain things have happened. Rather, it is necessary to inform them from a very early stage what exactly is going to happen and where they have a role to play in responding or leading the change, rather than being demotivated by factors which they perceive they cannot control. Team briefings are a key part of facing the challenge of change, and every sports organization should have well-briefed staff, whether paid or voluntary.

The old adage of knowledge being power can lead to managers not wishing to share their knowledge and understanding with staff. This is a sign of limited thinking and will lead to staid and restricted organizations which will not be able to respond well to the changes that face them.

As mentioned above, the demands of participants in sport tend to change in line with currently popular sports or trends in clothing or standards of equipment expected. Such change is almost constant, being driven by highly commercial agencies, and a key role of the manager is to attempt to foresee trends and patterns of participation and demand. As in any level of industry, the manager who gets in first with an initiative or reaction to changing trends will benefit both personally and organizationally.

In particular, in the public sector there has been a great deal of pressure to change the method of management and especially to make managers more accountable for their actions. This has led to the introduction of performance reviews (which are discussed in Chapter 7) and to tighter budget controls and cost examinations, as well as specific performance targets being set.

In addition, the following advantages are intended to come from such accountable management and more localized spending of the budget:

* a lessening of bureaucracy, which allows better response to localized environmental factors and more adaptability towards customer care and consumerism
* increased efficiency and effectiveness, which should bring about more economic working through localized setting of objectives
* the leaving of local operational management to lower-level staff while strategic planning is undertaken at a higher central level.

This trend to local accountable management is closely related to constant consideration of whether public management should be aligning itself to business management practices. In the recent past, the Thatcherite agenda suggested that it should and that too much thought was given to the public aspect of the management rather than the management aspect of activity. There was a strong belief that moving public services to business operation and thinking would be beneficial. There is, however, a strongly held local (politician and officer) view that the delivery of public services is in essence different because of the differing ethos, which makes it quite distinct from the business community beliefs. The overall goal to provide service is quite different from the ultimate goal of providing profit.

In the 1990s, government began to set very specific targets for local service organizations to raise their management standards – this was the main thrust of the Citizens' Charter announced by the Prime Minister in 1991. The intention of this was to give quality customer satisfaction and care through a detailed set of expectations that the customer could see fulfilled on all occasions. This would be the standard that organizations would be judged against.

Decision-making

He who hesitates is lost.

Anon

Interestingly, decision-making may be seen as a crucial factor in separating top-quality sports performers from the run-of-the-mill participant, and it is also a major distinguishing characteristic between top-level and mediocre management in the sports industry, as in many other industrial settings.

It is vital that staff are given the power to make decisions, the support to carry them out, and that they are dealt with fairly if the result of these decisions is not all one would hope for – again, very similar to the response one would hope to get from top players, coaches and team managers.

It appears that individuals tend to make decisions based on:

- experience
- judgement
- creativity
- innovation
- personal skills.

As with so many other abilities required by the manager, if an organization wants good decision-making then it has to train and support its introduction and adoption. It is wrong to assume that decision-making ability will naturally exist in all potential sports managers, and even if it is latent it will only be reflected or enhanced through significant training and encouragement of individuals. Additionally, the organizational structure must allow for decisions to be made at the appropriate level by the appropriate individual without fear or favour and without constant worry about retribution for errors – we are all human and errors of judgement are inevitable, but fortune favours the brave and he who dares wins!

Case study 8.1: Birchfield Harriers

Success comes with good development planning. Birchfield Harriers – one of the UK's most successful athletics clubs – has illustrated the need for, and the benefits of, planning for progressive club development (Tilling, 2001).

The club devised a five-year development plan by going through the process of:

- doing a current situation audit
- identifying the need for planning, how it is and who it is for
- examining the club structure
- specifying the key areas for attention and action
- detailing the key areas for development
- carrying out a SWOT analysis
- identifying aims and objectives for five years from now
- agreeing these and identifying sources of them
- costing proposals and identifying sources of funding
- building in monitoring mechanisms and review dates.

This type of businesslike approach is what underpins their success on the track – not just good coaching.

Self-assessment question

Which particular issues relating to organizational management listed in this chapter, do you see as most important? Justify your choice and proceed to consider any recent changes in a sport or in the context in which it operates that affect the management of the organization.

9 Management in practice

This chapter examines management in practice, starting with management processes and moving right through to the management of sport as a public service. In between, it considers financial management and the importance of monetary issues to sport, suggesting the particularly relevant issues and how they might be covered. It lists the massive legislation which impacts on sport and its management environment – added to enormously by, for example, the Disability Discrimination Act. The management of safety is mentioned and the Health and Safety at Work legislation and its implications are considered briefly. The management of support services and administration is elucidated, and public service issues are outlined.

Management processes

Many people within sports organizations see themselves as administrators rather than managers. This assumption fails to recognize the major changes facing sports organizations, which require management that has to be provided by the top people in the organization, whether paid or voluntary. People with ability must be found – the ability to make the most effective use of the available resources, to search for new resources, to innovate and take risks in stretching the organization in pursuit of new horizons.

Such change requires external awareness from everyone involved in the organization, beyond the very basic chalk-face operator. Effective officers must be oriented to working with people and drawing on their strengths, and be aware of the resources available outside their specific organization or limited role. Only by maximizing what is available internally and externally can progress be made in a time of seemingly constantly reducing resources.

Officers in any management role must be concerned with administering an ongoing effective service as well as being alert to the potential of collaborative problem-solving, which will ease funding through external sources. Such challenges demand two distinct areas of ability – a systematic approach to tasks and a creativity in developing opportunities.

Successful management depends on the ability to adapt management skills and organizational structures and practices to the demands of the agency's environment – both external and internal. It is important for sports organizations and their managers to be very aware of where the organization is functioning and to be active in the area in pursuing support for that activity. It is dangerous for any organization, especially sports organizations, to become insular and not to be responsive to external influences or at least be aware of any potential threats or opportunities.

It is common in voluntary sports organizations to see people dig in their heels against local authority or sports council action when in actual fact they should be looking for opportunities to manage the situation to their advantage.

Financial management

The raising, caring for, and spending of money is a constant battle for anyone involved in sport. This is probably true in a wide variety of business settings, but in the sports industry, which is often strapped for cash, working on tight margins and operating in the voluntary sector, money becomes a major consideration.

Two major concerns arise in particular about financial management in sport.

- The individuals involved in sport, whatever their role, are far more interested in sports participation than in looking after pounds and pennies. Financial management requires an attention to detail, and a regular and exact habit that to some extent is foreign to anyone involved in sport.
- For the voluntary organization it is very often found that the individual who spends all their working life handling finance is reluctant to spend their spare time doing the same; for example, the accountant would probably rather give their time to being a hockey umpire than being a treasurer. This reluctance to apply professional skills directly to the sports situation can give rise to some potential problems and can remove the highest level of professional skill to another role.

For sports organizations outside the private sector the first of these concerns is a real issue and should always be recognized. Within the private sector, the drive for a successful bottom line tends to ensure that finance is appropriately considered at all stages.

There is also a major contradiction about money within many sports settings – people who bemoan the lack of money are not prepared to spend their time trying to raise it or control it, so ensuring that it is used to the best effect. Consequently they may have to restrict their activities even further. In short, money management is often seen as a restricting requirement rather than something which can enable activity and is a key part of any sound planning process. Sourcing money is a key part of the work within sports administration, and looking after it once it is obtained is crucial to allow effective operation. The opposite situation is a lack of proper financial management impairing the functioning of the organization, reducing the opportunities it can provide, and ultimately restricting sports participation.

Failure to manage existing funds damages sports organization and individual opportunities, and can cause major damage to an organization's image. Such damage tends to multiply by creating a belief that money should not be directed to an organization because it previously failed to manage its existing finances properly.

Sports organizations do not require treasurers or financial controllers who are overly restrictive in their expenditure and use their control over money to limit the development of the sport, because they may have individual differences with general policy or they feel money is being spent wrongly. Equally, someone who is too lax with expenditure is not helpful, and such over-expenditure will return to haunt the organization in the future. The correct balance of secure financial control and ambitious development plans is crucial in a sports organization – a difficult, but essential debate to ensure progress based on a sound financial footing.

Often financial control in certain organizations is seen as something which is done for others, e.g. national governing bodies may feel that they undertake it for the Sports Council to justify the grant support from government funds. Such a belief is erroneous: financial control is key to any successful operation, and one only has to look at the major successful companies in the business world to see that financial considerations alongside strategic direction determine the ultimate success of the organization. This is equally true in the sports business – public, private or voluntary. Sports organizations must put in place systems and structures which ensure optimum use of finance to achieve organizational objectives. They should look upon finance as an opportunity rather than a threat, and realize that when money is available it is a major opportunity for enlargement of the scope of the business, and the obtaining of money is a vital part of allowing a sport to develop. Financial controls are good business practice; they are not a threat to existence, rather an enablement for further progression and development.

The scope of this text does not allow detailed consideration of financial management – there are many specialist texts for those charged with the responsibility of looking after the money and, indeed, raising the money. Some of the books listed in the bibliography and other non-sport financial management and control texts are worth studying. The necessity for professionalism and meticulous care in handling these matters cannot be over-emphasized, as the potential problems are enormous for both the organization and the individuals involved. Apart from lost opportunities, ineffective control can cause significant difficulties and embarrassment all round.

Due to the vast array of locations in which sport is delivered and practised, the requirements for financial control and management are extremely diverse. The following list indicates the difficulties in covering this completely, because many or most of these areas have to be considered in each case. The group or individual charged with controlling finances should perhaps look at the following list and identify the areas which concern them and seek appropriate further help or study sources. It is also advisable, where the sum of money is significant (as it is in many sports organizations) that professional help is sought at appropriate times in the establishment and monitoring of systems, as well as the assembly of end-of-year accounts and the auditing of these.

Among the areas which might have to be considered are:

- Accounting
- Analysis
- Auditing
- Balance sheet
- Book keeping
- Budgeting
- Business plan
- Capital costs
- Cash control
- Cash flow
- Cash holding limit
- Cash summaries
- Costs
- Equipment purchases
- Estimating
- Expenditure
- Financial statements
- Financial targets
- Forecasting
- Income
- Information technology
- Inventory
- Investments
- Limited company
- Organizational structures
- Petty cash
- Point of sale records
- Pricing policies
- Profit
- Profit and loss account
- Profit margins
- Recording
- Revenue costs
- Risk
- Sales
- Security systems
- Span of control
- Staffing
- Stock control
- Stock recording
- Stock taking
- Subscriptions
- Tax.

This list may be intimidating, but it indicates the many areas to be examined and the potential for difficulties. It exemplifies the necessity to ensure that appropriate structures and systems are in place to guarantee financial propriety and effectiveness. Missing or ineffective coverage of any specific area will potentially cause enormous damage to the organization, by undermining its practical efficiency.

> Sport is a business with a difference. The Board of Management usually do it for nothing and any surplus is usually reinvested in the sport.
>
> *Peter Lawson (formerly CCPR)*

Any sports organization, in whatever sector of the industry, must have a clearly laid out business plan and the financial targets to accompany it. Financial management is about assessing the success of the organization against these targets and monitoring its performance to ensure that any significant deviation is noted and acted upon.

To produce effective figures for presentation in a business plan, careful estimating and budgeting of expected income and expenditure must be done. The necessary financial research must be undertaken to ensure that these budget figures are as accurate as possible. Once again, significant errors in this area are all too easy to make for lack of consideration at the appropriate point. As in most situations, being conservative about income and pessimistic about expenditure is the best way for an organization to set its budget figures, while it is to be emphasized that they should be realistic and not artificially set. All too often, however, they are not based on past experience of the organization or the realistic situation the organization is currently in; or the figures don't reflect the practical situation for similar sports organizations in the country – this again is down to accurate research, which must be undertaken. It is a recipe for disaster to pluck figures out of the air which can then throw the organization off in the wrong direction.

Beyond setting the correct targets, the key issue is to ensure that the organizational set-up can deliver these targets and that the structure formed can implement appropriate controls and systems to deliver on the items identified as necessary (from the above list). An appropriate structure for many sports organizations should include individuals or groups covering the key areas identified in Figure 9.1.

While Figure 9.1 will not suit every situation, it indicates the kinds of thought processes and mechanisms that ensure appropriate financial control.

The key concepts about financial management in any sports organization are that:

- it addresses the issues that affect the business
- it is not ignored
- everyone takes a positive attitude to what properly managed finance can do for the organization
- the dangers of not facing up to such matters in a professional manner are recognized.

There are no second chances: a pound once spent is gone, and if it is not used for the correct purpose then the sport will suffer.

Legislation

A wide range of legislation affects the sports manager or administrator – it seems to increase almost daily. Areas such as health and safety, in the workplace in particular, increase in impact as sport and legislation become more demanding.

Figure 9.1 Financial management – a structure for policy and control

The operation of stadia and other sophisticated facilities entails more potential problems for managers. The frequency and volume of use can cause problems which are covered by legislation.

In general terms the professional sports manager/administrator should seek specialist advice from lawyers, health and safety experts, and others with specific expertise in areas in which they are unsure. The key point is that there are legal duties upon employers and organizers which must be met – failure to do so could lead to consequences which could permanently, or even fatally, damage the organization, and even have personal implications for management staff.

Where appropriate, further reference will be made to specific items of legislation throughout the text, e.g. the arrangements and implications under legislation introducing Compulsory Competitive Tendering for sports managing contracts as a part of government legislation on leisure provision by local authorities in the UK. Some of the less direct Acts that need to be considered by sports organizers and administrators are:

- The Health and Safety at Work Act 1974
- Offices, Shops and Railway Premises Act 1963
- Employers' Liability (Compulsory Insurance) Act 1969
- The Sex Discrimination Act 1975
- The Race Relations Act 1976
- The Unfair Terms Act 1977
- The Fair Trading Act 1973
- The Consumer Safety Act 1978
- The Consumer Protection Act 1987
- The Supply of Goods and Services Act 1982
- The Public Health Acts of 1875, 1890, 1907, 1925, 1936, 1961
- The Open Services Act 1976
- The Town and Country Planning Act 1990
- The Water Resources Act 1991
- The National Parks and Access to Countryside Act 1949
- The Wildlife and Countryside Act 1981
- The Countryside Act 1986
- The Gaming Act 1968
- The Lotteries and Amusements Act 1976
- The Licensing Act 1990
- The Trade Union and Labour Relations Act 1974
- The Employment Protection Act 1975
- The Employment Protection (Consolidation) Act 1975
- The Wages Act 1986
- The Equal Pay Act 1970
- The Local Government/Miscellaneous Provisions Act 1976
- The Local Government Act 1972
- The Salmon and Fresh Water Fisheries Act 1975
- The Safety of Sports Grounds Act 1975
- The Fire and Safety of Places of Sport Act 1987
- Fire Precautions Act 1971
- The Football Spectators Act 1989
- Football (Offences) Act 1991
- The Children Act 1990
- The Data Protection Act 1998
- The Disability Discrimination Act 1995

All these, in addition to, for example the Home Office *Green Guide on the Provision and Layout of Sports Grounds*, and the enormously (and almost daily) increasing body of European legislation, are affecting many aspects of life in the UK.

The impact of tax, in particular VAT, and the legal obligations of other relevant bodies with their appropriate legislation – the sports councils, National Trust, national heritage organizations, country parks and the Arts Council – can have an additional impact in the sports field where they are involved.

Obviously it is extremely difficult for any one sports volunteer to be expert in all or many of these areas, and it is essential that advice be sought before definite action is taken. This list of statutes does not cover every relevant government edict, but does serve to illustrate and back up the point that consulting the experts is advisable when legal issues are involved – take proper advice.

A large number of other rules and regulations can apply, depending on the precise situation, e.g. the various licensing and food hygiene Acts, as well as various laws relating to local government. There may be an obvious need to consider issues such as public entertainment and to follow the right legislation in certain situations; it is all too easy for issues such as alcohol licences and street collection permits to be forgotten, but this can prove expensive and problematic.

The sports manager/administrator may fill a number of roles, such as facility manager, event organizer or scheme promoter, but in all cases will have responsibility for considering relevant pieces of legislation. They must be aware of their detailed implications and try to keep up to date with the many changes that continually arise. It can be very difficult for the paid person to keep up to date; it is often verging on impossible for someone in the voluntary sector, but this does not make it any less essential.

It must always be remembered that, on occasions, the very lives of participants or spectators may be under threat if proper procedures are not followed and organizers must keep their knowledge current with regard to relevant safe practice and legislation. There are, for example, recent publications covering the health and safety of individuals at public performances and those at pop concerts or other outdoor events. This is in addition to the substantial legislation brought in as a result of the Taylor Report on the safety of stadia, after the tragedy at Hillsborough in Sheffield in 1989. Such legislation is designed to prevent any such disasters for spectators or participants in future, and is something that sports organizers should always be well aware of. In practical terms there are a lot of things that individuals can do to ensure that safety risks are minimal for event and sports participants. Sports organizers/administrators should cover and be knowledgeable about measures which help ensure that there will be no difficulty, such as:

- undertaking an appropriate risk assessment
- ensuring that appropriate first aid cover is available
- maintaining facilities to an appropriate and adequate standard
- ensuring that the rules of the competition specify a level of coaching qualification and constant coach presence during the competition or tournament

- good planning of a competition – allowing adequate warm-up time to safeguard against injury
- preparing participants to the appropriate level for the level of competition in which they are competing
- raising awareness of participants and everyone involved in sport about the inherent risks and the care that should be taken
- seeking legal waivers such as appropriate permission slips where necessary and ensuring that parents and others understand the potential dangers of certain activities.

Also:

- it is the duty of the sports manager/administrator to provide a safe environment for participants – the facilities and equipment should be safe, appropriate and correctly maintained; where risks do exist they should be kept to a minimum; defective or improperly designed equipment should never be used
- the organizers of the competition and certainly the facility manager, have a responsibility to ensure that maintenance and equipment are up to recognized international and national body standards, and that equipment is regularly inspected
- this duty of care is shared by everyone involved in sport – the facility manager, the sports organizer, the coach, the parent and indeed the participant
- coaches and officials should ensure that there are no mismatches in contact sport in terms of different ages, sizes, weights, skills or experiences being put in direct opposition, potentially causing significant damage to younger, weaker or less experienced participants (it is not the sole responsibility of the participants to ensure that they are not put in danger – everyone involved must take their share of the responsibility)
- participants and officials have certain rights to be allowed to express themselves in an appropriate manner and have freedom against discrimination – they also have a right to a degree of confidentiality of information which they pass to the organizers and they should have protection from intentional injury caused by the opposition or by bad procedures on the part of the organizers; the organizers should have adequate and properly circulated safety rules to avoid damage to any of the participants and they should inform the athletes and officials of what is expected of them
- officials at games should be aware that they have a role in ensuring the safety of all participants through correct and fair interpretation of the rules and having a good knowledge of the rules; they also have the role of ensuring that equipment and procedures in any event or tournament are safely employed – this is in addition to the competition organizers and coaches and others involved

- spectators and bystanders at events have a right to expect fair treatment from event organizers, who in turn must ensure their safety; equally there should be some rules for spectators and they should be advised as to what procedures to follow, especially in the event of any emergency, e.g. an outbreak of fire or a failure of floodlighting.

As mentioned above, a significant part of the legal implications is the necessity for organizers to keep records to ensure that all necessary legal requirements have been met, and are checked on an ongoing basis. This is vitally important; if the worst comes to the worst it may be necessary for such evidence to be produced in court. Failure to keep such records will also probably mean that incorrect procedures are being followed in that no regular checks are being made. Even if correct actions are being taken, it will be impossible to prove that this is happening (and that the staff are acting properly) if there is no record. For example, organizers should have a record or a checklist to be gone through when organizing an event so that they can brief all participants (and spectators) regarding fire and safety regulations.

As mentioned above, in the area of legislation it is always better for an organizer or administrator to check with experts to ensure they have followed the correct procedures. Additionally, it is essential that individuals consider all areas involved, for example:

- health and safety during the transportation of players and officials to and from a tournament or a facility
- insurance for people involved in organizing and setting up the event.

Insurance is an area often forgotten by sports managers/planning administrators. It relates to a wide variety of areas including personal liability, employee liability and employer liability, health and safety or health and accident insurance – another area well worth investigating.

It is essential to understand that all sports managers/administrators need to consider all the legal obligations of the vast operation they are involved in. They should not be expected to be expert in all areas, but should seek appropriate advice on all occasions. Failure to do so is in itself negligent. A good sports manager/administrator will always learn from the experts how to do things in the correct way. It is never advisable to think that they know it all. This is not an area which can be left to chance – the consequences are too frightening and potentially damaging to all concerned.

Sometimes, also, sports organizations need to be aware of the rules and regulations involved in running local lotteries and raffles, and the many regulations concerning the use of facilities such as public areas, rivers and footpaths. Additionally, since many sports situations require catering on either a commercial or a voluntary basis, the Food Safety Act 1990 and the Food Hygiene Amendment (Amendment Regulations 1991) as well as the regulations of 1966 for market stalls and delivery vehicles have implications.

The Lotteries and Amusements Act of 1976 is a key piece of information, and there are a significant number of additional considerations. The diversity of institutions causes all sorts of problems for sports managers, and they need to be aware and take appropriate advice while trying to get their thinking as wide as possible.

Management of safety

Safety management is a vital factor in sport. There are a number of legislative considerations under this heading that affect everyone involved, and additional concerns that arise through participation in sports. A number of sports are hazardous and by their very nature are challenging. The participants seek danger, thrills and excitement, and this can cause the manager or administrator major headaches. The organizer must aim to provide a safe and controlled environment for staff and participants, as well as spectators and anyone involved in any other role.

It may be thought that in relation to facility management, the management of safety is relatively straightforward, clear-cut and easily organized, but even there it can be difficult, and in some situations in the outdoors or the voluntary field it can be much more difficult to ensure.

The organizer's role is to ensure that all the participants, customers and employees are, as far as reasonably practicable, in a safe situation and are not putting themselves or others in more danger than the sport necessitates. This may seem an obvious statement, but is often difficult to put into practice, largely because the people we are trying to protect are being protected from their own or others' stupidity. In many sports, challenge, to the level of risking life, is a part of the sporting activity itself.

Legislation in this area is complex and manifold, and the advent of additional EU legislation has made it significantly more complicated for those involved in organizing sporting events.

Health and safety at work

It is essential for any event organizer to become familiar with the basics of health and safety legislation as they apply in such situations. There are a great number of items of legislation in the UK and the rest of Europe, all of which are designed to ensure the health and safety of participants and spectators in a variety of situations, with special emphasis on the workplace.

Significant pieces of legislation include:

* The Health and Safety at Work Act
* Food Handling
* Manual Handling Operations Regulations
* Display Screen Equipment Regulations (Computer and Word Processing Operation).

This vast array of legislation has been enacted to make the workplace and places of public entertainment safer for everyone. These regulations can be seen as limiting a manager's activities, but, as has already been highlighted, where there is any element of danger, public controls are essential and inevitable and should be looked upon as part of the organizational process, since they are vital to public health and safety. All managers in sport and recreation (as in other industries) must make correct health and safety arrangements, and undertake a risk assessment to ensure that there is no abnormal hazard or danger to anyone involved in the sport itself or the facility in which the sport is taking place.

The Health and Safety at Work Act 1974 lays down a number of regulations, but first of all it suggests that each facility should have a health and safety policy and this policy should have five key elements:

- planning
- organization
- control
- monitoring
- review.

The main focus of such legislation is that the manager of a sports facility, for example, has to ensure that to some extent individuals are protected against themselves and their own stupidity; for example, an unlocked door leading to a climbing wall might be seen as a chance for some individual to try their luck at this new and exciting sport. Obviously, potentially the results are extremely serious and it is essential that facilities are locked and access is available only on a planned and agreed basis. The Control of Substances Hazardous to Health (COSHH) Regulations are also a vital part of any sports facility staff guidance, because some of the chemicals used for cleaning could be extremely dangerous to individual and group health if incorrectly used.

It is important that all staff are aware of their responsibilities and the nature of these regulations – ignorance is no defence in law or practicality. Any such hazardous materials should be properly stored for the benefit of customers and staff alike.

The key items for consideration are that:

- a risk assessment must be undertaken on any work or participative area.
- potential activities must be given codings and rates against a frequency of risk – how often something is likely to happen based on past experience
- a safety audit related to all items of legislation should be carried out against the organization's current practice
- regular review of such a policy and how the regulations are implemented should be in place.

Another vital key issue in relation to health and safety is staff training – not just that it is done for their own and public protection, but also that it is logged and clear training records are kept showing the areas covered and when each individual member of staff attended any particular session. Staff should also be given updates, as sports facilities and equipment can change frequently as technology and techniques develop. It is essential that staff are aware of equipment, how it should be stored and set up, as well as practices in using that equipment which are seen to be potentially hazardous.

Examination of facilities, organizations and current practice by a new pair of eyes, from a safety point of view is an essential tool to minimize any possible risk through participation, and safe equipment and other such simple issues should be regularly attended to, maintained and an appropriate log kept.

Individuals can now be held personally responsible where the health and safety legislation is broken, and can be liable for allowing incorrect practices to proceed in events or facilities under their jurisdiction. This may be a little intimidating for some, but it puts the onus on all managers to avoid the continuation or development of unsafe situations for participation in sport. It also pressures individuals to assist in the formulation of the audits and procedures, necessary documentation and action frames for staff training.

It is difficult to exaggerate the absolute necessity for consistent quality safety management in all sports situations and for looking after participants (at all times, whatever their nature). This is because adverse publicity, apart from individual damage, can frighten people off certain sports and encourage the belief that these sports are in themselves dangerous and must be avoided. This could limit participation unnecessarily in a number of sports, such as gymnastics, diving and trampolining, and reduce individuals' enjoyment in these activities.

Coaches and organizers must also be aware of the increasing number of cases of litigation which have been seen in North America and in the UK. This may not necessarily be a constructive trend for the sport in general, but it means that managers, coaches, administrators and everyone involved in any sport must ensure that any duties they undertake are correctly carried out to ensure that there is no damage or potential damage to participants or others involved. Such a concentration on health and safety and ensuring that every possible step is taken to avoid ending up in litigation concentrates the mind of organizers to ensure that they think in a more decisive way about safe practice and carry out all steps necessary to guarantee, as far as humanly possible, the health and safety of all participant groups.

It is absolutely essential that all staff are adequately trained in appropriate procedures in terms of running an office or an event, including appropriate first aid knowledge, health and safety roles, emergency procedures and any facility regulations and roles laid down. In the sporting context there can be an added potential danger and the need, for example, for resuscitation to be applied in certain situations. The issue of health and safety is live, growing and will continue to grow, and needs to be closely considered in the establishment of any facility or any development scheme with sport. Not only local and national legislation are involved, but increasingly European legislation has to be considered due to the significant impact it can have in sporting situations. The Health and Safety Executive in the UK has been, and continues to be, extremely helpful in terms of educating individuals through providing educational booklets and pamphlets to everyone involved in situations where health and safety has a part to play, and certainly this is true of sport. Sport coaches, managers and administrators are well advised to make use of all the information they can obtain from such sources, as ultimately, being well versed in this vital area will be beneficial to all the groups of participants in sport.

It is always worth remembering that ignorance is no defence in the eyes of the law.

Managing support services

Often there is an erroneous concept in sports management that we are solely concerned with technical sports facilities, their provision and a high level of knowledge in their utilization. Realistically, nothing could be further from the truth – many of the organizational and motivational skills of the sports manager or administrator are common to managers in a variety of industrial spheres, especially in the wider area of leisure.

Additionally, the role of the sports manager is often largely taken up by provision not seen, initially, to be directly sport-related. The required back-up services for sports participants are an essential part of any manager's operation and must be seen as such – the typical facilities here are crèches, cafés, dressing rooms, toilet areas, meeting rooms, physiotherapy clinics, drug-testing facilities, etc. This list is extensive, but not exhaustive; it means the manager must be alert to the many requirements of supporting sport.

The management of a crèche can be a complex issue with legal requirements and other needs which must be thoroughly examined before such a facility is established. It is, however, increasingly essential to any sports facility, and can be beneficial to participation levels in a wide variety of events, from half marathons to water aerobics. The complications of running a crèche are enormous and should be very carefully examined by management staff before embarking on this project.

There is a necessity to consider almost everything in this provision in terms of location, interior layout, windows, doors, storage, toilet provision, kitchen facilities, baby changing area, safety, overall space, specific equipment, both large and small. In addition, the staff and their training and abilities must be closely examined and checks undertaken with the criminal records office as to their suitability.

A crèche is just one of the additional facilities that sports participation requires, and while it is one of the more complex, it just highlights the many other areas that the sports provider must know about.

Administration

Henri Fayol looked at administration and came up with a strategic view of the organization (Brodie, 1967). He argued that the administrative functions of any organization could be divided into:

* forecasting
* planning
* commanding
* co-ordinating
* controlling.

He stressed the need for clear objectives, authorities, decisions and tasks, and for a unity of command from top to bottom. All personnel should be linked into a clear hierarchy and chain of command. The span of control of managers should be limited so that they supervise a limited number of subordinates to get things done.

In practical sporting situations, administration is a hands-on delivery of sound procedures and systems to ensure that sport in all its aspects happens as it should. Administration focuses on the organizational practices and procedures which ensure that the day-to-day competitions, tournaments and events happen as they should, as well as making the overall organization function as it should. The list of duties involved in this sort of administration is almost endless, but would include:

* book-keeping
* handling entries
* arranging fixtures
* organizing transport
* keeping members informed
* arranging venues
* organizing meetings
* applying for grants
* keeping records
* paying expenses
* arranging events
* organizing international events
* supporting committees
* preparing development plans
* assisting coaches with training arrangements
* liaising with the media

- arranging team uniforms
- selling tickets
- inviting VIPs
- liaising with sponsors
- recruiting volunteer support
- selling programmes.

It is about the practical, vital minutiae of sport, and ensuring that it is organized.

Participants in sport need everything done for them (except to perform) or else they turn up at the wrong venue, at the wrong time, dressed wrongly. Careful attention to detail is the key to good administration, as is consistently applying quality standards in implementing the agreed policies of the organization.

Administration – delivering flawless organization – is every bit as crucial to the development of sport as quality management or coaching (Figure 9.2). Top-class arrangements are needed for top-class sport – poor administration will tend towards poor sport in terms of performance and development.

All too often the administrator is seen as the poor relation in the 'sports organization triangle', but this is quite, quite wrong – a good argument could be put that they are in fact THE most important. Sound administration is the basis for all top performing sports organizations.

The management of sport as a public service

While change has been the constant theme of many aspects of industrial operation and has affected sports management as other industrial sectors, nowhere has it been more noticeable than in the management of sport in the public sector.

The public sector in UK sport is a major player through national organizations such as the Sports Council and the home nations sports councils, but also through the massive spend on sporting activity by local authorities.

Figure 9.2 The sports organization triangle

The funding of sports activities, both local and national, has been dramatically affected by the limitations set on public expenditure by recent governments – a trend likely to continue well into the twenty-first century regardless of the political hue of the government concerned. The pressure on the public finances brought about by growing expenditure on the ageing population, social security and health payments has meant that all other sectors have had to take a significant cut. The effects of this have been seen in the leisure services generally and in sport quite noticeably. While the lottery income has brought about a massive increase in the funds brought into sport and sporting activity overall, this has been matched by a significant cut in the core funding of sport at local and national level by local and national government.

The impact of Compulsory Competitive Tendering has also been marked in changing the focus of sport from participation, enjoyment and community benefit towards the need to ensure that performance measures are met and that financial returns guaranteed by contracts are achieved. The impact of contract culture has been sizeable in both the short and medium terms, as well as potentially in the long term, but councils have begun to realize that the need to meet contract demands does not necessarily militate against developmental work in relation to sport, and indeed effective contract tender specification can enhance sporting opportunity and development work rather than always being seen as damaging to it. The efficient contractor will also see that being developmental and progressive can in fact lead to improved performance in contract terms.

The drive for Best Value, and the need for continuous improvement to deliver it, is likely to place more strain on public sector managers. They need to provide services as part of councils' corporate objectives of social inclusion, but against a backdrop of ever-reducing resources.

In public provision, as in any other sphere of delivery of sports services, good leadership and effective planning will consider marketing and customer care issues as well as other more modern management techniques. These matters have often been thought to be solely private sector issues and not so clearly identified with public provision of sports services. It is essential, however, that these services are in fact delivered in a well planned, well managed and customer-focused way. The national government would maintain that all the initiatives it has identified in this area have been focused on encouraging such thoughtful planning and efficient delivery for the benefit of the consumer. Some local government politicians, particularly those in an opposition party, would feel that many of the suggestions on how public leisure services should be provided have been imposed for reasons of governmental cost-cutting rather than for customer benefit. Recent years have seen public services inundated with a wide variety of measures aimed at improving the quality of service, and these have had an impact in sports management. Among others, these issues have included:

- quality management
- quality standards, e.g. ISO9001
- Investors in People
- Citizens' Charters
- Compulsory Competitive Tendering
- Best Value
- vocational qualifications and other training initiatives.

Some of these initiatives are considered in the next chapter and elsewhere in the text.

Self-assessment question

'For sport to be delivered effectively, top-quality management must be practised; often the level of achievement – at all levels – corresponds directly to the quality of the management.'

Comment on the accuracy of this statement and justify your comment on the basis of practical examples. Look particularly at financial and administrative delivery.

10 Management challenges

This chapter covers a range of varied issues which face the sports manager or administrator and considers their impact. It attempts to identify some of the key challenges at the time of writing – the balance or future impact of each of these is difficult to predict.

The issues covered include:

- Citizens' Charter
- competition
- financial control
- national standards
- voluntary input and management
- philosophical issues
- leisure trusts
- facility ageing
- performance indicators.

There are many aspects to all of these challenges, and they don't all apply in all situations. In some cases, however, they are of major importance to the sports manager.

Citizens' Charter

The main thrust of government thinking is that the management of public services in general, and sport within them, needs to be improved. To achieve this it is seen as important that customers get a clear statement of what they can expect from any public organization. Such a clear statement or promise to customers means that the organization becomes much more accountable to the clients and will have to introduce control mechanisms to ensure that it delivers what it promises.

Customer charters started with national organizations and organizations such as the Health Service, and have percolated down to local authorities, individual leisure departments, sports sections and individual sports facilities. It is not uncommon when entering a sports facility to see clearly listed a number of promises to customers in terms of a detailed charter of what they can expect within the facility, backed up by a brochure giving the full charter, and often by a defined complaints procedure so that any customer can raise an issue if they feel the customers' charter is not being fulfilled.

Competition

The 'threat of competitiveness' has also been used through Compulsory Competitive Tendering and market testing to give a more real challenge to the public service sector – especially at local government level. In practice a good deal of competition has come from the private sector through private clubs, hotel health suites and other such provision in the sporting area; however, research by the Centre for Leisure Research in Edinburgh has shown that competition for local authority sports and leisure management contracts in the first round of tenders in 1992–93 was extremely limited throughout the UK and very patchy indeed in its distribution. The private sector became more confident in the next round of tendering, although in many ways the context has changed. Many councils have become more aware of examining the methods of service delivery, and not just because the government has imposed Best Value procedures.

The biggest motivation for sports managers to change and develop facilities and services has been direct competition from the private, commercial and sometimes the voluntary sector for the finite number of customers in the market. The opening of new fitness suites with a very high standard of provision has meant that, to succeed and compete in the market, public facility managers and development officers must be able to provide something additional or at least of a similar standard to that which customers now expect. As with all provision in our modern society, customers' expectations are high and their experience through television, and other technological developments, is of a sophistication which many sports facilities have to struggle hard to match.

This drive to succeed in a competitive market has led to an improvement in the standard of many facilities, both new and refurbished, particularly in areas such as health suites and fitness training facilities where there is substantial commercial competition.

The push for competitive success has led to the introduction of quality management techniques which were first seen in Japan and the USA. This has placed additional pressures on managers in all organizations to come up with quality practices and procedures. This concept is considered at more length in Chapter 8. The movement towards quality operation and delivery has caused considerable additional work for the sports manager and administrator. While the end achievements of clearly understood working practices and correct procedures may be beneficial, the economic and social benefits have to be balanced to see whether the impact of the quality concept has been worth the time and effort it requires.

Best Value

The Labour Government, under pressure from its allies, the trade unions, devised a scheme to replace Compulsory Competitive Tendering (CCT) and its potentially punitive penalties. The unions felt that their members were losing out in terms and conditions of employment.

The government placed a responsibility on local authorities to ensure Best Value in the delivery of all their services – meaning that the local authority had a duty to provide them in the most cost-effective manner available. It further insisted on a programme of continuous improvement to ensure that innovative and efficient ways are found of providing its services to its customers while not overcharging local council-tax payers.

The government has continued its drive to enshrine this initiative in law, and in 2002 was in the process of finalizing its intentions and passing the necessary legislation through parliament in London and Edinburgh, and the assemblies in Northern Ireland and Wales.

Best Value is now clearly defined by all relevant government departments as 'a duty to deliver services to standards – covering both cost and quality – by the most effective, economic and efficient means available' (DCMS website). It will mean that local authorities will have to undertake fundamental performance reviews, set targets for sustained improvement in all their services and take into account the views of the local community and any nationally set government standards.

The government is also keen to establish a set of performance indicators that measure both output and outcome of local authority work, but this is complex and demanding and is taking some time to complete.

As far as sport is concerned, there are some real benefits to this drive to Best Value. Efficient and effective delivery of sports services must help everyone involved.

The need to measure outcomes as well as outputs is also of potentially enormous benefit to sport in the UK, especially because sport has often been subject to short-term thinking and project delivery, whereas to produce significant change, development or improvement is usually a lengthy process.

Very often, for example, in sport the emphasis has been on qualifying coaches and the output statistics. It may seem a really great output to qualify 50 new assistant club coaches in a year – but what is the actual outcome?

- How many people do they coach and what age are they?
- Are they still coaching three years on?
- How do they progress up the coaching ladder?
- Do they undertake further training?
- How many new clubs are formed?

- How many were previously unemployed?
- What is the real impact on the sport over a longer period, and in actual participation or performance?
- Was this a cost-effective use of the allocated monies?

Facing up to the demands of Best Value will be intimidating for some local authority officers, but, if positively and properly handled, could well enhance the long-term impact of the sport services.

Financial control

Central government has also used financial control to limit and dictate the activities of local authorities and other organizations such as the sports councils. This has been most effective in determining what activities these organizations will perform, and controlling staffing levels, otherwise central government funding, which is crucial, has been withheld. The claim of government has been that this will lessen the amount of, and the interference of, bureaucracy and get the money directly to the required areas – in truth, this requirement often tends to be what is perceived a priority at any given time by central government within financial limitations set by the Treasury (Figure 10.1).

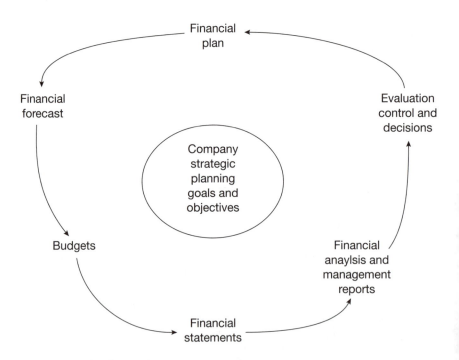

Figure 10.1 The financial management cycle – organization

National standards

The government continues to seek more ways of reviewing of performance and delivery by the public sector. it has increased the activities of the Audit Commission and the role of the office of the Deputy Prime Minister to monitor the performance of public sector management in a number of spheres, as well as keeping tight control over local government spending. It has been keen to introduce a number of national tables or standards, which must be met or measured by local authorities laying down a national curriculum and examination and testing structure with league tables to show clearly how schools are performing, though obviously this is only one area of their performance. This move is accompanied by the introduction of national performance indicators and public measures of the standards of provision. Designed to give the consumer more information on which to base choices, they are also intended to forge efficiency on public bodies and local authorities.

Generally speaking, any rise in the standard of provision for participants and others involved in sport must be welcomed and always aimed for, while there must be some type of real cost/benefit analysis to see whether the concept can actually work.

Pressure for change

Perhaps the key issues in relation to the management of change in sport, as in other settings, are:

- who makes the change
- whether it is imposed externally or brought about after a real consultation period
- where the power to make the change actually rests.

One of the major areas of difference, and perhaps confusion, within sport is the differences in working methods between the public, private and voluntary sectors. Change in the public sector is often imposed by national or local politicians, with officials left to carry it out and (where necessary) pick up the pieces, making the best use of limited resources in terms of cash or other requirements. They are sometimes left with little real power over the decisions made, so changes can be forced upon them.

This is the difficulty that some of these officials have in relating their situation to the private sector, where individual managers may well have significant power to make changes and to alter working practices. Managers must learn to recognize these differences, and perhaps be more tolerant of them when dealing with colleagues from other sectors. The voluntary sector, on the other hand, operates on a democratic basis and with committees and group decisions. This mechanism is not flexible enough to react quickly to change.

Voluntary input and management

Very often in voluntary bodies the power lies with committees rather than individuals, and even paid employees have very little real executive power in practice. One of the major changes being put in place by many governing bodies and being considered by others is in their management structure (which is referred to at various other points in this book) – aiming to make them more able to initiate changes they feel should be happening, rather than merely following sports participants into a change process.

This is a major consideration for governing bodies, which often react rather than lead sporting change, even in their own sport. The consultation periods undertaken by bodies, such as the Sports Council are often too short to be practical for many of the voluntary groups involved in the sports industry, and this often leads to a reaction against new initiatives by sports bodies that struggle to keep up with the pace of change. True consultation with voluntary agencies is difficult because of their extended operational structures. This is a major issue since governing bodies really should be taking the lead in their sport and yet, by their very organization and structure, often play the following role.

There is continuing government pressure to reduce the spending of money, through the sports councils, on governing bodies' general activities – the move is to eliminate as much bureaucracy as possible and fund to youth sport and excellence directly, so that the money goes to other more general activities or administrative activities. This is a move that many in sport support, while the long-term effects of such initiatives are not known.

There are also claims that too much money given to the sports councils is spent on bureaucracy – a view which may have some substance – but it is difficult to see how direct funding from central government to governing bodies, facilities or activities could function without an intermediary body such as the Sports Council. Also, the more money it has to allocate (e.g. through the lottery) the larger its bureaucracy must inevitably be. This issue is live and will continue to be so for the foreseeable future, especially if a government of a different political view comes along.

Certainly, the government sees the Sports Council role as one of empowering other people to spend money to achieve sport participation and performance. It is likely that this perceived role will not change significantly, especially as it is widely shared by those participating in sport who do not like to see the Sports Council spending money on marketing itself.

Philosophical challenges

Undoubtedly the key issue for sport facing change is the need to ensure that its philosophy and concept are kept intact and that no damage is done to the fundamental belief in sport which keeps sports managers, administrators and participants going.

This conviction that the provision of, and the participation in, sport is vital to our health individually and culturally makes it worth facing up to challenge and change, making progress and leading the way for the benefit of all involved. With this positive philosophy in place, change will throw up many more opportunities than threats, because it will be met face to face by individuals with a commitment to the cause, taking positive steps, seizing the initiative and charting a way forward.

Sport is all about ethics and philosophy linked to belief and commitment – anything that undermines such concepts has the potential to damage sport, in the public or other sectors.

Investors in People

Investors in People (IIP) is a government scheme which aims to encourage organizations to take their people seriously as the key aspect for the improvement and development of the organization. The scheme sees a personnel development programme as key to improving industry quality delivery.

The four principles are as follows.

1   An 'Investor in People' makes a public commitment from the top to develop all employees to achieve its business objectives.
2   An 'Investor in People' regularly reviews the training and development needs of all employees.
3   An 'Investor in People' takes action to train and develop individuals on recruitment and throughout their employment.
4   An 'Investor in People' evaluates the investment in training and development to assess achievement and improve future effectiveness.

A variety of sports organizations have become involved in IIP and have had either an initial, or in some cases, concluding assessments by the independent assessor provided by IIP. As in so many systems, the key issue is not the certification but the recognition of the crucial nature of staff and staff development to successful organizations.

This initiative has, however, as in a number of other industrial settings, proved so onerous that the numbers coming forward are still small.

Leisure trusts

Many local authorities have, in recent years, moved the management of their sport and leisure facilities (and in some cases, services) into an independent (to a greater or lesser degree) leisure trust. This has largely been done to save money and to benefit from certain tax breaks, particularly in relation to VAT. The change is also intended to create more commercial opportunities and foster the adoption of good business practice to reduce over time any council grants.

A number of smaller leisure trusts have also been formed to allow local communities to run their own sports facility or facilities. This has facilitated localized democratic control and input to the management process. The accountability to largely 'amateur' voluntary boards has become an issue under this sort of regime; again, different stresses and strains can appear and delivery can be affected.

Only time will tell whether the trust approach to sports provision has been successful, but the focus has been on saving money and necessarily improving service in the short term. The increase in commercialization may also mean that trusts will compete with the private sector for the better-off customers. In an attempt to maximize income, they may exclude some of the poorer members of society – the precise group local authorities are meant to be supporting and providing for.

It does seem that there will continue to be a drive towards the leisure trust delivery mechanism in the foreseeable future – for better or worse.

Ageing facilities

A major issue in UK sport over the next decade will be the growing age of the facilities, particularly those under public control. The bulk of the facilities in the country are reaching their 'sell-by' age, supposed to be 30 and for many now approaching 50, and for some even passing this.

This ageing process brings massive cost implications in terms of maintenance, refurbishment and replacement. Most public agencies simply can't finance these capital costs, even where lottery funding is available in support.

There is a growing challenge in keeping these facilities operational, and there is a real possibility that some will close or at least start to offer reduced provision.

Performance indication

In a number of settings, the levels of service delivery and their measurement have become increasingly important. Some believe that the public sector has become almost fixated by them.

The government has imposed statutory performance indicators on local authority provision in leisure and recreation, including sport. These are limited to basic percentages of the local population participating at the authority's facilities. Various initiatives have suggested ways of making these indicators more appropriate, but it is always difficult to identify ways of gathering the information on performance which we would like to know across the country. Sport England has recently produced a range of recommended performance indicators, of which local authorities can choose to adopt one or all. This leaves the situation somewhat *ad hoc*, but at least it gives a clear picture of what should be considered important in delivering local sport services and what should be measured.

The fundamental and difficult task is to make what is important measurable, and not just measure what we can – i.e. make the measurable important. Ultimately, the impact of the sports provision on the local community and its population is what is important.

Self-assessment question

In your situation in sport (or in one with which you are familiar), which are the key challenges to be faced and what are the specific issues relating to them? How will these challenges be addressed, and what will be done to meet them?

---

11 Marketing

This chapter covers the important, if often misunderstood, area of marketing. It starts by emphasizing the need to be businesslike and to take a wide view of marketing – seeing it as integral to the management process, not as just an 'add-on'. It expands on this ethos and gives a number of practical illustrations, both positive and negative. It then establishes the marketing mix of the four 'p's seen as relevant to sports marketing. Each of them is explained and illustrated in the context of sport. Later concepts such as marketing ethics and participation are considered, before looking at how the process is implemented and what activities are undertaken. It is suggested that an organizational SWOT analysis may be helpful. Public relations, fundraising and sponsorship are then examined, with examples.

'Brusque to the point of being businesslike.' This statement reflects a British viewpoint that being professional and businesslike means being curt and short with customers and clients. In a true customer-care focused business this is exactly the opposite of the truth; being businesslike is about spending time with clients, getting to know what they want and meeting their needs.

> Business has only two functions: marketing and innovation.
>
> *Peter F. Drucker*

Marketing is a key area of operation for all modern-day businesses. It must be seen as a process, not a theoretical concept, and must be a shared concept for every one of the staff. Marketing should be seen as the responsibility not of one individual but of every person working in the business of sport. It is often believed that marketing is the weakest part of some sports operations. This may well be due to the fact that the term is not understood by many and so is not implemented by everyone as it needs to be.

The definitions of marketing are many. However, all of them place the customer as 'king' and emphasize that the manager's job is to ensure that this is the case on every occasion, and in every circumstance. Sports administration is a client-led business.

There can be little doubt that the function that people in sports management and administration do least well is marketing. As suggested above, the problem often originates from a misunderstanding of what marketing is, and this filters right through the organization to cause poor provision of the practical requirements in the implementation for sports management.

Marketing is a much abused word in many aspects of modern business and, indeed, some blame has been directed to the marketing professionals themselves for being seen as more interested in show and a 'razzmatazz' profile than in the delivery of a quality product. This misguided effort and the growth of the marketing industry, and all its spin-offs, have given some people a false impression of what is meant by, and what should be implemented under the heading of marketing.

In any industry, marketing must be seen as a process and a practical approach to apply throughout the organization, and not just as a clever concept or 'the showy bits' of presenting a finished product. It is as important for sport to consider marketing, thinking back from the eventual product and the end client, as it is to consider sports policy. The analogy of genuine marketing starting on the factory floor where workers put bolts into cars is sound – marketing pervades the whole business. Everyone involved in the sport, including (and sometimes especially) the performers, must see themselves as part of the marketing of the sport and must make an effort to make the sports product attractive, if it is to be sold to potential supporters and customers.

Marketing is about the whole package, not just advertising. It is about the way everything is packaged and presented from idea to implementation. Part of marketing will be to produce an attractive product which is then sold to appropriate groups in an appropriate manner. Consideration must be given by everyone involved to their part in the whole marketing process.

The biggest task, then, in the area of marketing is to convince everyone that they have a role within marketing, and to get everyone working towards successful, genuine marketing of the sport. This may sound easy, but for many traditionalists it is a whole new approach and a considerable amount of effort will be required to get any real movement in this direction. This change of thought process is absolutely essential for the marketing approach to work. To implement such a major change in thinking is very difficult with people who have often felt that participation in sports organization just happens for a small number of people who want to play the game, and there is no need to extend beyond the basic provision for the committed person.

In the mid-1990s, an official of the Rugby Football Union, speaking to a parliamentary committee, said that he saw no major problems for his sport in terms of attracting sponsorship. It was a well supported game which was currently thriving. This type of complacent approach may mean that in a few years sports with such an attitude will not continue to thrive. This optimistic outlook can be justified in the periods of success, but to have genuine prolonged progress, sport needs to have a firm foundation which can sustain its growth even through leaner periods. To be complacent because of what may be transient success in a specific sport is to 'fiddle while Rome burns'.

The structures of sport need to be able to withstand any fluctuations in success and to ensure lasting benefits in the future. Sports also have to recognize that good management practice will allow them to benefit from monies which may from time to time become available. If good practice is not in place then they may well suffer. A case in point could be said to be tennis in the UK. A lot of money has been available over a prolonged period, but the necessary marketing and the development of mass activity as well as the support structures for a number of talented individuals have not been properly in place to allow for the growth of standards or the production of quality players in the UK.

Money, while a major bonus, is not the sole contributor to sporting organizational success, nor is it a guard against external fluctuations. For example, it may be that rugby would suffer quite substantially if tennis were to get its act together in terms of producing quality in Britain and more public interest, or if one of the home nations were to be highly successful in the soccer World Cup then the interest in participating in rugby might fall dramatically, leading to a drop in standards possibly followed by a spiralling effect of continually reducing participation. This in turn could lead to less money and other support coming into the sport. Coupled to the 'club versus area' professional team debate in Welsh rugby union, there is a serious threat from a successful soccer team tempting potential players and backers away from the game. Professional sport needs to balance the books while maintaining longer-term interest for future investment.

A genuine marketing approach means that sport will do its best to guard against fluctuations in performance and external factors to ensure the standard is consistent by targeting the sport to attract new participants, satisfy existing ones, and develop the highest possible standards. There can be, especially, for the smaller sports, no opportunity for a 'sit back and watch' approach while the world is changing around them and other sports are growing. Clinging to the status quo is a recipe for death.

The aim must be to deliver a quality product in a form that is attractive to everyone involved. Even to participants, sports must be well presented and offered in a way that is attractive. This becomes increasingly important as demographic and economic movements mean that fewer people can afford to play more than one sport seriously; or some choose a sport for life or a range of sports for different levels of participation and commitment. An obvious example of how the product can be substantially changed is the many games that have introduced mini versions in order to please, suit and attract potential participants, especially young people, and tailor the product to the demands of these groups. Indoor bowls fundamentally changed its whole format and rules in order to attract television, sponsors and participants.

The Institute of Marketing has defined marketing as 'the management process responsible for identifying, anticipating and satisfying customer requirements profitably'. This concept has been widely accepted in private industry, but not so wholeheartedly in the public sector. A significant educational and motivational input would appear to be needed in both the public and voluntary sectors to get more effective marketing put in place for a number of activities, including that of sports management and administration.

Marketing is ultimately about an organization, whether commercial or not, identifying exactly what it is trying to do and who it is doing it for, and then doing this efficiently and effectively. It is necessary for the end-product to be widely available, and to be seen to be available, whether it is a service or a manufactured product.

The process of considering who the customers are and what they want will help focus the operation of the sports management service and will result in an improved product for the customers.

Effective marketing will also be very necessary for organizations in sport, because they too are in a competitive environment and must compete for customers and clients, whether they will be paying or not. The demands on young people, for example, mean that governing bodies must effectively compete for their interest and participation if sports dealing primarily with young people are to survive and thrive.

There is little doubt that marketing is the thing that sports organizations, particularly in the voluntary and public sectors, do worse than almost any other activity they undertake. This is not uncommon throughout industry, but sport certainly must languish near the bottom of the pile in terms of marketing acumen in the UK.

The problem is that the concept of marketing is not comprehended. The process of marketing must pervade the whole organization at all levels and be seen as a total process rather than as an initiative taken by one individual, or a group of individuals.

In order to embark on effective marketing one has to look at the current situation and consider users and non-users of the available sports facilities or services. This must be done by significant neutral market research. Research is essential, of both existing and potential customers, before goals and, more particularly, exact objectives are set for our organization.

The whole group of managers in sport must begin to see that marketing is an overall concept and relates to all aspects of the organization. They must begin to understand marketing in terms of the marketing mix and produce a marketing plan bearing all these factors in mind.

In the traditional combination or marketing mix there are four 'p's:

- product
- price
- place
- promotion.

Modern thinking is that one or more 'p's should be added to this list, these new concepts being:

- people
- physical evidence
- process.

In sport the following 'p's are also relevant:

- programming
- packaging
- presentation.

In 'people' we are referring to the key marketing tool in terms of implementation and face-to-face contact. They are the number-one determinant for the quality of the individual customer's experience on visiting a facility or coming into contact with any service provision.

The physical evidence is an area which is significant in sporting terms, because the physical experience will be a large part of what people see and experience and will affect their opinion as to whether they want to return in the future. The presentation of facilities, events and services is very important from a marketing point of view.

'Process' underpins service delivery in that the quality of the personnel and their delivery of the service in a helpful way is a major marketing bonus. If customers are to genuinely benefit and enjoy the experience then the process of staff involvement must be of prime importance.

For certain areas of sport and leisure facilities, the programming of facilities can become the eighth 'p' in the marketing mix, because the timing and presentation of a varied programme of activities for different levels of performer are key in increasing numbers and commitment of customers.

The balancing of a full and varied programme is a major factor in successful sports provision. Offering the right activities at the right time with the right leadership will determine substantially what type of uptake any provision obtains.

Examining all these factors will lead organizations to produce a marketing plan which puts in place the approach that has to be taken to increase customer uptake, market share, or organizational image. There may be other aims depending on the specific situation, but these three are often shared by a variety of organizations.

Very simply, the marketing plan, having identified the aims and objectives to be achieved, will look at all the factors in the marketing mix and specify a strategy for achieving them. There are perhaps three key issues: staff training, involvement and understanding of the marketing process and the part they play in it; a SWOT (strengths, weaknesses, opportunities and threats) analysis of the situation as far as marketing is concerned; and the production of a promotion plan for the facility or service on offer. This is a very basic guide for the considerations in drawing together a marketing plan; it is a very specialized and challenging task, but one that should be undertaken by all sporting organizations, as with other industries.

There are many sources of further information on how this can be done, and the number of books on marketing is enormous. All managers should study this topic, make themselves more market-aware and understand fully how they may get involved in developing the market to its fullest extent (a number of suitable texts are listed in the bibliography).

In practice, sports managers must first of all examine the location of their product or service, and where possible this should be made to be most suitable to potential customers. However, it has to be recognized that it may not always be possible to move this product. A sports centre cannot be moved to another part of town where customers might have different concepts and more money. It may be possible to open a new sports facility only in a limited space where there is enough land to make it viable. However, in terms of the internal place and finishes and furnishing, we should do everything we can to make it attractive and appealing to the consumer, present and potential.

One must realize that we are in a very competitive market and customer expectation is generally high. Many facilities in the public sector suffer because of a lack of refinement or polished finish when compared to high-spending, high-profile commercial facilities.

In terms of product, sport has to examine exactly what it is offering its customers, both present and potential. The quality of the product is often not considered, especially in terms of changing it. Rather it is presented to the potential user on a 'take it or leave it' basis.

At a very basic level, sports organizations have to consider whether their product is genuinely the type of thing that potential customers really want; is it the most suitable to the customers or is it the one that people tend to think of as most suitable? This would relate to things like mini games for under-twelve-year-old performers. Many sports see this as some type of extra rather than a total necessity if youngsters are to be attracted into their game. Children given the choice will not play games which they think too difficult or demanding with equipment which they cannot adequately handle.

The product, then, must be analysed and designed or altered, as appropriate to fit the customer's desires.

The price of sports activities is, in many situations, outside the control of the facility manager or the individual closest to the shop floor. In some other sectors, such as the smaller commercial gyms or snooker clubs, the manager may play a key role in the setting of prices. The price factor is the key issue in making things appealing to people, and its importance should not be forgotten in terms of siting facilities and user patterns. People should not see pricing as separate from marketing, but should look at what monies can realistically be taken in at specific prices.

Eli Callaway was a successful entrepreneur who turned his hand to golf-club production – starting famously with metal woods. He had an interesting belief as far as price was concerned:

> You cannot sell anything too expensively.

He thought that people valued and cherished expensive items and would pay for them. Cheap items were believed to be shoddy and undesirable: high price = high value = high quality.

This proved an extremely successful strategy for him in selling golf clubs – probably quite cheap to produce – for a very high price. Perhaps giving tickets a low price, as many administrators do, indicates a low-quality product to strangers?

Promotion is another aspect of marketing, much talked about and very often done poorly. Indeed, it is what many people see as marketing, perhaps because it deals with the more visible aspects. Promotion is wide-ranging and includes publicity, media relations, press conferences and other areas. Much of promotion can be done on a high-spending commercial basis, or even substantial things can be done at minimal cost, especially by voluntary organizations.

'People' is the most important 'p', as mentioned above. It is not always added to the marketing mix, but it should be because ultimately, in sports terms people are the most important commodity both as customers and as clients, and indeed as factors attracting other people to take part in sports or in specific sports facilities. The way in which people react as management or frontline staff will determine very largely how well a facility is marketed or used.

We must always, always, always remember that we are operating in a people business where personalities can make or break impact in both a positive and a negative way.

As mentioned above, when dealing with sport there are three other 'p's which perhaps can be usefully considered. First, programming is important in how any particular sport fits into the timetable of a facility or even the social life of participants. The timetabling of the busiest periods for the sports club or organization will be crucial – everyone wants to take part between 7p.m. and 9p.m., and creating programmes round these times is the secret to success, even if it is extremely difficult.

In terms of packaging sport has often been criticized for not presenting itself well enough, for example, to be attractive to the family in user-friendly language and information targeted at that particular group. The presentation of sport in terms of events and even publicity materials can be limited. It is unrealistic to believe that you will increase the participation levels if the presentation of sport, both on paper and on the playing field, is not of the appropriate standard. It is often, and correctly, said that all consumers, including children, are becoming more and more sophisticated each year in the UK, and if sport is not presented in a professional and attractive manner then it will not be taken up by many. This is particularly true as the number of young people to target is falling dramatically over the years.

Marketing ethics

In recent years a number of considerations have become more important in terms of marketing. These are issues that have to be addressed now, for the first time in many cases. Ethics is certainly one.

A specific prohibition, in most cases, is sponsorship advertising by tobacco and alcohol manufacturers. Only a few sports will escape severe criticism for becoming involved with such companies. In addition, the 'greenness' of products and the social image of sponsors is important to consider for sports getting involved with specific commercial interests.

Consumers are now worried and put off by high prices, deceptive practices, high-pressure selling or marketing, shoddy or unsafe products, planned obsolescence, cultural pollution, excessive political power, etc. There is a new marketing force in the air: marketing for the 'thinking customer'. A major concern is the image of sport generally and of individual sports organizations. For all marketing activities – internal and external – image is all-important.

The impact of 'drugs' on the public image of sport has been considerable and can cause significant problems to individuals trying to promote sport and the commercial benefits it can offer.

As well as positive image, marketers must limit negative image and potential damage. There is something called bad publicity – just look at the Millennium Dome!

Marketing participation

A lot of the time in sport we talk about encouraging participation, and marketing and promoting this concept. It is interesting that many such campaigns, such as Sport for All, 50+ and other targeted groups have been relatively unsuccessful, because of the lack of effective reinforcing factors.

Ultimately, participation in sport will be increased by potential participants seeing some greater benefit for participating – this may be in the form of health or fitness or some other reward which suits their purpose.

They need to see that participation in sport is supported by government, local and national, by public attitude and indeed by the public purse. It is pointless to ask people to take part in sport if it is going to cost them too much for the initial participation.

Possible actions of positive reinforcement could be in the income tax system, or some other concrete method of encouraging participation not yet identified or practised in the UK. If taking part in sport is genuinely good for health and this can be proved, perhaps participants should have a lower national health service contribution. Indeed, it may be that the government should encourage sports participation because such health benefits are a long-term saving for the public purse, and to encourage participation it should pass on these possible economic benefits to the individuals concerned.

This type of thinking may be radical but, until some such change comes, it is difficult to anticipate further dramatic rises in baseline participation just for the sake of it. If the government truly wants us to take part in sport and believes it is very important, then it must be positive about tax benefits or find some other basis of supporting this participation.

Additionally, the whole issue of school sport needs to be addressed with a view to encouraging schools, especially in this time of devolved school management, to consider school sport as important and to fund such activity appropriately. The future of school sport will be left in the hands of head teachers, and they must see some encouragement for this participation in terms of health and potential support funding.

Again, if the national government believes that sport is important then it should be specified quite clearly within the national curriculum and enforced through government pressure in all possible ways. The benefits to the school system through reduced absenteeism, truancy and social misdemeanour could make any money spent in encouraging involvement in sports very well worthwhile, not just from a performance point of view.

Marketing sports participation is not just about telling people; it is also about creating the correct environment and resource conditions in society.

Implementing the marketing process

It is important that the whole of the association or organization sees marketing as important and realizes that everyone within the organization must be involved if it is to be effective. In a sports centre, for example, the frontline staff (the reception and leisure attendant staff) are a key part of the organization marketing from the presentation and image point of view. Such staff must clearly see that they have a role in marketing the organization, and not feel it is an activity related only to advertising and promotion.

Obtaining such a positive belief on the part of all staff is extremely difficult, but should be undertaken since the benefits are considerable in terms of customer return; more intimidating is the prospect of negativity to all customers if this marketing role is not seen by all staff.

The practical overt steps of marketing, such as market research, advertising and mailshots, should not be seen as the only marketing duties undertaken by any organization. The holistic approach, which involves all the staff in an ongoing process, is crucial to effective marketing.

Case study 11.1: Marketing Manchester United

People often wonder why Manchester United are so successful, both on and off the park. There is absolutely no doubt that the marketing of the club, in terms of exploiting opportunities and maximizing profile, is quite superb.

Recently they have launched a credit card taking the club into the provision of financial services (with MBNA Bank). This is built on the back of their strong image and encourages supporters to support the club further by using its branded credit card.

United caused turmoil a few years ago by dropping out of the FA Cup to go and play in the inaugural World Club Championship. This move was not about football, but rather based on their desire to build their worldwide profile to an even higher level. A commercial branding exercise. Similarly, people wonder why Manchester United go on a Far Eastern tour each year – easily explained if you see the club shop in Singapore! Manchester United have saturated the market in the UK and in Europe, and they now have to look further afield. Soccer is a world brand and they are the brand leaders.

It is interesting to consider all the other activities which they will embark on. These will include:

- player appearances
- corporate hospitality
- developing new team uniform
- supporters' newsletters
- charity work
- TV appearances and interviews
- junior football development
- steward training needs analysis
- supporters' packages
- developing the image
- stadium tours
- merchandising
- website developments
- media relations
- local visits
- foreign tours
- stadium refurbishment
- advertising
- ticketing
- sponsorship.

For a large commercial sports business like this, the list is almost endless. There is a question over what impact any future lessening of standards on the park would have – how would the marketing personnel and activity have to react to that?

Marketing activities

The action dictated by marketing as an ethos and an organizational concept means that many additional activities have to be undertaken. It means that *ad hoc* decisions should not be taken in terms of organizational planning or action, but rather that significant research and analysis is necessary before any commitment is made which affects the whole marketing approach.

It is essential that all the staff put marketing into practice and use their joint expertise to consider, and where necessary search, the market they are in.

There are a number of steps to be undertaken to put a more active marketing strategy in place. In particular it is important that the organization undertake a SWOT analysis. This means that the organization should examine its strengths, weaknesses, opportunities and threats. This analysis, if realistic, will help identify where exactly the organization is in terms of facing up to the competition and moving forward to capture more of its potential market.

The typical strengths and weaknesses, opportunities and threats in a sports organization could be:

STRENGTHS	WEAKNESSES
Enthusiasm	Lack of knowledge
Commitment	Poor co-ordination
Technical knowledge	Untrained staff
Teamwork	Lack of management

OPPORTUNITIES	THREATS
Public interest	Other attractions
Positive image	Poor public image
Wide range of potential participants	Lack of understanding
	Lack of direction
	Competition

It is important that, following on from the internal analysis, the surrounding environment that the organization operates in is examined, in particular identifying the competition which faces the sports organization. It is also essential that potential and existing customers are clearly identified to see who they are at present and who they may be in the future, and what may be done to service their needs.

Overall the self-analysis process is to provide a better product for existing customers, and a more attractive one for potential customers.

If this marketing analysis is correct then the number of participants in any given situation will probably increase, though if a significant mistake is made in terms of the presentation of the facility, operation or service on offer, then damage can be done and the proposed beneficial marketing could in turn become detrimental.

Public relations

Over many years sport could be rightly criticized for having a generally poor image with the public, and this is something that it must work hard to improve. It is true in all sectors of the sports industry, and the poor image continues to the present day with the high public profile of the few athletes who take drugs as opposed to the millions who don't.

Sports organizations and institutions must work hard at their public image to minimize any negative effects. There is little doubt that this is one area of major failure of sport in the UK. The arts appear to have a fair amount of public and political sympathy, though not necessarily money, whereas sport tends to be the relatively poor relation in terms of such support and public awareness, and in fact government financial support – running at about 30% of that of the arts. This is particularly true of the amateur scene within sport, but is also true of all but a very small minority of professional sport teams or individuals.

Public relations (PR) is not just about publicity; it is to do with image, with comparing yourself to competitors; it is to do with public perception and is a process that should pervade the whole organization. It should start with an assessment of the current situation, and continue with production of a specialized public relations plan to improve image (and thinking) and the detailed consideration of how to implement this plan; there should be an evaluation at the end of the plan.

Such a plan would have the clear goal of ensuring that a positive image for the sporting organization was established and maintained through many items of promotion and a full ongoing marketing overview.

For example, many clubs have worked hard to change their image to a multi-purpose family venue rather than the hard-nosed game only for the working men. Strangely, rugby league fought such a battle for many years before soccer, and has probably been more successful in its results.

It is also arguable whether the family aspect of soccer is a real contributor to improving support or merely a cosmetic image frill. False imaging is long-term poor PR, as it will inevitably be found out.

The need to change the general public attitude to sport is well identified but is difficult to achieve, and certainly relates to a wide variety of issues including culture, family, religion, education, age, gender, social and ethnic groups, as well as socio-economic status.

Public relations is a process that must be worked at; it is not an afterthought but an ongoing issue of considerable importance.

Case study 11.2: The All Blacks brand

Gilson *et al.* (2000) researched the New Zealand Rugby Union with particular reference to its brand image and activity. They conclude:

> The NZRFU has been able to establish brand identities and equities [at high speed]. How have they achieved such a rapid transformation? In terms of its overarching purpose, the organisation quickly realised that, following the advent of professionalism, the maintenance of the inspirational dream – to keep rugby union close to the heart of the nation – required the sharing of new dreams, additional to the All Blacks. The NZRFU is now a burgeoning house of brands. The NZRFU is also able to point to its other domestic and regional brands as evidence of its success. The focus now involves relentless brand building alongside extensive player and organisational development. Through these activities the NZRFU is creating the future today.

This statement exemplifies how important the marketing image is in making a sport organization successful. This is true at local as well as international level.

Fundraising

Sport and recreation are highly popular in the UK – many people take part, show tremendous commitment and derive enormous enjoyment from their activity. There is, however, something of a reluctance to subscribe to this participation or to support financially, both individually and organizationally. In comparison with many other countries, there is no large sum of public money pumped in by the government to support activity and development in sport in the UK. This means that many, if not all, sports bodies seem to be constantly searching for money to enable participation, promote awareness and improve standards of performance.

Inevitably, this means that within any sporting organization someone or a group of people will have fundraising as their duty. Only in very few sports will money be easily found (relatively speaking) because of the high media image and the perception of it being good to be associated with that particular sport, e.g. rugby and soccer. Some sports will have support at certain times when they have a high level of success or public image, but this may wane and the television exposure, for example, may be reduced significantly due to the rise of other sports, or the whim of TV programmers. For example, until recently athletics had a very high profile and successfully attracted sponsorship (even if not at the lower level of participation) but this has passed as the high standards of achievement were not maintained and its image was damaged by a perceived poor reputation for drug use. Sports such as darts and snooker have also reached a peak and then fallen away – every sport must be wary of this and its financial and participation implications.

Regardless of the amount of sponsorship money coming into a sport, there will be levels – very often the base level and early participation stages – which will require substantial amounts of money to function and yet will not benefit from major sponsorships. The largest part of any sponsorship in soccer, for example, goes to the professional game, not to the local amateur teams struggling to survive.

This means, as mentioned above, that fundraising will need to be undertaken by the sports body in order to continue to survive and, hopefully, to progress. There are many possible schemes of fundraising, but regardless of the scheme, the commitment of the fundraiser(s) and the novelty of the scheme will probably be the two key factors in obtaining any significant income for the organization.

It is also necessary, obviously, to get some commitment from the potential customers for the scheme, and it is important that club or association members themselves get involved and act as sponsors or supporters of the scheme. On the most basic level, there is no point in someone trying to sell local lottery tickets to friends and colleagues if the club members themselves are not willing to buy them and support the initiative. A united effort is essential to have any sustained success in fundraising, and to continue to keep the individual involved interested and not totally frustrated by the lack of support and enthusiasm of others.

In organizing any fundraising effort it is essential to consider the estimated net profit, assessing whether this is going to be worthwhile for all the effort expended.

The degree of difficulty in establishing the operation must also be considered, as what is desirable may be too difficult to achieve. It is not, for example, realistic for a single local club to organize a major national raffle or promotion without other partners or some significant base of support outside its own limited membership.

The timing of the fundraising effort can be crucial, both from the organizational point of view in leaving enough time for success, and in relation to other competitors in the field. To launch a major promotion when everyone in the local area is about to go off on their annual holidays, or just before Christmas, when there is little spare money around, is not a recipe for success. Close consideration must be given to the actual ability of any organization to set up a fundraising scheme and the planning must allow sufficient time for success.

The fundraising resources needed, such as facilities and equipment, initial outlay, and publicity and promotion, must be closely considered. More particularly, the number of people required to support the initiative must be closely considered. If there is not going to be enough support from the relevant personnel, then the effort may well be doomed to failure. A surprising number of successful fundraising events, however, rely almost exclusively on one person; where this is all that is required, or there are relatively few demands on personnel, it may be possible to proceed.

There must be detailed examination of the risks involved, i.e. any losses that may be incurred or any potential legal costs that could result from certain projects. It is always worth considering the 'worst case scenario' that could arise before embarking on efforts to raise funds.

Legal requirements mean that individuals or organizations should be aware of the permits and licences they may require, e.g. for a sportsman's dinner in a tent or a raffle. There are often more permissions required than realized at first glance. It is usually advisable to seek advice in this area.

Generally, it is very useful to speak to others who have embarked on similar projects before or who are aware of some of the advantages and disadvantages of various fundraising projects. It is never sensible to 'reinvent the wheel'; it is always better to learn from their wisdom or their mistakes than from your own.

Having examined some of the general rules and considerations, here is a list of the type of fundraising promotion that sports organizations might consider. These are based on personal experience and also some of the ideas listed by Stier (1994):

- annual ball
- bob-a-job
- car boot sale
- car wash
- car raffle
- celebrity autograph and photo session
- celebrity sports dinner
- deed of covenant scheme
- donkey derby
- race night
- publishing a cook book
- bring and buy sale
- sale of work
- merchandising
- jumble sale
- life insurance policy naming your organization as a beneficiary
- pro-celebrity golf tournament
- selling badges and pins
- selling raffle tickets
- selling programmes
- sponsored walk, run or swim
- lottery or raffle

- wine tasting evening
- swim marathon
- celebrity coaching clinic
- sponsored sales table
- personality appearances.

These have varying degrees of staff input and complexity.

Regardless of how we set about the process or which particular project(s) we choose, one key issue is identified by Stier (1994): 'many fundraising projects involve selling'. It is important that we teach relevant staff and volunteers how to sell successfully. Stier suggests the following guidelines:

- identify potential customers
- approach them
- explain the product
- emphasize the benefits to the purchaser
- explain the nature of the non-profit sponsoring organization
- clarify how the money will benefit young people and sport or recreation programmes
- handle objections
- thank the prospect whether or not a purchase was made
- maintain accurate records
- over-aggressive hard-sell tactics should be strongly discouraged.

These guidelines are very helpful, as we often leave people to fundraise or to sell items on our behalf without giving them any indication of the type of thing they should do or not do, say or not say to potential customers. This often reflects badly on the individual and the organization, as well as damaging future prospects for fundraising. As in all sports administration, professionalism in fundraising will result in more success and be more beneficial to the organization's reputation.

Tax relief for voluntary sports clubs

In his budget speech in March 2001, the Chancellor of the Exchequer announced that the government would review the taxation of non-profit-making amateur sports clubs, with a view to giving them 'further support' and recognizing their 'contribution to community life'.

This news followed months of concerted behind-the-scenes lobbying by (among others) Sport England, the Central Council of Physical Recreation and the National Playing Fields Association.

The review is expected to consider whether 'community amateur sports clubs' should be exempted from a range of taxes (including income tax and VAT) to (1) help cut their tax bills and (2) increase their ability to attract voluntary donations from members of the public.

At the time of writing, Sport England is working with the CCPR, NPFA and DCMS to help determine which clubs should qualify for any such exemptions, and recommend how a reformed tax system could be policed.

Sports sponsorship

Sponsorship is the hardest part of all.

Robin Knox-Johnson

Many people would think that sailing round the world single-handed was pretty difficult. Knox-Johnson, who did just that, suggested that his search for sponsorship was harder than that! Perhaps that sets the real hard work required in context.

Sport is struggling for support; without sponsorship sport would wither.

Peter Lawson (formerly CCPR)

McCarville and Copeland (1994) examine exchange theory in relation to sports sponsorship. They suggest that: 'Partners exchange to enjoy benefits that cannot be attained in isolation'. Their idea is that people seeking partners should discover exactly what the potential partners are looking for and how the sponsorship seeker can satisfy these desires.

They further suggest that 'new sponsorship initiatives are likely to be undertaken when placed in the context of past successes and present priorities'. They continue that events should be aimed to meet a number of objects, including the success of the sponsorship and that outcomes should be realistically in line with what all concerned are hoping for. Ultimately, happy sponsorships are built on co-operation and mutual dependence: 'Those involved in sponsorship should offer a variety of benefits to their exchange partners'. McCarville and Copeland's conclusion is that 'it is important that those who seek sponsorship partners first discover those resources most valued by their potential partners'.

Much of this may seem straightforward and something we all know already, but there has been limited investigation into sports sponsorship especially in relating it to academic theories such as exchange theory. The lessons may be learned by experience, but it is better to learn from others' words and experiences than from your own misdemeanours. Many people have made mistakes in the field of sports sponsorship, and, unfortunately, some continue till today.

Value for money! You bet. There is no other promotional area on which we can get such a bang for the buck.

Leo Mehl

The sponsorship of sport provides a service to the whole of sport and to the community which sport serves: in this respect therefore it also serves the public interest.

The Central Council of Physical Recreation Committee of
Inquiry into Sports Sponsorship (the Howell Report), 1993

For most sponsors, sponsorship is part of the marketing budget. Sports organizations should also be aware of companies and their own marketing practices and targets in seeking and delivering sponsorship. It should be a highly publicized and high-profile relationship where the correct public image – of harmony and joint effort – is portrayed.

Sponsorship is a mutually beneficial arrangement fuelled by publicity. There are many examples of quality sponsorship arrangements in sport – some of great longevity. The ones which work best are those in which the partners both work very hard to deliver their joint objectives – the more they put into the sponsorship, the more each can hope to get out of it.

Case study 11.3: Small-scale sponsorship

A lower-league rugby union team obtained a sponsorship from a local further education college. The figure – a few thousand pounds – was sizeable to the club but, throughout the relationship, it saw this money as a donation which it didn't have to work very hard on cultivating for the future.

Wrong! They lost the sponsorship because they just took the money and didn't consider how to deliver up to – and beyond – the sponsor's expectations. They fulfilled the minimum terms of the agreement and no more – indeed, they needed prompting to do even that.

The college got involved partly because of the principal's personal interest, but largely because it wanted to increase its local community profile – where its students came from. It wanted positive stories in local papers, photographs and community networking opportunities – few were delivered, and only if set up by the college itself. The club was not innovative or proactive in seeking out ways to support the sponsor.

Astonishingly, the club approached the sponsor at the end of the year looking for more money for a bigger package – having failed to deliver the small one as a beneficial package for the sponsor.

Naturally, the college went elsewhere and signed with one of the other local clubs!

Case study 11.4: Large-scale sponsorship

Bank of Scotland (now merged with Halifax in HBOS) sponsors the Scottish Premier League (SPL) in football for £10 million over seven seasons, plus £250,000 per annum support funding.

The thinking behind the bank's involvement clearly establishes the business thinking, the need for the 'bottom line improvement' case to be justified, and the absolute link to the bank's marketing strategy.

General benefits

- credibility
- emotional buy-in
- association
- change perception of bank

Sponsorship objectives (for BOS)

- increase in sales
- developing customer loyalty
- growing brand awareness
- internal communication
- business-to-business relationship
- good corporate citizenship
- commercial opportunities – product sales in the boardroom

Research

- preliminary research
- quantitative
- qualitative

Sponsorship objectives (BOS and SPL)

- to improve the quality of Scottish football
- to build a league competition with standing and recognition throughout Europe
- to encourage attractive and entertaining football
- to commit to youth football development
- to develop a suitable image for the league and the sponsorship partners

The SPL 'offer' to sponsors – 'sponsorship as a marketing solution'

- proven research
- proven brand awareness
- corporate hospitality
- creative promotion
- powerful link to the world's most popular sport

Why choose the SPL for sponsorship?

- football massively popular
- SPL dynamic organization
- hospitality
- media
- 'good fit'

Evaluation

- meeting corporate objectives?
- monthly media monitoring
- equivalent costing of adverts – approximately one-third of cost of advertising
- sales promotion

I know that half of my advertising budget is wasted, but I don't know which half.

Variously attributed including Lord Lever

Self-assessment question

Think of a sports organization you know and consider it from a marketing point of view. Look at each of the seven 'p's listed in this chapter, and make a short assessment on how it performs under each heading.

12 Event management

This chapter looks at the area of event management, which is a major one for many sports managers and administrators. It goes methodically through all the stages in the process and suggests the key issues and questions to be considered, including:

- event feasibility
- trends
- what are events?
- the purpose of events
- event objectives
- fundamental planning
- basic questions
- event planning
- event requirements
- timetable
- implementation plan
- structure
- people
- funding
- sponsorship
- evaluation
- key considerations.

A range of practical tools and checklists is given, and there is a case study on planning the Commonwealth Games in Manchester, 2002.

Event feasibility

A crucial part of any sports organization's management operation will be its organization and administration of the sporting events that are part of its sphere of operation. It is sometimes assumed that sports people, almost automatically, know how to organize events. However, any casual visitor to most sporting events would identify some potential changes that would benefit the event and consequently the sport itself.

A large part of the public image of sport is sporting events and their organization. Much of what we see on television or read in the newspapers relates to the special events – the showcases of sport. This may be a slightly artificial picture of what is actually happening in sport, but it is the shop window, so when looking at major national or international events, it is essential to ensure that they give the correct and, hopefully, favourable image of sport.

As mentioned above, there can be a worrying impression that people who come into sport automatically have the skills, knowledge and background to organize events – this is not necessarily the case and very seldom is project organization the business background which people come from. Certainly there is often an element of organizational ability inherent in the games player, and an element of teamwork is expressed in many sporting activities, but many people come into sports and sports administration through the involvement of their children, and their own sporting exposure may be quite limited. Additionally, it is always worth remembering that sound organizational skills are given to few, let alone the enormous amount of knowledge and commitment that is also required to do a sports event organization job effectively.

Another major difficulty for sports bodies is that very often the individuals concerned are not actually trained in organizing events, even after they have begun to work in the area of sports administration. Given an interest and some ability, potential organizers should still be supported and helped through appropriate training and support at relevant stages in their work in this area. It is difficult enough for somebody to be plunged into an area where they may not have enough knowledge or experience, but it is verging on the negligent not to give them some proper training and help ensure that they can fulfil the tasks better, so lessening the pressure on them. This is particularly true in the area of events because of the time and task pressures that can build up on individuals as they move towards event competition or embark on major projects, especially for the first time.

Trends

The growing recognition of the importance of events has been identified in a number of ways. Many local authorities, and not just the large cities, have appointed events officers. Even some of the UK's smallest local authorities have identified events organization as at least a part of the job role of one of their employees. This has happened as local authority managers have begun to realize that events are a big part of the work they do and key to the operation of the sports industry, in its widest sense.

They have begun to understand more fully that events are a major part of all aspects of the sports business in relation to marketing, promotion and public awareness, as well as being universal across the aspects of their department. If a department is going to start a new service then it will be necessary to have an opening launch for the facility, a press conference to let people know what is happening, a seminar for local councillors, or an open day for potential public users. All of these are events which require planning and implementation, even where they are going to be aimed at establishing, prolonging or publicizing a well-used service which will remain on an ongoing basis. Events can be used to set up services, to test the market, to create customer awareness, and can fulfil a host of other strategic purposes. One major trend in the UK over the past 15 years has been the recognition and use of events by politicians and others looking to urban regeneration in areas previously considered to be deprived in some way. This has especially been noted in the larger cities of the UK, all of which have set out their stalls to attract major events because of the economic impact of attracting visitors and, it is suggested, some potential long-term investment. It is noticeable that major cities such as Glasgow, Manchester, Birmingham and Sheffield were among the first to set up events departments, and now go round Europe and the wider world trying to attract sizeable sports events to their cities. The most notable such effort recently was Manchester's (disappointingly, failed) bid for the Olympic Games in the year 2000.

One could argue that, in itself, the effort to bid for the Olympics has been of immense benefit to the city, and the publicity gained can only benefit the north-west in general, by attracting media interest and public awareness worldwide. In addition, Manchester was selected as the host city for the Commonwealth Games in the year 2002.

Sheffield, in bidding for and hosting the World Student Games in 1991, stated quite clearly the following objectives for the Games.

1   They would play an integral part in the economic regeneration of the area.
2   They would heighten Sheffield's profile nationally and internationally.
3   They would identify Sheffield's potential as a major sporting venue.
4   They would encourage local participation in sport and collaboration in the Games themselves.
5   They would promote the concept of a relocation to Sheffield for seminars, conferences, etc.
6   They would leave the city with a legacy of world-class facilities as it headed into the twenty-first century.

There was therefore a clear set of objectives, most targeted at economic development, urban regeneration and long-term legacies rather than the short-term benefits of participation in the Games.

For any incoming event, such as a major international tournament, it is likely that there will be a major short-term economic benefit for tourism through participant spending in the locality. This indicates that events may be worthwhile in themselves, regardless of any long-term benefit. The hope is that some of the sports people will later return with families for a holiday, again bringing money into the area.

This recognition of the importance of events is a significant and relatively new trend; while they have been used as a focus for attention on occasions such as the Olympic Games in London shortly after the Second World War, the real, localized benefits of such significant spends before, during and after events have only recently begun to be truly realized.

In addition, the identification of events' importance has meant that quality event implementation and provision has become a more essential issue, partly because there is such competition between major cities to act as potential venues for almost every major event or international seminar.

Events – what are they?

One of the definitions of 'event' in the *Shorter Oxford English Dictionary* is 'something that happens'. While this is very wide, it has to be all-embracing to allow for the innate universality referred to above. Events can range from a local competition to a ten-day international championship featuring teams from all parts of the world.

> A special event is a one-off happening designed to meet specific needs at any given time.
>
> *David C. Watt*

> Local community events may be defined as an activity established to involve the local population in a shared experience to their mutual benefits.
>
> *David Wilkinson, The Events Management and Marketing Institute*

Goldblatt (1990) notes that 'a special event recognises a unique moment in time with ceremony and ritual to satisfy specific needs'.

The definition can be flexible to suit different situations, but exactly what is meant in terms of a special events department, or an events officer, or an organizing group must be defined before starting work on specific events. Events are important, and need to be planned and delivered with care and attention to detail.

The purpose of the event

Consideration of recent trends has identified quite clearly that the major cities, among others, have been able to identify specific purposes for holding events. This is the crucial point to all good events – having a genuine reason to hold them. Even a fairly small event will require a significant commitment by staff or volunteers. This is not going to happen for an event which is not seen as genuinely worthwhile, beneficial and serving some useful purpose within a wider scale of operation. According to Goldblatt (1990), 'there must be a clear purpose which is clearly understood by all participants'. This aim may be quite general and long-term, but it should be public and widely supported, for example:

- to encourage the identification of . . . as a venue for events in the sports field
- to encourage visitors to come to . . .
- to boost the participation levels of the local population in . . .

All these, and many others may be worthwhile aims in setting up sports events. The key point is that there must be a clearly stated aim, otherwise the event should not happen.

Events demand a lot of concentrated effort and commitment. This commitment can only come out of a genuine belief, in all the participants, that they are worthwhile and they will be beneficial in the long term.

Event objectives

As well as an overall purpose, any event must have its own set of objectives. They will number around three to five; they must be clear and be set down in a way which will allow us to judge the success of our event after completion.

Objectives must be:

- specific
- measurable
- agreed
- understood
- clear
- achievable
- realistic
- simple
- unambiguous
- timed.

If we check this list, we will have objectives against which we can measure our event when everything is finished. This will be important to keep us working in a constructive planned manner, for effective evaluation after the event, and for better targeted events in the future.

Examples of event objectives might include:

- to increase the numbers playing volleyball locally by 10 per cent in the next year
- to raise the venue's public profile through ten pieces of media coverage – one TV, three radio and six local newspapers
- to involve 100 local sports people as volunteer helpers.

Fundamentals

Basically, events need to be organized in exactly the same way as any other project in any business or industrial field. The same thought processes, planning and meticulous attention to detail are required to produce successful events as are evident in good project management in other commercial fields.

Often, because of the voluntary nature of sport, some of these principles are ignored, but when the suggestion of re-examining them is made most people are very positive and appreciate that extra thinking and planning are worthwhile in this demanding area. The key rule is that relevant principles, policies, practices and procedures should be identified, laid down and followed so there is no doubt about what course of action is to be followed.

We must identify what has to be done to get the event achieved successfully, and then allocate roles and tasks to those who are going to do it properly.

The basic questions

Like so many other business (and life) activities, it is essential to approach the planning by asking some fundamental questions about what has to be done, why and how. The feasibility questions in sports event organization would begin with simple ones, moving on to the more complex ones which may only be applicable to the more complex events.

The questions to be asked include the following:

Why?

This is **the** fundamental issue when one is looking at events in sports or any other leisure area. If there is not a clear purpose and a set of parallel objectives, there should be no event. In particular, there should be a reluctance to hold any event just because it was held last year or because it is part of our annual calendar – this is not sufficient reason to hold a sporting event and takes up the organizers' much-valued time, which could perhaps be better spent. Events are a very important part of sport, however, and if they are well thought through can be a major bonus – a development incentive to performers and, indeed, to sports organizations themselves, nationally or locally.

The potential impact for Malaysia or Manchester of holding the Commonwealth Games or any city going for the Olympic Games is enormous. As well as serving major national and economic purposes, such a major event will benefit sport in the city, region and, indeed, country if successful. On a lower level, the running of a local tournament for badminton clubs or an inter-district championship for gymnastics may well be a major improvement in the competitive and development cycle for the sport itself, helping give a focus and incentive to everyone involved.

Significant events give training targets and development milestones for individuals and organizations to develop to their own level of potential within a given sport. Events are fundamental to sport, but only beneficial if they are the right events for the right purpose and delivered in the right manner.

What?

Having decided that there is a purpose for an event, the next decision is what form exactly the event should take; should it be a championship, tournament, knock-out or festival type of event?

Is it targeted at the appropriate age group and does it meet the purpose outlined? The precise details of the event should be specified and then followed through. Having the wrong type of event can be as bad as having an event with no purpose.

Where?

It is essential to ask whether the necessary facilities are present to host the chosen event. The obvious example here is that of Manchester, which had to provide, with government support, a velodrome and build other venues to improve its sporting facilities significantly in order to be taken seriously as a bidder for the Olympic or the Commonwealth Games. It is quite normal in the UK for people to want to hold events even though there are inadequate facilities, just to show that the UK can host major events. Realistically, until recently, there were very poor sports facilities and, even now, we lag considerably behind many other countries throughout the world. The notion of the UK – even London – hosting the Olympics seems fanciful, not just because of facilities but because of the lack of transport infrastructure.

It is essential also to ensure that all the facilities required to stage any event including ancillary rooms, medical facilities, training facilities, etc., are available. The requirements for many events are now enormous: for example, to hold the world gymnastics championships requires up to six adjacent training halls as well as a significant competition venue. Precise specification of facility needs must be clarified at early planning stages to ensure that these needs can be met.

When?

The timing of an event can be crucial, and is determined by many factors. The local, national and international sporting calendar will be a major factor in determining the timing, as will the availability of facilities and the general sporting calendar in the UK, if significant interest is to be generated and event clashes are to be avoided.

For a large-scale event, perhaps the most important question is when it will fit in to the television or media programme, and close consultation must take place to see if dates are suitable for TV coverage if that is a major purpose of the event and will be key to attracting a sponsor. Indeed, this is where the organizers should start for any major event – with the broadcasting companies and their schedules.

Who for?

This is another fundamental question, because if no one is interested in participating in an event, is it worth trying to organize it? There may be a place for organizing an event to attract money into the sport, or increased publicity, but generally speaking there has got to be some market of involvement that is satisfied, otherwise the effort will not be worthwhile and the event itself will be poorly attended. There can also be a tendency to organize events for the wrong people (in other words, the organizers rather than the participants) or to do it to keep a group of politicians happy though it is not the most appropriate development for the sport at a specific time. To be worthwhile a sporting event needs a group of participating customers.

Who by?

This can be problematic in that an event can only be staged if there is a group of available and able organizers for it. Organizing events is demanding and needs some special characteristics in organizers, whether paid or voluntary. There is always a danger of a governing body of sport, for example, offering to host an event when it does not truly have the necessary expertise or personnel available. It should never be assumed that because a group of people can organize the district or national championships they will automatically be able to organize the European or Commonwealth championships.

It certainly will be possible to buy in event agencies' expertise or advice, but this can be expensive and certainly would have to be part of any initial budgeting exercise. If there is no one able to do the event, don't try.

Who watches?

It is a common assumption among people involved in sport that if they organize an event then lots of people will rush out to watch it – this is certainly not true. Apart from the major manifestations of sport, such as the Six Nations Rugby Championship or the Premiership football matches, the numbers of people attending is not large. In fact, the number of people watching most sporting events would go a very small way towards meeting the cost of the event – this is even true of rugby or football in most cases, throughout the UK.

Furthermore, because sports administrators are desperately interested in (to the point of being fanatical about) their activity, there is a natural tendency for them to find it much more interesting than almost anyone else. Because they have this interest and would be willing to pay to watch, they assume that others will; very often this is not the case.

Spectators usually only turn out at the very top, or the very bottom, of sport since only supreme expertise or being a total novice tends to attract the interest of the non-expert or, particularly for the novice, all the family. As you develop up the excellence tree you will gradually find that fewer and fewer people will in fact come to watch you until you reach the very top in your chosen sport, and even there only in a certain number of chosen sports. Added to this, certain sports, e.g. archery and shooting, by their very nature are not spectator events.

The lack of people watching is not necessarily a major concern for the sports event as long as it is not relied upon to produce money to make the event viable, or assumed to attract sponsors on the basis of unrealistic spectator figures.

What will it cost?

This is a fundamental issue which is sometimes not examined carefully enough. It is absolutely paramount that all the potential costs are identified and that potential sources of income are clearly matched against them. Failure to produce a detailed budget in advance is a recipe for worry and potential disaster. It is crucially important to be pessimistic about income and realistic about expenditure.

Who leads?

Is there an individual or group who can lead the organization in the direction of achieving this significant commitment to organizing the event, carrying out the planning or implementing the event? The type of leadership required to build an effective team, which can work under the extraordinary pressure that it may be subjected to during an event, is not easy to find and should not be assumed, even in the natural environment of leadership which is sport.

Who pays?

The funding for sports events is often difficult, especially with larger events where it can be extremely difficult to find the necessary finance to make them viable. It is very important that, before embarking on any major project, a detailed budgeting exercise is carried out so that all the costs can be established accurately and precise methods identified as to how these costs will be met. Many events have come to grief in the past because realistic budgeting has not been undertaken in advance.

It is common, for example, to assume that sponsorship can be found when this can be extremely difficult, and can end up being impossible. The nature of many sports events does not necessarily make them attractive to sponsors, and relying on such income can be a home-made recipe for disaster. There are people who may well support the event, such as local authorities, voluntary groups and other interests but the key step is that these potential sources of funding are identified clearly in advance.

All these questions, then, need a positive and detailed answer before we embark on trying to set up what may be a significant commitment in time, money, staff time and resources. Sports resources tend to be limited – events may not be the best use for them.

Event planning

Events are important to sport, and they need a professional and thorough approach to planning. Earlier, we gave a somewhat simplistic view of events when defining them as something that happens. This is not all bad, but it suggests that they happen by themselves – nothing could be further from the truth. People will be required to make them happen.

Additionally, perhaps, the crucial difference between what one might call 'routine' events and 'special' events is that the latter must always be planned or they will not end up being 'special'. This planning will fall into a variety of stages: it must be stressed that, regardless of the size of event, each of these stages must be gone through. Obviously, depending on the size of the event, the length of each planning stage will vary.

Event planning stages

 1 determine aims and objectives
 2 formulate policy
 3 carry out a feasibility study
 4 make decision to go ahead
 5 compile budget
 6 identify personnel
 7 identify resources
 8 identify event requirements
 9 identify tasks
10 define structure
11 communicate structure
12 detail plan and time-scale
13 establish control systems
14 plan event – presentation, preparation, implementation and recovery
15 finalize accounts
16 hold debriefing
17 compile and circulate final evaluation report.

Event requirements

Having identified the overall planning progressions, it is necessary to be more specific and identify the precise process by detailing all the requirements for the event. This can be a time-consuming procedure, but should involve a number of people who can think in the widest possible way in an attempt to consider all the possible items which will be required to execute a successful event.

This list, which can never be all-encompassing, is necessary to allow detailed planning and implementation to go ahead. The aim here is to identify every single heading that needs to be covered and, within it, every single item that will be required to produce an efficient, effective event of a quality appropriate to its level.

This means going through a very precise thought process for every event, no matter how large or small, endeavouring to ensure that nothing is omitted which may ultimately be required. Having gone through this process, you will end up with a significant list of items that need to be considered and must then be double-checked against other events and/or by other people to ensure that nothing is omitted. For example, Figure 12.1 shows a checklist for organizing a community fun run.

Having identified the specific requirements for your run, you will have to:

- analyse costs
- identify necessary personnel
- specify the timetable
- construct the plan
- implement the plan.

The next stage is to fit this set of requirements into a time-scale of action.

Timetable

It is going to be important, in any successful event, to make sure that there is a time schedule where important items are set to be achieved by certain dates. For a major event, this may be quite simple on paper and often very difficult in practice. Ideally, every item to be achieved should have a time-scale attached to it, but, in practice, it is more likely only to be done for the major points or major items that have to be achieved: funding, securing necessary equipment, etc.

This should be set up in some sort of diagram and supplied to all the staff. The diagram can vary from simple to complex, depending on the event. A relatively simple chart is shown in Figure 12.2.

Personnel

Race Director	Course Manager	Medical Co-ordinator
Publicity Officer	Media Liaison	Police
Athletics Club	VIPs	Volunteers
Runners	Stewards	Announcer
Starter	Timekeeper(s)	Technician(s)
Photographer	Car Park Attendants	VIP Stewards
Drivers	Local Authority Liaison	Permits
Licences	Approvals	Administration
Support (political or other)	Media	Organization Structure
Souvenirs	Work Schedule	Support Services
Post-Event Services	Press Launch	Post-Event Evaluation
	Legal Advice	Contingency Plans

Finance

Controller	Systems	Petty Cash
Contingencies	Estimates	Accounts
Appeals	Sponsorship	Sales
Patronage	Traders' Stands	

Health and Safety

Medical Cover	First Aid Provision	Fire Precautions
Safety Certificates	Stewarding	Traffic Control
Emergency Procedures	Radio System	Ambulance(s)
Emergency Services	Health and Safety Legislation	

Warm-Up Area Facilities

Crèche	Transport	Marquees
Registration Desk	Telephone	Ancillary Activities
Entertainment	Notices	Exhibitions
Press Facilities	Waste Disposal	Car Parking
Catering	Spectators' Seating	Hospitality
Changing Accommodation	Start/Finish Areas	Lost Property
Runners' Clothing	Access	Toilets
PA System	Electrical Supply	

Course

Route	Maps	Signposting
Equipment	Direction Marking	Spectators
Policing	Cones and Tapes	Radio Communications
Stewarding	Running Surface	Clock(s)
Disabled Access	Fencing and Barriers	Mile Markers
Equipment Hire	Advertising	Fun Sport Prizes
Invoicing & Invoice Payment	Cash Security	Banking
Receipt System	Steward Bibs	Start/Finish Arrangements
Banners	Course Access Passes	Maintenance

Administration

Stationery	Check-lists	Entry Procedures
Planning Documentation	Logo	Planning Meetings
Event Timetable	Posters	Publicity

Figure 12.1 A fun run checklist

Timescale Event Requirements	2 years	18 months	1 year	6 months	3 months	1 month	Event	1 month after	3 months after
Market research									
Secure finance									
Book venue									
Arrange catering									
First aid									
Safety check									
Detailed costing									

Figure 12.2 A simple schedule chart

Implementation plan

With the identification of requirements and the compilation of a time-scale to go alongside them, we are now in the business of producing a detailed implementation plan to get everything up and running. This will be our implementation plan, which, depending on the level of event, may be simple (one sheet of instructions to staff and volunteers) or, for a major international event, be extremely complex (many handbooks to VIP hosts, stewards, catering staff, etc). The possibilities are endless and, for an event like the Olympics, so too is the planning and the paperwork.

For most events, however, it will be a fairly routine document, which may just be a checklist (such as Figure 12.3) which shows who does what by when, etc.

Structure

This implementation plan can only be made to work within an appropriate structure for the event. This again may be very simple and straightforward,

Event Requirement	Detail	Timescale	Undertaken by
Book venue	Confirm suitability Fix date	18 months ahead	Venue manager
Arrange main speaker	Sufficient standing in profession Pencil in alternatives	12 months ahead	Conference director
Arrange venue layout	Space for working groups as well as listening	3 months ahead	Venue manager
Confirm catering arrangement	Final confirmation after delegate numbers	1 month ahead	Catering manager

Figure 12.3 A simple implementation plan checklist

coming through an existing staff structure or voluntary committee. It could, however, be very complicated and be developed over a period of time for a major event. It will need to allow for individuals to work their best to get things done, while ensuring that everyone knows their role and how they relate to others within the structure.

Three examples of possible structures are shown in Figure 12.4. They serve only as rough templates that may be appropriate to an event in certain areas.

People

Probably the key factor in achieving successful events is getting the right people in the right positions to get things to happen in the best possible way. As every sports organizer is aware, the necessary commitment is considerable and cannot be limited to 9a.m. to 5p.m. The demands on personnel, whether paid or not, will be extraordinary and they must be willing to face up to these challenges. This is the type of person that events require – someone who is committed, who is willing to work very hard and who doesn't panic if anything goes wrong.

It is also important that everyone involved is fully aware of the objectives of the event and is clear about their role within the event achievement plan.

It is essential in major events that every single person, from the car park attendant to the chairperson of the organizing committee, is completely

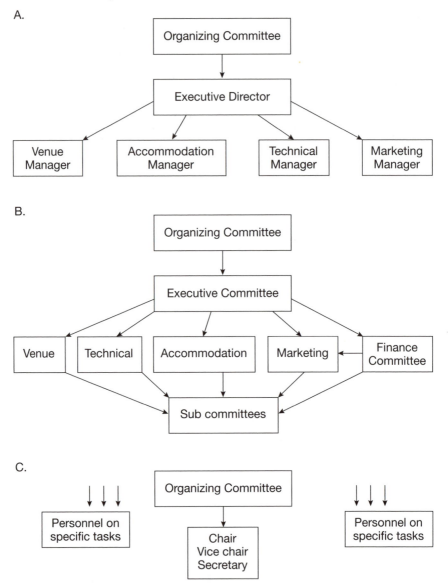

Figure 12.4 Alternative event structures

sure of their role and has a **written** job remit (or specification), clearly showing:

- whom they are responsible to
- whom they are responsible for
- what specific tasks they have to achieve.

It is to be emphasized that every individual involved in the event has this clearly specified job remit, regardless of their level. The job remit should not be dictated but should evolve in discussion with the individuals involved and then, when agreed, be made widely known, so that there is no doubt as to who undertakes what particular duties.

This clear demarcation avoids confusion and staff conflict and gets things done. It is the best way forward for everyone involved.

The personnel who will be the 'key performers' in event implementation must be clearly identified and it is important that there is a support system for them, giving training as well as rewards, in whatever way appropriate, to ensure that they are aware of all procedures and are well motivated (it's great what people in sport will do for a T-shirt!).

For example, 'front-of-house' personnel are the ones who will meet all the event participants, VIPs, officials and spectators and give the whole project its atmosphere. They must be trained in a way which will equip them to handle all the varied groups of customers properly during the event.

It is wise to remember that money is not a major motivator for people involved in events; indeed, in many cases, money will not be available and the effort of many key personnel will be voluntary and amateur. This means that they cannot be tied by definitive contracts and payments. A special effort must be made, then, to get cohesion and commitment, through good staff management and building on the interest that the volunteers have already shown.

During any event tremendous demands will be put on volunteers and other staff in many situations. To be fair to them, there must always be a clear indication of what they are required to do and they should be consulted and involved on every possible occasion, to ensure that they always feel part of the event and its organizing team.

Funding

For many events finding the funding is the crucial item and the one which requires most work; it causes most headaches and worries leading up to any decisions to proceed with an event.

Given the correct event, the correct aim, with the correct objectives, funding can be found. It must be a package and not an afterthought; there must be a clear mission and purpose to the whole operation from the start.

Many agencies can have a significant interest in supporting events to ensure they happen successfully in a given location. The more obvious are local authorities and local tourist boards, but there are others, for example:

- local enterprise agencies
- tourist associations
- hoteliers
- local chambers of commerce

- national agencies, e.g. Arts Council, sports councils
- major local employers.

Remember, sports events can have a significant effect on the local economy by promoting 'sports tourism'.

Sponsorship

There is a belief that sponsorship will easily be made available for events; sadly, this is not the case and only if it is handled in a professional and appropriate way will sponsorship be found in most cases; it will seldom be 'easy'.

Many sponsorships are still found through personal contact and this should be exploited to the full, though obviously it cannot be relied on. Thereafter, preparing the necessary documentation for presentation to a sponsor, with follow-up phone calls, can sometimes produce sizeable amounts of money to support worthwhile projects. This must be targeted at sponsors that are generally likely to be interested in the particular project concerned. For example, a baby food manufacturer may be interested in crèche provision or the extension of an activity programme to cater for young children. This targeting is important as, ultimately, commercial firms will want to see some return for their investment – sponsorship is a business arrangement, not a charitable donation.

Perhaps the most crucial step in the area of sponsorship for events is to involve the potential sponsor from the very early days when the initial concept is suggested, and not to present them with a completed fixed package. There is little point in taking a totally inflexible finished package to a sponsor and saying 'take it or leave it'. If they are expected to put money into a project, then they are certainly entitled to make some comment on the construction and the detailed format.

Throughout the event, successful sponsorship will be a partnership and this process, started at the conception, should continue in every aspect. This will produce the best benefit for everyone concerned in terms of a successful event for the organizers, and a good return on sponsorship investment for the sponsoring agency.

The next key is to establish exactly what each partner wishes to gain from the project, and how this can be done together. There may be occasions after initial discussion with the sponsor when it proves impossible to reconcile the partners' desires. This is the time for the relationship to stop, rather than trying to stumble through further problems that will inevitably arise with a lack of total commitment on both parts.

Consistently throughout the projects, sponsors and organizers need to work closely together and to keep each other informed, especially of any problems that arise – there must be a full and close communication at all times.

Ultimately, if we can deliver an event which becomes identified with the sponsor then we are beginning to get places. There are many famous examples of this in nationally covered events, e.g. the BBC's sponsorship of the Promenade Concerts, the Royal Bank of Scotland's sponsorship of rugby, Embassy's sponsorship of the World Darts Championship: the list is endless. Product identification and public awareness are the primary aims of most sponsors and, if the organizers wish to keep their support, these must become event objectives.

Characteristics of the best events

Good events have most, if not all, of the following:

- definite purpose
- market research
- customer care
- feasibility study
- committed personnel
- clear objectives
- co-ordinated effort
- quality leadership
- appropriate structures
- business planning
- good communications
- resources committed
- appropriate management
- political support
- flexible systems
- public support
- accurate budgeting
- financial control
- detailed evaluation.

How, then, do we do it?

1 Have an aim and a set of specific objectives.
2 Examine all the event questions and issues.
3 Identify all the right requirements.
4 Recruit the personnel and take all the necessary steps to get these items carried out.

You need to obtain the appropriate:

- funding
- people
- structure
- systems.

Event evaluation

Many events struggle through lack of learning from previous mistakes due to insufficient evaluation, monitoring and feedback from past events. Event evaluation should be marked by the following characteristics.

- *Compulsory.* It should be done for every event, large or small.
- *Concise.* Should not be any longer than it needs to be.
- *Concurrent.* It should go on during the event as well as after it.
- *Constant.* How we are going to evaluate success (or explain failure!) should be a consideration throughout the event and even in the earlier planning stages.
- *Customized.* Even though we may have a specific checklist for evaluation, each event should have an additional set of criteria because the objectives were probably different from others in the past.
- *Consultation.* Evaluation involves seeking the opinions of as many relevant groups as possible: participants, officials, VIPs, sponsors, etc.
- *Canvass.* It is necessary to canvass opinion and not just wait for it.
- *Circulation.* It is necessary to circulate opinions gathered and also to circulate the debriefing document as widely as possible to help everyone involved build for the future.
- *Customers.* Whatever the nature of the customers for the event, they must all be asked for an evaluation through, for example, an exit survey, or questionnaires placed on seats.
- *Colleagues.* All staff, paid or voluntary, should be involved in the evaluation process for their part within the event.
- *Collected.* Care should be taken to collect confidentially appropriate information.
- *Catalogued.* It should be recorded in an appropriate way and filed for future reference, with due regard to the Data Protection Act.
- *Complete.* It should cover all aspects of the event from early arrival to departure.
- *Communicated.* It should be communicated to relevant parties during the debrief process and at the end of the debrief process.
- *Copied.* Successful evaluation methods should be reused in order to emulate their success in the future.

Event management: key considerations

Remember, before embarking on an event it is going to be necessary to examine a number of key issues which will clarify whether the event is actually possible. This is best done by asking a series of questions. Some of these questions are as follows.

- Why do we need to hold an event in the first place?
- Is it the best way to achieve what we want to achieve?
- What will be the exact form of the event we are going to stage?

- Is there a range of options, and, if so, which one will we choose?
- When is our event going to be held?
- Have we checked with all relevant people?
- Have we checked with television companies or the national arts calendar for the performers' agents?
- Where will our event be held?
- Do we really have suitable facilities for it?
- Would it be better being held in a more suitable facility that we can provide?
- Do we have everything that is required in the facility we intend to use?
- How can it be achieved?
- Is it possible for the mechanisms to be set up which will enable the event to be successfully completed?
- What will be the cost of running this event?
- Where will any monies come from?
- Who will organize?
- Who will attend?
- Who will watch?
- Who will participate?
- Who will pay?
- Will the media be interested?
- Will a sponsor be interested?
- Will the politicians (or superiors) like the event?
- Are there lots of events like this?
- Where do we go from here?
- How do we get started if we go ahead?

Event preparation

We all turn up at large events and take the preparations for granted. For example, at the much publicized World Snooker Championships, the preparations start early.

The World Championship was first staged at Sheffield's famous Crucible Theatre in 1977; the venue is now as famous for snooker as Wembley is for football, Wimbledon for tennis and Lord's for cricket.

Six days before the championships start, the World Snooker Association moves into the theatre to prepare for the event. The theatre floor is lowered by three feet to install the set and a series of 16 jacks is installed under two tables which each weigh one and a half tonnes.

The stage is carpeted, and the snooker arena is installed complete with press seating, boxes for the BBC commentator and photographers and TV cameras. Meanwhile, behind the scenes, the rehearsal room is converted into the press room and the band room is transformed into an interview area.

Case study 12.1: Commonwealth Games – Manchester 2002

The following information related to the Manchester Commonwealth Games of July/August 2002 gives an indication of the scale and thought behind a major event – the biggest multi-sport held in the UK to date (see Figure 12.5). (This information was issued in advance of the Games.)

The Manchester 2002 mission

- To deliver an outstanding sporting spectacle of world significance, celebrating athletic excellence, cultural diversity and the unique atmosphere of 'The Friendly Games'.
- To deliver a successful Games on behalf of all competitors, spectators and stakeholders.
- To leave a lasting legacy of new sporting facilities and social, physical, and economic regeneration.
- To set a new benchmark for hosting international sporting events in the UK and the lasting benefit they can generate for all those involved.

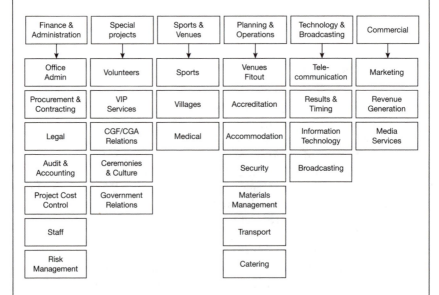

Figure 12.5 Manchester 2002's organizational structure

Manchester's key goals in bidding for the Games were:

- To play a central role in the successful delivery of UK policy for national and international sport.
- To heighten the profile of the city at national and international level.
- To give impetus to the regeneration of East Manchester through the creation of a major sporting and commercial development with the new City of Manchester Stadium as its centrepiece.
- To produce other economic benefits for the city and wider region.
- To create a wide range of social legacy benefits through the cultural and educational programmes associated with the Games.

Funding and sponsorship

- The cost of providing new venues for the Games is £170 million.
- Public sector funding for the Games has been provided through a partnership between Manchester City Council, the government and Sport England.
- Official sponsors of the Games are Manchester Airport plc, Adecco (UK Ltd), Guardian Media Group plc, Microsoft Ltd, Cadbury Ltd, Cussons Imperial Leather and Addleshaw Booth & Co. Official partners are United Utilities, Bruntwood, Xerox, Guilbert Ltd, Claremont, First Group and Boddingtons.

Long-lasting benefits

- Approximately 4,500 new jobs will be created.
- 40 hectares of land have been reclaimed for Sportcity, which is acting as the catalyst for a major regeneration programme in East Manchester.

Sport

- 5,250 athletes and team officials.
- 17 sports: aquatics, athletics, badminton, bowls, boxing, cycling, gymnastics (artistic), judo, shooting, squash, table tennis, triathlon, weightlifting, wrestling, hockey, netball, and rugby sevens.
- The first time at a major event that élite athletes with a disability are fully integrated into the sports programme, with 200 sportsmen and women participating in ten events over five sports.
- Innovative sports programme setting a new precedent – athletics will begin the programme, ensuring that public attention is secured

immediately with a very strong first weekend of sport. The pace continues with finals every day until the climax of the Games, the popular rugby sevens competition.

- Expected competitors include GB Sydney Olympic 2000 medallists such as Jonathan Edwards, Steve Backley, Katharine Merry, Tanni Grey-Thompson and Simon Archer as well as the North-West's local heroes including cyclist Jason Queally, shooter Ian Peel, sprinter Darren Campbell and swimmer Matthew Walker.
- Superstars from the world of athletics such as Australia's Cathy Freeman, Ato Boldon of Trinidad and Tobago, Maria Mutola of Mozambique and Obadele Thompson from Barbados are hoping to be going for gold in the stadium too. Canada's Simon Whitfield, who won an Olympic gold in the triathlon, is expected to be competing, as are Australian swimming sensation Ian Thorpe and New Zealand rugby legend Jonah Lomu.
- Three events at the Commonwealth Games will be virtual world championships: netball, lawn bowls and squash, which are sports exclusive to Commonwealth countries.

Venues

- 15 venues in Manchester and the North-West as well as the National Shooting Centre at Bisley, Surrey.
- Situated two kilometres from Manchester City Centre and the largest sport development to be built in Britain, Sportcity will include:
  - The City of Manchester Stadium
  - Indoor tennis centre
  - The National Squash Centre
  - Outdoor athletics track with stand for 500
  - Indoor athletics facility
  - Sports hall to provide regional performance centre for netball and badminton
  - Sports science and medicine facilities
  - Office accommodation.

Accommodation

- Sportsworld has been appointed the official accommodation management company with accommodation ranging from youth hostels to luxury 5-star hotels. The company now has over 4,500 rooms on its list.
- Sportworld also sells tickets as part of inclusive travel packages, and it is the main ticket and tour operator for the Games in key Commonwealth countries.

- For more details contact Sportsworld via email on travel@sports-world-group.plc.uk.

Volunteers

- With the help of Adecco, official staffing sponsor, the Games volunteer crew is almost complete but we are still looking for volunteers with specific skills such as medics, drivers and IT specialists.
- The Games welcome applications from people with disabilities to count themselves in to these inclusive Games. Wherever possible we will offer them roles compatible with their ability.
- The volunteers will work across all areas from the Athletes' Village to all sporting venues and will be trained in a range of roles.
- The volunteer line is 0870 241 7374.

Merchandising

- A wide range of products is already available in Manchester stores in the Arndale Centre and the Trafford Centre, as well as from Tourist Information Centres: from exclusive collector's items in bone china, pewter, gold and silver, through to pin badges, coins, stamps, clothing, toys and stationery.
- A further outlet at Manchester Airport will open shortly.
- In 2002, the range will expand and a selected range of products will also carry the Manchester 2002 Games logo, along with the Official Golden Jubilee mark.

Media

- The BBC is the host broadcaster and UK rights holder.
- Overseas broadcast rights have been sold to major TV channels including BBC Television & Radio, Channel 7 (Australia TV), New Zealand Television, South African Broadcasting Corporation, Canadian Broadcasting Corporation, Asia Pacific Broadcasting Union (covering India, Pakistan, Brunei, Bangladesh, Malaysia, Singapore) and ABC (Australia radio).
- 4,500 press and television media representatives are expected to visit Manchester during the 10-day Games.

Spirit of Friendship Festival

- The Spirit of Friendship Festival will run from 11 March to 10 August 2002, coinciding with the Queen's Golden Jubilee and ending with the 40th Jamaican Independence Day celebrations.

- The festival will combine sports, arts, culture and education.
- The festival will involve communities throughout the UK, show-case artists from five continents and use new media and the Internet to embrace countries from across the globe.

What the games mean to the UK and the North-West region

- The XVII Commonwealth Games will showcase Britain to a worldwide audience.
- The opening ceremony in July 2002 will be watched by 38,000 people in the new City of Manchester Stadium and millions more worldwide on television.
- A successful Manchester 2002 Commonwealth Games will encourage other international events to come to the UK.
- The Games will have significant economic impact and strengthen and establish new trade links across the globe.
- A substantial international boost will be given to the image of Manchester, the North-West and the UK. In the North-West, more than 5,681 direct jobs and 751 net additional permanent and ten year equivalent jobs will be created.
- Sportcity at Eastlands will stimulate the regeneration of the Eastlands site and the wider East Manchester area.
- Sportcity is Sport England's largest ever investment in sport. The development at Eastlands, part funded by Manchester City Council, will be a focus point for local excellence and will provide the local community with access to outstanding sport and leisure facilities. It will also be a regional, national and international showcase providing the highest quality, state of the art training and resource facilities.

Self-assessment question

Examine an event you have been involved in – as an organizer, a participant or even just as a spectator – and ask some of the feasi-bility questions about it that the organizers would have had to. Assess the outcome of the event, and suggest whether it delivered against these questions.

13 Education and training

This chapter highlights some of the main issues and agencies concerned with education and training for sports managers and administrators – both paid and voluntary. Having emphasized the importance of education and training, it considers coaching awards. The existence or, perhaps more accurately, the lack of, and need for, sport management education is identified. The role of national vocational standards and qualification is examined, as is the role of the national training organization – SPRITO. Finally, the training of volunteers in sport is discussed and the Running Sport programme is outlined.

> Education and training should be designed to meet the needs of the people you are there to serve – the customers!
>
> *George Torkildsen*

One of the key areas for sports management and administration in the UK, in all its guises, is education and training. Apart from very specific organized coach training, there has been, until recent years, little significant input to the training of people who wanted to work in sport as organizers and administrators. Thankfully, recent initiatives have seen a significant turnaround in this area, and the signs are that many more people working in sport, including the voluntary sector, will be trained in the skills of sports administration.

The driving force for this movement towards better administrative and management training is difficult to identify precisely, but it relates to a movement in political thinking, the incorporation of colleges of further education, and a combination of sports' circumstances and the requirement for administrative professionalism, led by the professionalism of sport itself. All of these factors are combining to produce a growth in courses and qualifications in sport, recreation and related subjects which will prove to be of significant benefit to the management and administration of sport. This has moved the profession from the days when all the managers came from the ranks of physical education teachers. A discrete new profession has developed, and a PE teacher would find it hard to break into the paid side of management and administration.

> Learning without thought is labour lost; thought without learning is perilous.
>
> *Confucius*

The arrival of vocational qualifications (now with a specific qualification in sports administration) has had an impact, but much less than the government had hoped for, although their influences on existing courses and training practices has been considerable. Vocational qualifications have been beset by many implementation problems, but the impact across the whole field of sport and recreation has grown. When the issues of awareness and implementation are resolved, the proliferation of such competence-based qualifications will be helpful in all aspects of sport. In particular, the assessment of ability to perform at present being able to lead to a qualification will be very appropriate for a number of sport settings, where people have done the work before but have not been fully recognized for it, and often without possessing any specific qualifications.

The impact of training, qualification and recognition must be helpful to the individual, the organization and the whole industrial attitude towards sports management and administration. Hopefully, this combination of commitment and qualification will have a beneficial effect in producing improved organization for the sports participant, and regard from the sports participant for the sports organizer.

Coaching awards

The UK has a long history of the training and certification of coaches. Most governing bodies of sport have undertaken this role, with varying degrees of enthusiasm and commitment. There is a need to ensure the continual flow of suitable individuals to help produce their sports' performers for the future, as well as the need to introduce new participants to the benefit and joys of their particular sport. There has also been a financial implication – charging people for courses and certification has been a significant income earner – while there has also been the concern (most importantly) to ensure that correct and safe techniques to educate participants and performers are followed, so ensuring correct and safe performance.

An element of coach education has been missing, in that many coaches have to take on administrative roles within sport, in the voluntary sector in particular, but very often there has been no recognition of this in their training. In terms of club, district, regional and even national associations, coaches are expected to perform a number of important administrative tasks. This is inevitable and necessary, because sport requires a degree of technical input to guide the direction of thinking of sports organization in administrative terms as well as in sports participation and performance terms. Such administrative requirements have, however, left coaches overstretched, and to some extent individuals who have much to offer in the non-technical administrative areas have been underestimated and underused by sports organizations.

While extensive coach education schemes have existed, there has been very little significant input from governing bodies to developing these coaches or any other volunteers into administrative or organizational skill enhancement. This has led to a great deal of coach wastage due to the pressure and stress of the issues surrounding the day-to-day coaching, and a feeling that the coach has to do everything while not necessarily being trained to perform organizational roles, or losing motivation since they are acting in areas in which they feel they have no special skills or knowledge. Someone who comes into sport to work with a team or group of individuals to enhance their performance will not necessarily be highly motivated to spend a lot of time and pay attention to detail in delivering organizational and administrative roles with a sports body.

It is to be hoped that current developments in sports administration training can rub off onto coaches and give them some of the added skills they require, while not detracting from the quality of coach education and development directed specifically at the coaching tasks they have to perform.

In this area, the impact of vocational qualifications is and will continue to be significant. Hopefully it will lead to higher and more equitable standards of coach education throughout sport in the UK. It is to be hoped that a significant number of coaches will feel it appropriate to obtain vocational qualifications in coaching, and indeed will see it as relevant to encourage others to look for vocational qualifications in sports administration. Such an assessment of operational roles and the work to be done will be of significant benefit to sport, and the whole process of working to national standards and competence assessment will benefit everyone concerned, making them think and become more aware of the needs and the necessities of the professional operation of sport as a business.

It is also hoped that coaches will be able to spend less time on the administration side of sport so they will be able to become more focused, while others take the pressure from them for organizing events and other duties. It is important to see that the administrator's job is in many ways to back up the coach, to support them rather than have conflict with them or endanger the coaching process. They are in fact enabling an effective coaching process in many cases. At no time should the strengthening of sports management and administration be seen as a threat rather than an assistance to coaches.

It has been suggested that until recently many sports coaches probably needed administrative as well as technical training, because for many of them the administration is a sizeable part of their work, along with promotion and development. It often seems that the more organizational demands are put on sports coaches, the less coaching they do.

Education versus training

> All education is, in a sense, vocational, vocational for living.
>
> *Sir John Nessom*

There is some debate about the difference and relationship between education and training, though few doubt the necessity for both. The actual differences can vary depending on the specific situation, but the most commonly perceived difference is that education is about the process, while training is about the product – the ability to perform is often seen as the end-product in terms of training, while knowledge can be seen as something accumulated through a learning process in education. Such differences should not be seen as derogatory comments on either side of the argument or as implying that one is better or more necessary than the other. It is essential that both occur in the area of sports management and administration because both have a part to play in guiding a professional approach to the industry and practice within in it.

> Experience is the best teacher
>
> *Proverb*

The profession of sports management needs people who have come from a practical background with additional training, as well as those who could be perceived as academics who have come from an educational background. In many situations the difference may be seen as more to do with attitudes than with specific skill-based training – most industrial settings, and sport and recreation is no different, would prefer an open-minded wider-thinking person whatever their background, so this is perceived to be one of the benefits of a more academic education.

> Education is leading human souls to what is best . . . the training which makes men happy in themselves also makes them more serviceable to others.
>
> *John Ruskin*

Fundamentally it is much more important for people to have the enthusiasm and empathy for sport and its participants than any written qualification, but it is important that they have the ability to think widely enough to consider everything that may impinge on the operation of sport in their country as well as their specific situation in a club or national body. The width of education, perhaps from a degree or some other general management qualification, may well be effective for someone in sports administration if it is coupled with commitment and enthusiasm for the activity of sport – the characteristic that distinguishes it from other management situations. Interpersonal skills and interest in sport are, however, more important than any qualification or educational background.

The need for training is relevant regardless of whether a person already possesses a qualification, a degree or even a postgraduate award. Training can provide specific skills, knowledge and expertise that will not come from degree-level courses and will be essential for sports managers in the work situation. For example, a degree in sports management is never going to train one precisely how to handle volunteers in some of the situations that can arise in the day-to-day sports arena. Specific consideration has to be given to the practicalities that face people working in sport and how they are going to cope with them – this is normally best achieved through a progressive and well-established training programme.

The training itself should be designed to allow the individual, group or team to better face up to the challenges around them at present and prepare them to face the future. It is vital that training is started by assessing the needs of everyone concerned both in a personal and an organizational way, then building on these identified needs and desires to produce an effective training programme which is self-managed by each individual as well as overseen by an appropriate supervisor or organizational leader. It is crucial that training is seen as an ongoing process which does not just relate to individual skills or short-term development through one-off courses, but rather is a full development process which leads to an effective organization through producing highly skilled and well motivated individuals.

An effective organization will come through individuals feeling that their personal development is valued and seen as crucial to the organization and the working of the staff team, including themselves. The staff must be seen as individuals worthy of education, training and development for their own benefit as well as that of the organization. Ultimately an organization is a set of individuals, and the development of their personal needs and skills will lead to an improved operational system.

It is often said, with some justification, that the UK has fallen down in industrial competitiveness due to its lack of attention to education and training. If this is true in industry then it must be especially true in sports management and administration, because training for full-time, part-time and voluntary personnel has, until recently, been limited to the point of being almost non-existent.

Over the past few years, the UK sports councils have been actively developing a volunteer development programme called 'Running Sport', aimed at training volunteers who have been attracted into sport and giving them a better idea of how to operate and perform the many roles they are required to meet within sport in the UK. The existence of these courses reflects the importance of the volunteer and the need to support their actions rather than leave them feeling unwanted and unrewarded.

This programme is still relatively new, but it is an important initiative which should be a significant help to the operation of the voluntary sector in particular. This is a massive area in terms of sport in the UK – between 1.5 and 2 million people according to 1995 figures. Too often in the past the training of these individuals has been ignored. Hopefully through courses such as Running Sport and related initiatives such as the Barclaycard Volunteer Investment Programme, the standard of support for these hard-working individuals will increase, so enhancing their skills and ultimately benefiting everyone involved in sport.

Training must not be seen as solely for leaders but is required for everyone involved in sports administration, even if they are working for only a few hours a week. It is certainly absolutely vital for the full-time sports administrator. For them it should really be compulsory and, however achieved, should be provided as a matter of routine operational practice.

Sports management education

> The goal of education is the advancement of knowledge and the dissemination of truth.
>
> *John Fitzgerald Kennedy*

US research by Masteralexis and McDonald (1997) has produced some significant recommendations on sports management education and suggested some key points: 'sports management educators must recognize that the opportunity exists for an international dimension to be included in sports management education'. The authors also quote Kelley *et al.* (1994) as noting the need for

> bold, assertive sports management programmes to go beyond departmental boundaries to enlist expertise of academics in other departments to create inter-disciplinary programmes. Sports management programmes could take this advice and encourage students to take language and cultural courses in liberal arts and international management in business schools to create international sports concentration.

Masteralexis and McDonald also note that in the USA the survey results indicate that there is interest from practitioners in enrolling in executive education programmes focusing on international issues in sports management. They further state that 'the international frontier will create challenges for sports managers; sports management programmes ought to be able to respond to the needs of these practitioners with training sessions specifically tailored to address the needs of individual sports managers'.

Such issues and research exist largely in North America, but as programmes develop in the UK and other parts of Western Europe there will be a need to take these issues on board, particularly in relation to the ever-expanding European sphere of management operation. Sport must react to the European dimension and the international opportunities in the more globalized world, just as any other industry has to.

Academic qualifications

Education is an ornament in prosperity and a refuge in adversity.

Aristotle

It is quite surprising, considering the relative size of the sports administration field, that relatively few academic courses are offered to provide for the needs of this occupation. There tends to be an assumption that administration is generic and that people with these skills and an interest in sport are the suitable people to work in sport. This is an interesting and ongoing discussion point.

Most people involved in sport, whether they be coaches or development officers, need administrative and management skills to varying degrees – some to a very high degree – and it is surprising that Stirling University is one of the few that have put the two subjects together to any significant extent. There is some development at postgraduate level for those already practising, but at higher national or undergraduate level there is a slowly growing provision. This is a very interesting European situation when one looks across to North America, where courses in sports management are many and varied. There is obviously a gap in the market which will be filled as demand grows through increased expenditure, particularly from the lottery and the private sector, producing a need for more and more professional people with a knowledge of sport, allied to high level management and administration techniques.

In the past decade, both higher and further education establishments in the UK have seen a massive increase in the number of people studying sport. Particularly popular have been practical courses on sports coaching and sports science, but the study of sports management is growing as well (albeit more slowly). It is now possible to study sports organization in late secondary school right through areas such as sports development, to advanced strategic management at masters and postgraduate level.

The numbers involved now are growing, and while relatively few may find jobs in sport, their education and interest should benefit everyone in sport.

Professional institutes

The professional institutes in the sport and leisure areas – particularly ILAM and ISRM – provide a variety of education and training opportunities, ranging from one-day specific skill sessions through to one- or two-year distance learning diplomas. They are all run under the banner of continuing professional development and/or professional qualification schemes.

This work has proved immensely useful to, and popular with, the practising professional.

SPRITO

The most important and exciting development in the field of education and training in sport in recent years in the UK has been the arrival of SPRITO – the National Training Organization for Sport, Recreation and Allied Industries.

SPRITO is fundamentally about representing the views of industry on relevant education and training matters to government and other decision-makers so that the correct provision for practising industrialists at all levels is the underlying principle of policy-making.

Having suitably influenced policy-making, SPRITO is now taking the lead in delivering appropriate mechanisms for overseeing, quality monitoring, and in some cases provision, of education and training opportunities for those working in the sport and recreation profession throughout the UK.

The organization is made up of a range of relevant industrial bodies: the professional institutes, the UK and national sports councils, the private sector (including the fitness industry and outdoor education), Sports Coach UK, the British Institute of Sports Administrators, the Institute of Groundsmanship and a range of other relevant bodies. The purpose is to act as a genuine voice for people working in the sport and recreation business. The importance of training has to be advocated, both within the industry and outside, and this role is also taken on actively by SPRITO, especially in terms of training support and resources internally and externally. It also encourages players in the business to join SPRITO, which is in essence a membership organization.

Examples of the type of work in which SPRITO has become involved include:

- Investors in People in the sport and recreation industry
- national traineeships
- modern apprenticeships
- graduate recruitment survey
- review of vocational standards.

Occupational standards and vocational qualifications

One of the major developments in training in all industries in recent years has been the development of occupational standards leading to vocational qualifications in a range of industrial sectors. Sport and recreation, previously through the industry lead body and now through SPRITO, has developed, is reviewing and will continue to develop appropriate occupational standards on behalf of the sport and recreation profession. These standards should be seen as measures of competence at various levels for people working in the sport and recreation industry. Over a considerable period of time a number of industrialists operating in various areas have produced occupational standards leading to vocational qualifications in a

wide range of areas – sports coaching, sports development, facilities operation, spectator control, outdoor education, playwork, supervision and sports
administration.

These vocational qualifications are offered at a variety of levels, starting
at Level 1 for an introductory qualification, up to Level 5 for a course
that could be judged to be around the standard of competence required
to do a postgraduate qualification. In terms of sports administration, a large
number of areas have been identified as units of competence for a sports
administrator to gain a vocational qualification, as follows.

Level 3

- prepare a programme of activities
- co-ordinate a programme of activities
- contribute to the planning, monitoring and control of resources
- maintain financial systems for an organization
- contribute to the health and safety of others
- provide information and advice for action towards organizational objectives
- promote and evaluate services to maximize participation
- contribute to the planning, organization, and evaluation of work
- maintain services and operations to meet quality standards
- contribute to the provision of personnel
- contribute to the training and development of teams, individuals and
  self to enhance performance
- establish and maintain relationships with organizations and individuals
- create, maintain and enhance productive working relationships
- service meetings
- assist in regulating sport
- contribute to frameworks for participation and progression in sport.

Level 4

- provide sports-related planning and co-ordination for a major sports
  event
- recommend, monitor and control these resources
- seek, evaluate and organize information for action
- exchange information to solve problems and make decisions
- promote and evaluate services to maximize participation
- contribute to the implementation of change to services and systems
- maintain and improve service operation
- contribute to the recruitment and selection of personnel
- develop teams, individuals and self to enhance performance
- plan, allocate and evaluate work carried out by teams, individuals and
  self

- create, maintain and enhance effective working relationships
- enable committees to make decisions to further organizational aims
- contribute to the formalization of policy
- contribute to the implementation of policy
- contribute to the regulation of sport
- develop a framework for participation and progression in sport.

With each of these units containing an average of four elements, and each element in turn having around four performance criteria, these standards are extremely demanding and indicate the vast range of work that sports administrators undertake. Partly because they are so demanding, the uptake for this particular vocational qualification has been less than might have been anticipated judging by the number of people operating in the area.

The review of the occupational standards has started and will shortly cover all levels, including 3 and 4.

Running Sport

The Running Sport programme is designed to improve the knowledge and skills of everybody working in sport, both voluntary and professional. It is targeted at sports administrators at all levels, ranging from the local club treasurer to the chief executive of a large governing body. Many of the resource materials will also be appropriate for coaches, match officials and sports development officers.

The Running Sport programme:

- was originally a GB Sports Council initiative developed in partnership with the British Institute of Sports Administration, the British Olympic Association, the National Coaching Foundation, the National Sports Development Centres, the Sports Council for Wales, the Sports Council for Northern Ireland, the Scottish Sports Council and the respective sports associations
- provides a series of publications, courses and workshops covering a range of sports-related management skills
- is led by accredited, trained tutors who have been selected because of their strong sports administration background knowledge and their learning facilitation skills
- is now forced forward largely by the resources of Sport England, although the other national sports councils are involved in some delivery and promotion.

Booklets

A series of short booklets has been written in a straightforward, friendly and practical way. They are designed to cover a range of topics for those who need some basic help with the jobs that they have to carry out in sport. The titles available include the following.

- *Running Meetings* acts as a guide to chairing a sports organization. It discusses issues relating to meetings, along with the role and skill required of a chairperson.
- *Running a Club* focuses on the role of the secretary in a sports organization, addressing aspects such as qualities needed, correspondence, agendas, AGMs and records.
- *Looking After the Money* focuses on the role of the treasurer in a sports organization, examining aspects such as paying the bills, accounting for the money, petty cash, budgets, income and expenditure and balance sheets.
- *Raising Money* acts as a guide to raising money for a sports organization, providing guidance on donations, grants, fundraising, marketing, promotion, publicity and sponsorship.
- *Managing Events* focuses on the basic requirements for putting together small-scale sport tournaments, championships and events. It looks at some of the key planning issues and helps organizers plan more effectively and comprehensively.
- *Volunteering Matters* looks at volunteers in sport – their importance and the roles they play. It considers how we find them, keep them interested and can encourage them.
- *Planning for Sports Development* looks at the sports development pathway – from getting started to being the best. It focuses on who can help, what is to be done, and planning principles and practice.

Resources for club and people management

Resource materials at this level have been developed to provide individuals with the opportunity to improve their knowledge and competency in specific areas. In some cases, courses have also been developed to support these resources. Courses will help people (especially administrators, coaches, officials, and development officers) to gain some of the underpinning knowledge and gather the necessary skills in a range of areas.

Personal Effectiveness. This pack is intended for sports people who wish to run their sport, business and home life more effectively and with greater enjoyment. It includes practical advice on communication, running meetings, office administration (or personal administration) and report writing. In particular, it will help you to:

- deploy the principles of effective communication (oral and written) and appreciate its importance in fostering productive working relationships

- assess strengths and weaknesses in written and oral communication, and identify strategies to develop these skills
- assess personal administrative skills against recognized principles of good practice and devise action plans to increase work effectiveness and efficiency
- understand how meetings should be run and how to contribute positively to meetings.

Time Management. Again, this pack is intended for sports people who wish to run their sport, business and home life more effectively and with greater enjoyment. It includes practical advice on goal-setting, prioritizing and action-planning, and offers guidance on selecting strategies to reduce stress and gain greater satisfaction. In particular, it will help you to:

- evaluate how you use your time
- recognize where you are being less effective with your time
- prioritize tasks and set achievable goals
- set specific tasks to increase your work efficiency
- plan, organize and evaluate your work better
- identify strategies to improve your time management
- manage your time-related stress better.

Leadership and Delegation. The pack is intended for sports people who need to get things done by managing, organizing or influencing others, or simply working effectively alongside others. It includes practical advice on leadership and management styles for employees, colleagues and volunteers; and strategies for making delegation both effective and rewarding. In particular, it will help you to:

- understand a range of leadership/management styles
- identify when to use different styles
- appreciate the advantages and disadvantages of delegation
- identify and plan how to delegate tasks to other people
- plan and organize the distribution of tasks
- monitor to ensure that delegates' tasks are achieved.

Motivation and Team Building. The pack is intended for sports people who need to get things done by managing, organizing, or influencing others, or simply working effectively alongside others. It includes practical advice on motivational strategies for employees, volunteers, and colleagues; and ways to make the team function more effectively and with greater satisfaction. In particular, it will help you to:

- understand different theories of motivation
- identify the strengths of colleagues, staff and volunteers

- identify ways to develop more motivated colleagues, staff and volunteers
- identify the characteristics of successful working teams
- rate the effectiveness of any teams to which you belong
- identify ways to improve the way in which their work teams function.

Balancing the Books. The pack is intended for sports people who have to handle money for their sports organization, handle their own finances or wish to understand financial accounts of their organization. It includes advice on book-keeping and accounting for revenue. In particular, it will help you to:

- understand the importance of keeping accurate accounts and budgets
- handle and account for cash transactions
- prepare and analyse a receipts and payments account
- maintain basic financial systems for an organization.

Managing the Money. Again, the pack is intended for sports people who have to handle money for their sports organizations, handle their own finances or wish to understand the financial accounts of their organization. It includes practical advice on budgeting, balance sheets and accounts. In particular, it will help you to:

- calculate the accruals and prepayments relevant to each financial period
- prepare detailed income and expenditure accounts and balance sheets
- analyse an income and expenditure account and a balance sheet
- prepare and adjust budgets and financial statements
- operate stock control procedures
- apply the taxation levels relevant to your situation.

New modules in various stages of development have been added to the range of courses available. Topics include the following.

Funding and Promoting Your Club. This take-home study pack and possible accompanying course combine these important areas for sports clubs and their administrators. The idea is that the reader (or the tutor on a course) can 'pick and mix' the most appropriate lists for them and their club. Areas covered include:

- the meaning of promotion and marketing
- the importance of effective planning
- assessing financial requirements
- sourcing funds
- completing appropriate forms
- sponsorship proposals and grant applications
- planning for promotion and fundraising.

Volunteer Management. This very important pack looks at ways of 'making the most of your sport workforce'. It considers a number of vital issues about volunteers in sport and suggests how they can best be managed – or at least co-ordinated and supported. The issues covered include:

- recruitment
- retention
- rewarding
- action plans for improvement
- developing appropriate goals and targets
- which structures and mechanisms can be used.

Other resources and home study packs are available covering:

- *Employment Matters*
- *Sports Development Planning*
- *Sports Facility Development – Planning a Building Project*
- *A Club for All*
- *Developing Sports Partnerships/Developing Junior Clubs*
- *Girlsport* (only with a workshop).

For most of these packs, a facilitated learning workshop exists or can be developed to assist in assimilating the topic and the materials.

In addition, an accompanying suite of materials has been devised (in conjunction with Sportscoach UK) covering child protection – obviously an essential knowledge area for administrators as well as coaches. This includes:

- *Safe and Sound* – an introductory leaflet
- *Good Practice and Child Protection* – a workshop
- *Protecting Children* – a home study pack
- *Keeping Children Safe in Sport* – a distance learning pack.

In summary, Running Sport is about helping people, particularly volunteers, to help their sport as effectively as possible by addressing key issues such as volunteer management, club finances and development planning. The focus is currently very much on supporting club development, recognizing the importance of this level of sport and the need for helping volunteers at this level.

Following up on Running Sport is easy – the best way to get involved is to contact your national sports council (addresses at the back of this text) and they will tell you more about resources or setting up courses.

Volunteering in sport

Government sport strategy

In April 2000, the government published its strategy for the development of sport in England over the next decade. An implementation group made up of leading figures from sport education, local authorities and the national governing bodies (NGBs) of sport was charged with agreeing practical ways of achieving the strategy recommendations. A subsequent action plan, *The Government's Plan for Sport*, was launched in March 2001.

This action plan highlights the government's commitment to school sport, developing a system for identifying and supporting top UK athletes, and to the training, development and recognition of volunteers. The action plan states that sport relies heavily on an army of volunteers and that NGBs need to be supported to develop and implement volunteering strategies through which they can provide direction and support, and offer sound volunteer management.

The government believed that Sport England should be the national advocate of volunteering across sport in England. It asked Sport England to:

- raise the profile of volunteering in sport and highlight what sport has to offer volunteers
- develop a website that is effective in the promotion and support of volunteering in sport
- ensure that the strategic management of volunteers is integral to all relevant Sport England programmes
- lead research, monitoring and evaluation of the effectiveness of volunteer management throughout sport
- advise and update NGBs on the impact of new and changing legislation on volunteer management
- take the lead in researching and establishing links between sport and volunteering organizations and initiatives at national and regional levels
- identify and support effective pilot projects.

The action plan also states that 'Sport England will consult with all NGBs on a flexible, cross-sport strategy for volunteering'. Key principles of this common strategy include the following.

- NGBs will be encouraged to identify and appoint a national volunteer manager to implement the strategy throughout sport. That role will include the recruitment and management of volunteers' raising the profile of volunteering within the governing body and identifying training, support, recognition and reward need of volunteers through sport.
- At regional level, volunteer management should be a key part of a sport-specific development officer post. The key tasks of regional officers

will be to co-ordinate the implementation of the volunteering strategy and support voluntary county and club co-ordinators.

- Volunteer co-ordinators should have key roles within county associations and clubs where they will raise the profile of volunteering and bring the strategy to life at grassroots level.
- All volunteer co-ordinators will be linked into the Volunteer Investment Programme network to be the first point of contact for volunteer management issues and advisory services and to play a key role in attracting volunteers into sport from all sections of the community.

In order for all this to happen, adequate training is essential. The Department for Culture, Media and Sport (DCMS) allocated £4m to underpin training and support for young people aged 14–19 to develop leadership skills and to volunteer in their communities. The scheme, which is running from 2002 to 2004, builds on work already done by the Youth Sports Trust (YST) and Millennium Volunteers, and the Department for Education and Employment (DfEE) Citizenship and Sport programme linked to the Commonwealth Games in Manchester 2002. An additional £3m from the government's Active Community Fund will develop a nationwide implementation strategy, and train adult volunteers to mentor, lead, officiate and coach sport locally.

Volunteer Investment Programme (VIP)

The Running Sport programme is now being supported by a programme called the Volunteer Investment Programme. It emphasizes the importance of volunteers to sport, and suggests practical ways in which they can be recruited, retained and rewarded.

Sport needs people who are skilled not only in the knowledge of the sport itself, but also in the delivery of quality service to all the participants at whatever level. They will have to have the necessary job skills for the post and have them updated and enhanced through training on an ongoing basis. This will be true whatever post individuals occupy, and whether this post is voluntary or paid.

Training is one of the few areas where government ministers and trade unionists always agree there is a major priority. However, in the past, neither have put their money where their mouth is and promoted training in such a practical way. There is some evidence to suggest that the UK has one of the more poorly trained and underskilled workforces. We constantly face change, and a major push to upgrade skills is required in sport and recreation as in other industries.

There must be a constant and consistent drive to get people trained, educated and qualified to the highest possible level to help keep their motivation high and increase their ability to perform the jobs they undertake. Investment in the education and training of administrators will ensure that everyone involved in sport benefits. The benefits of good practice are not limited to the highly competitive business environment but can greatly enhance voluntary and public sports management and administration situations as well.

A website to support volunteers in sport has been set up by Sport England. It includes good practice guides, tips, volunteering in sport updates, VIP factsheets, advice, contact details, links to other websites, etc. The site address is www.sportengland.org.uk/vip.

Self-assessment question

What type of training have you done or are you aware of in sports management? Some opportunities are identified in this chapter, but there will be others. What do you see as most appropriate for (a) volunteers (b) paid staff, and why?

14 Personal skills

This chapter looks at the personal skills of the sports manager and administrator – their ability to manage their time, meetings and their own schedule and space. These personal organizational skills are vital given the pressure and the pace of the work role of the sports administrator. In this role, an individual is up against demands often based on the fact that sports participation, and planning for it, is led by volunteers outside the normal 9a.m.–5p.m. working day. To respond to such calls on their time, and still to have a life outside work, people in such roles must be well organized.

Covey (1992) pursues these themes:

- be proactive
- begin with the end in mind
- put first things first
- think win/win
- seek first to understand, then to be understood
- synergize
- (vitally for this chapter) 'sharpen the saw' – meaning improve your personal skills to deliver effectively.

It is fascinating to note how often Gilson *et al.* (2000) refer to individuals – their skills, drive and commitment, and how essential they are to the successful sports organizations. Time and again, in organizations such as women's hockey in Australia, Netball Australia and the Williams Formula One Team, Gilson *et al.* note key individuals who 'copy the dream forward'.

Individuals and their skills and commitment are key to successful sports organizations. Sports administration, like any other business, is about people and their performance. Improved performance comes through increased personal knowledge and skills, particularly the very practical skills of managing time, managing meetings and managing yourself.

Time management

All managers in work situations feel stress and pressure due to perceived lack of time. This is particularly true in the sports industry, where one is dealing with many others' often conflicting demands on one's time, and with a range of very enthusiastic people coming at the manager or administrator from a wide variety of viewpoints, each demanding that their view be supported and that work be done for them.

Additionally, the manager/administrator in the sports situation will be dealing with time during the unsocial hours, which many people see as their recreation hours – while for the sports manager it is probably paid work time. This necessity to work unsocial hours creates even more pressure for the manager/administrator and conflicts with other demands on their time such as home life. This means that effective use of time is particularly important – time lost between 9.00a.m. and 5.00p.m. cannot be caught up in slacker periods when people are not taking part in sport, because there are no such periods.

Time management action plan

In order to find more time, the manager must take some action to identify where time goes at present, set targets for its use, and the steps towards improvement. Having devised these targets, an action plan needs to be established to achieve them.

In particular, steps must be taken to remove 'time wasters' and bring in 'time creating' moves. 'Time wasters' include:

- stress and strain
- crisis management
- procrastination
- poor prioritization
- doing everything oneself
- lengthy phone calls, meetings, face-to-face conversations
- conflict
- poor communication
- lack of preparation
- poor use of paper
- taking work home
- only doing easy tasks and allowing inadequate time for major tasks.

The following creative 'time makers' can assist in 'making' more time and compensate for the incorrect use of time, which is so common.

- ranking task priority
- setting appropriate deadlines

- setting realistic schedules
- saying no where appropriate
- estimating time realistically
- delegating appropriate tasks – with direction, authority, power and support
- setting clear goals
- identifying better working practices in terms of efficiency and operation
- stopping procrastination
- managing meetings properly
- prioritizing phone calls and paperwork appropriately
- using time, such as travel time to undertake suitable tasks
- setting time aside each week for major project work
- leaving spaces in the diary – daily, weekly, monthly, etc.
- giving clear signals to colleagues as to when there is time available for them
- using information technology.

There are countless books on the subject of time management, naturally of varying quality. It is a subject that should be studied in depth by the sports administrator due to the enormous pressures on their time. In particular, the sports administrator is plagued by this imbalance of the normal working period of 9.00a.m. to 5.00p.m. Monday to Friday, versus the desire of sports participants to see their administrators at work outside these hours.

There will inevitably be work to be done by the sports administrator between the hours of 9.00a.m. and 5.00p.m. during the week, as they will have to deal with the suppliers and other routinely operating organizations, but they will also have to meet the 'spare time' demands of sports people who participate and attend meetings after 6.00p.m. and during weekends. To respond effectively to these conflicting demands, the sports administrator needs to prioritize tasks and manage their time effectively in completing them, otherwise they will crack under the strain of constant working hours and pressure from all angles.

Managing meetings

The length of a meeting rises with the square of the number of people present.

Anon

A meeting is a group of people that keeps minutes and loses hours.

Anon

There are some who believe that sport survives on fitness and exercise, and numbers of participants – there are others who believe, more realistically, that sport survives on meetings!

This phenomenon of meetings, meetings, meetings is not unique to the sports business, nor indeed is it limited to the voluntary sector. There is a culture of meetings in business and industry, and the sports voluntary sector suffers from this as do many other organizations. There is a strong argument that a large number of meetings are important in areas of the voluntary sector because of their involving role – people come to meetings to be involved in the whole process of running their sports club or organizations. Inevitably, in the voluntary sector, there is a need to let people have their say and play a part in the actions of the organization, but this has to be moderated by some organizational practicalities and common sense on the part of the organization and the individual.

There is no doubt that many of the meetings held are necessary and, if conducted properly, can in fact be beneficial to the future development of projects and, indeed, the organization itself. The following general guidelines, however, are essential if real, effective progress is to be achieved.

Theoretically, meetings on sport, particularly in the voluntary sector, are about planning and achievement, but realistically they are often about social gatherings, discussions of current controversies and building informal interpersonal relationships which serve to keep the organizations going.

It is noticeable in the voluntary sector that people see meetings as their opportunity to express their strongly held views on issues affecting their sport. It is perhaps a reflection of their profound commitment and enjoyment of their sport that they attend many meetings, and so feel that there is the opportunity to consistently repeat their views on such occasions, whether they are relevant to the business of the meeting or not. Very often, such views are repeated constantly on a similar basis and do not lend anything new or significant to the proceedings. This may appear a somewhat cynical view, but it is often reflected in practice.

Minimizing meetings and being more businesslike in the approach to procedures would considerably improve the achievement of many organizations and associations in the sporting world. Problems at sports meetings often arise because the first and fundamental consideration is often not examined closely enough, i.e. is the meeting necessary and what exactly is its purpose? This is undoubtedly the most crucial issue and the one most often ignored by a wide range of organizations and individuals. If a meeting does not need to be held, and there are other ways of achieving certain tasks, then such other methods should be used first – there is absolutely no point in having unnecessary, time-consuming meetings which achieve nothing and tend to create resentment and frustration at having to attend, often during unsocial hours, with no relevant perceived outcome.

If there is a real purpose to the meeting then the correct procedures should be followed so that progress is made towards the necessary purpose and the agreed set of objectives. It is essential to ensure that the following points are implemented.

- All necessary preparation for the meeting is done by all those attending it.
- There is a clear pre-arranged agenda, a specified chair for the meeting and someone taking minutes or at least action notes.
- Notes taken for action are circulated to others as soon as possible after the meeting.
- Everyone present is given the opportunity to participate.
- All the people in attendance need to be there and have something to offer.
- The meeting is appropriately formal in terms of following the agenda, but not so formal as to limit meaningful discussion.
- All background papers are read before the meeting.
- Meetings are adequately planned and properly controlled.
- The chairperson prevents rambling discussion and keeps everyone focused on the correct agenda.

Sporting people at meetings tend to be quite fanatical about their activity, and apply this also to getting their own specific view across. This, coupled with informal meetings and a lack of respect for the chairperson (often known from another sporting situation on an informal basis), can be a recipe for chaos. Such almost inevitable informality creates its own problem for the chair of such meetings and they need a sufficiently strong personality to handle it sensitively, yet firmly, while allowing people to express their views, but not rambling on indefinitely on the same topic.

In essence, in terms of such meetings it is vital that there is something that everyone wants to achieve from the meeting; that the group fits together well; that all the information required is to hand; that all the people around the table can get on well together or at least consider the views of others; and that each person listens as well as talks.

Sometimes sports meetings have the added pressure of poor or inappropriate facilities due to the lack of resources within the organization, and meetings having to be squeezed into the homes of individuals or inadequate back rooms of sports facilities. Such a situation puts an added pressure on everyone involved, even though initially it may be seen as a more convenient and cost-effective method of meeting.

While meetings must be kept to a minimum, they are the lifeblood of the sport in the organizational sense. Undoubtedly many are necessary, but equally many are not – the benefits can only accrue if they are appropriately planned, organized, arranged and chaired.

When meetings fail it is generally due to a lack of:

- preparation
- purpose
- communication
- resource utilization

- decision-making
- implementation
- clear objectives
- time keeping
- suitable physical environment
- written agenda
- strong chairing.

Most sports administrators complain that they have to attend too many meetings, and this is often justified. Often it can be beneficial to communicate in other ways. For example:

- by meeting people on an individual basis
- through informal meetings
- by telephone, fax or e-mail
- by writing directly to an individual
- by issuing a memo to several people
- by getting involved in video conferencing or electronic conferencing.

However, there are still occasions when it is essential to have a more formal meeting, and these often prove useful mechanisms if used properly. Also, as mentioned above, the process of communication is often aided in the meeting situation.

The necessity for a meeting, however, depends on its purpose and it involves concepts of control, communication, problem-solving and decision-making. It is often a useful exercise to think back to recent meetings and consider whether any of these processes are actually undertaken.

Voluntary organizations can survive on meetings but they do not always achieve a great deal. Positive planning to get a more useful way forward will help everyone.

Meetings in practice

God so loved the world that he didn't send a committee.

Anon

Meticulous preparation for a meeting in terms of sending out papers etc. will help to make sure that everybody is there on time and understands what is going to happen. Additionally, however, it is vitally important that the chair or whoever will lead the meeting has all their planning done before the meeting in terms of paperwork and issues to be raised, that there is a definite purpose to the meeting and that everybody understands what it is. Meetings also have to be structured, and that structure needs to be followed.

It is essential that the agenda is circulated to all participants in advance and they are all made aware of any information which is required before the meeting; it is all too common for necessary information not to be made available to all parties sufficiently in advance of the meeting for it to be studied – this leads to people fumbling through unread papers at the meeting and causes an enormous waste of time.

Additionally, it is important that only relevant points are placed on the agenda and discussed at the meeting. This can be enforced by making sure that only current issues are covered in the pre-meeting papers, and that the chair prevents unnecessary items from being discussed – they should rule such irrelevancies out of order, as they can significantly delay the proceedings.

It is essential also that agendas are not too long – having many more than ten items is asking for trouble, and indeed even this number may be too great.

There are a number of formal agendas for annual general meetings etc. and these will be prescribed in the constitution of the organization; otherwise common sense should be used and only appropriate items included. Every meeting should have some record of what took place and what is to happen after the meeting. This may be in the form of formal minutes written by someone, normally the secretary, and agreed by the chair of the meeting before circulation. Whatever form these minutes take, they should:

- be accurate
- be clear and unambiguous
- be properly organized
- be brief
- be agreed
- be non-personal
- be a joint responsibility (e.g. chair and secretary)
- state clearly what has been decided
- state what has to happen as a result of the decisions
- be circulated promptly.

There is a tendency in sport for minutes to be too verbose and too personalized. This causes a waste of time. To indicate the decisions of the group is helpful; to indicate who initiated such decisions can be disruptive and damaging. Decisions of committees once agreed must be acted upon in a unified manner; to cause divisions by allocating responsibility to one individual for any decision is not helpful and can in fact be quite detrimental to organizational efficiency.

In order to get good organizational involvement it is important that the minutes of meetings wherever possible are widely circulated. They will not tell everyone an enormous amount, but they will make it clear what has been discussed and decided, thus fulfilling the need to keep everyone informed and involved. This will not allow anyone to make the usual plea of ignorance of what is going on within the organization. There may be some occasions, e.g. in the case of disciplinary proceedings, when minutes should be very brief, and certain minutes may be confidential for legal purposes. Wide circulation will still be the general rule.

In a sporting setting, especially where volunteers are involved, chairing the meeting can be quite a difficult task. Everyone will want to have their say, but the chair must push the meeting towards achieving its objectives and getting finished in a reasonable time. This is not to deny individuals the opportunity to put their point of view across, but this should only be done briefly and on a specific subject, rather than being a reiteration of long-held strong opinions.

Ultimately, the chair takes the responsibility for structuring the meeting and ensuring it is carried out and recorded through the minutes in a proper way. Chairing a meeting can be extremely difficult and requires special skills of personality and awareness, which can be sharpened up with practice and most importantly by preparation – it is vital that the chair is well informed about all the items likely to arise at any meeting and has thoroughly gone through any papers to be presented. Failure to do so will cause embarrassment to the chair and possibly others present, as well as significant delays in the proceedings of the meeting. It may be difficult to have a full knowledge or understanding of every topic on the agenda, but it is essential to know who will talk to a specific point and what should happen in relation to all the items on the agenda.

The chair will benefit from some support, and indeed training, in performing this function as they need to have a considerable range of skills in order to be effective. Such skills include listening, questioning, encouraging and conciliating. All too often in sport these skills are expected to be present as soon as somebody is appointed, and we are not always very good at helping people once we have put them in such posts. Programmes such as Running Sport can be of significant assistance in giving individuals the basic skills required to take on such a role.

The principle of training in meeting behaviour should be carried to all committee members as soon as they are appointed (or even to prospective committee members). Such action will mean that sporting organizations will function a great deal more effectively and, indeed, enjoyably for all concerned.

Fundamentally, successful meetings need:

- minutes, with an action-by column
- agenda and objectives
- feedback and contributions
- to be well led
- written reports
- a venue with all necessary equipment
- appropriate atmosphere
- to be kept to time
- a timetable for each item and overall

- clarity of expression and purpose
- members with necessary skills and knowledge
- decisions made leading to action.

Personal management

> Desire to have things done quickly prevents their being done thoroughly.
>
> *Confucius*

The business of sport requires managers in all sectors to be doing their work at a time when most other people are taking their recreation. As mentioned above, it is not a management role that can be confined to certain hours or shifts, but requires seven-days-a-week, 24-hours-a-day commitment and a considerable dedication if it is to be performed effectively and to the satisfaction of, at least, the majority of customers.

This necessity to work long hours, coupled with the almost inevitably short time-scales and tight deadlines, exerts enormous pressure on managers and administrators, and their ability to respond successfully will depend largely on their own personal organization and management. To be personally effective in the sports business one has to be efficient in personal management. This skill has a number of aspects, some of which are considered below.

Some might argue that this section is the most important of the whole text. The issues considered here include time management, personal organization, managing meetings, and considering the job role and responsibilities.

> To do two things at once is to do neither.
>
> *Publilius Syrus*

It is a long-held belief that someone cannot be an organizer or an efficient administrator if they are unable to manage their own behaviour and organize themselves. Basically, to organize others one must be personally efficient and not continually have to rely on everyone else to do things or to find things or to arrange things or to know what is going on. This in essence must be the job of the administrator professionally, and therefore they must take steps to handle all the challenges that may face them individually.

Sports administrators must be able to:

- get control of their own time
- avoid procrastination and take action promptly
- manage interruptions to the work schedule and deal appropriately with inevitable social contacts
- develop a telephone manner to shorten telephone calls

- prepare for every meeting they attend
- preserve personal time
- devise appropriate methods of personal time management.

There is little doubt that there is a frequent tendency for individuals to get snowed under by a massive amount of paperwork, and this must be managed effectively if any progress is to be made individually. A paper-handling system must be developed, otherwise bits of paper will be handled countless times.

Sports administrators should consider a number of items in dealing with the organizational and administrative tasks which face them. These include:

- appropriate record-keeping systems
- learning from others in similar situations
- keeping appropriate diaries
- organizing the desk appropriately
- developing relevant filing systems
- keeping appropriate records, such as health or absence records
- recording incoming and outgoing mail
- developing a file of resources and contacts.

The keeping of appropriate financial records is absolutely essential in terms of banking, invoice paying and issuing, extracting appropriate records from the financial statements for submission to the relevant committees, and dealing with potential investments and banking systems to the benefit of the sports club or organization.

There is a wide variety of other personal, even domestic, arrangements that an efficient administrator could consider in the search for efficiency and ease of operation. The more that any individual can do to bring their personal time management into efficient operation, the more they, and ulti-mately the organization, will benefit.

As mentioned above, Covey (1992) lists seven guidelines to enhance personal effectiveness. These are as useful to the sports manager/adminis-trator as in industrial situations, and the text is well worth reading by anybody who wants to increase their effectiveness.

Covey suggests that people begin by being dependent, move to inde-pendence, and should ultimately move to a situation of interdependence. This reflects the fact that individuals can strengthen their own roles and actions, but ultimate success will rely on working happily with others – this is seen in sports administration in the networking situation mentioned elsewhere in the text. This is a vital part of sporting structures everywhere – working together for mutual benefit is very much what it is all about, and combining limited resources makes this most effective. Being person-ally effective is as much a case of who you know as what you know.

Covey's seven habits are listed at the beginning of this chapter, but are worth repeating:

1 be proactive
2 begin with the end in mind
3 put first things first
4 think win/win
5 seek first to understand, then to be understood
6 synergize
7 sharpen the saw

Quick tips for managing your personal life

This list may seem a little patronizing, but in the drive for time and organization to allow for sports involvement, it can be helpful.

- *Things others can do* – make a list of things it's better not to do yourself, but rather to pay others to do: car repairs, DIY jobs, etc.
- *Use the post* – why pay all bills in person? You can pay bills and indeed shop by using the post, the phone or the Internet.
- *Avoid peak hours* – do your shopping on a Monday morning. It is much quieter than a Saturday afternoon.
- *Organize your finances* – have a financial file at home. Keep all your money and related items in it. Make sure you have a bills-due folder and set definite times to pay them.
- *Don't get glued to the tube* – limit your television to a few shows of special merit each week; don't flop down and watch whatever comes on. Far better to use this recreation time to read something, do some exercise or just catch up on mental rest.
- *Keep a spare set of keys* – duplicate keys for home, car and office should be kept in safe, handy places. This is a real timesaver.
- *Forget perfection* – especially in household management, perfection is probably not possible so simply strive to make everything reasonably clean, comfortable and complete.
- *Keep in touch with the family* – make sure you keep a notice board or a phone message board at a suitable place in the home where everyone knows things will be posted.
- *Crowd your appointments* – make sure that you get all the appointments you can for yourself and your family as close together as possible, rather than having to go once a week for four weeks.
- *Have a master list* – put down items to buy at shops or work to do as they arise or come to mind.
- *Keep paperwork under control* – at the very least sort through your mail and other papers at least once a week, otherwise you will create a monster. A home filing system can be very worthwhile.

- *Shop only twice a year for clothes* – this can be done at sale times and we can save money and a lot of inconvenience.
- *Keep repairs under control* – make sure that clothing, equipment and home repairs are done as they arise. Don't put things away that need to be repaired, as they will be broken the next time you look for them.
- *Keep an accurate professional and social diary* – everything must be on it. Perhaps a desk and pocket copy is the best system as long as they both say the same thing.
- *Accept invitations or meetings selectively* – if you can't go or really don't want to go, be sure to say that your time is valuable.
- *Make sure a holiday is a holiday* – don't take work away with you.
- *Keep your eyes open for time management tips* – you can always learn from others on new improvements that are being made.

Self-assessment question

Consider the time and meeting demands on a sports administrator you know. Make a list of these, and suggest approaches to handle these demands. Devise an action plan for the person involved to maximize their effectiveness.

15 Into the future

This brief chapter takes a look at the future and asks a few questions about what might happen.

At the time of writing it would probably help to be an astrologer to predict exactly where sport will go over the next few years – there are so many questions in the air which will have a major impact on what happens.

1 Will the vast sums paid to some sports people continue?
2 What will be the impact of the National Lottery's declining revenue?
3 What will be the impact of the UK Institute of Sport?
4 Will pay-to-view television produce the anticipated sums?
5 What area will the private sector move into next?
6 What is the next boom sport?
7 What will be the ongoing impact of the fashion houses and clothing manufacturers?
8 How will sports providers cope with the demographic changes in society?
9 How will education and training developments in the area of sports management and administration impact on sports provision?
10 How will the growing professionalization of sports administration impact on sport?
11 What will be the impact of information technology, in particular virtual reality, on sport,?
12 What additional environmental considerations will develop to encourage activities such as cycling and walking, but perhaps work against activities such as skiing and mountain biking?
13 What impact will the rapidly changing technological society have on sport?
14 Will the change to home-based leisure activities continue?
15 What will be government's ongoing commitment to and views on sport?

The answers to these and other such questions are not straightforward, and no-one knows any definitive answers at this point in time. However, a professional sports administrator must be keeping an eye on them and ensuring they are not caught out by changes of which they are unaware. For example, they should have foreseen the political step to remove tobacco company sponsorship from the sporting arena. This had been widely promoted in advance as party policy, and the professional administrator should have been looking to set in place replacement sponsorships long before any change of political power. Anticipation is essential for any professional manager and as society – politics and its technology – changes ever more rapidly, the need to take a forward-looking approach is all the more essential.

To assess what might happen in the future it is always wise to look to the past and examine how change has affected organizations: be a student of sport and sports management. This can be done through relevant journals and texts as well as the developing academic knowledge, but sports administrators can also learn from more general management thinkers and their potential view of the future.

For example, Naisbitt (1995) gives useful insights into how our world and country may develop in the future. It is not necessary to accept everything that any management guru says, but it is certainly necessary to consider it. Getting it right is difficult, but getting it wrong, for sport as well as for other businesses, can be fatal.

Handy (1997) suggests that we must look forward to uncertainty in the future and not seek the comfort of a sure and steady situation. We must make the best of the chaos and change that exists around about us, try to keep ahead, and recognize it rather than fight it. This concept is very pertinent to sport since the old cosy clique is a thing of the past and traditionalists trying to cling to old methods and behaviours must step aside for innovative leaders who will be proactive in facing up to a changing future.

There is a need to carve a positive direction for the future, with sports organizations being responsive to others' initiatives – to do otherwise could lead to withering on the vine and could cause fatal damage to some sports.

The future is not just going to be based on the past; change in society today works at a multiplier effect – as technology reinvents itself more rapidly than humans can extend it, computers double in power every two years. Having moved in 30 years from the first computer to computers appearing on every desk in industry, it has taken only two or three years for them to appear in many many households. Progress is extremely rapid in technology and related areas where we come to rely on such factors – this has a spin-off effect for all individuals and organizations, as well as society as a whole. Even to assess the work implications for such changes is difficult and has led to company downsizing, early retirement and major social impact. This has left the way open for more sports participation and made people more available to provide administrative support on a voluntary basis having given up their jobs relatively early.

As all these changes happen, the fundamental thing for a consumer business like sport is that the needs, expectations and desires of the customers will change radically and these must be assessed and matched. Like society, our customers will change.

It will become more important for sports administrators and everyone involved to be more aware of what is happening in other industrial settings. Industrial change has a massive impact on sport, as indeed does, for example, the expansion of tourism, the development of the Internet, etc. – sport must get in early, responding on its terms and leading the way where possible. Innovation that can be shown on the sports field needs to be shown in administrative terms as well.

The growth of the Internet throws up major opportunities for sports organizations to improve their communications network, improve public awareness, and sell their goods and services nationally and internationally. This opportunity will be exploited by others if it is not seized by sport itself.

There is a common phrase used by many management gurus at present: 'think globally, act locally'. This phrase is vitally important to sport. It must take into account the wider picture while putting together the practicalities of sport on a local basis where it has a real impact.

The future then, as ever, provides opportunities and threats, necessitates action on the part of individuals and organizations who want to be truly successful and will be quite radically different from the past, even the recent past. Sports administrators and leaders of the twenty-first century must be more dynamic, forceful and proactive than in the past if they are to maintain and increase their share of an ever more challenging market place.

Conclusion

The aim of this book is to enlighten, educate and assist all of those involved in the management and administration of sport. It is hoped that this has been achieved to some degree and what is contained is of significant help to everyone involved.

Like any area of management or business operation, learning – to improve performance – must be an ongoing process, and must be constantly updated and reviewed if genuine improvements are to be seen in the function of the organization and the effectiveness of individuals. The author has devised leisuretraining.com to help with this continual development on an ongoing basis.

The general management concepts examined are valid in many contexts, and it is felt that the sports scene is no different in that respect. However, the author believes that there is a fundamental difference in the sports scene from that of the highly commercial, high-speed business scene and from most other areas of management operation – even other areas of leisure such as the arts.

Throughout the book an attempt has been made to apply theory and good commercial practice to situations which exist in sport, but no attempt or intention has been laid out to lessen the 'specialness' of sport and the unique nature of the situation and the staff operating in it. Anything that lessens the empathy of everyone involved for the special commitment (almost to the level of fanaticism) of those involved is damaging to sport in the long term. So, while enthusiastically embracing management concepts and placing them in a context which is helpful to sport, the author does not underestimate the special nature of sport – quite the contrary, having spent my lifetime in its participation, administration and organization. It is to be hoped that this book will make that path easier for others in the future and that the thoughts contained in it will assist effective operation in a wide variety of sports situations.

There is always a danger of becoming a fanatic through involvement in sport, in any role, simply because of the commitment it requires. This single-mindedness must not be allowed to let anyone in sport ignore correct practices and procedures. The fact that the sports setting is unique should be a strength and not a weakness, but it can become a weakness if the difference is pushed to the level of believing that proper management practice is not appropriate in that unique situation. On the contrary, the special nature of the activity makes the need to link closely to 'good management and leadership' all the more important.

Hopefully, this book has been a small step along the way and has helped lay down some guidance and guidelines which apply to this special situation. It is to be hoped that the author's enthusiasm for the subject has shown through the words, and that enthusiasm will be encouraged in others by the views expressed throughout the book.

The key point is that sports staff, voluntary and paid, should press on and continue the good work they are already involved in with renewed, more focused and so more effective enthusiasm, channelling in a sensible predetermined direction.

A final word to all sports administrators:

Please keep up this vitally important work. It is the lifeblood of sport itself and all its accompanying benefits and pleasures. Without competent sports management and administration, there is no sustainable sport.

Self-assessment question

What are your predictions for the future of sport and its administration and management? Justify your opinions with relevant facts from this book and your experience.

Appendix: Useful sports contacts and addresses

It was decided not to list the hundreds of national governing body addresses because of space considerations and their sometimes rapid turnover. The first point of contact for these should be the appropriate national or regional Sports Council.

Locally, don't forget to look in your telephone book, Yellow Pages and other local directories (often handed out by the press or other advertisers). They can be invaluable for contacts and increasing your networks.

Government agencies – local and national

Association of County Councils
Eaton House
66A Eaton Square
LONDON
SW1W 9BH
Tel: (020) 7 235 1200

Association of District Councils
Chapter House
26 Chapter Street
LONDON
SW1P 4ND
Tel: (020) 7 233 6868
Fax: (020) 7 233 6551

Association of Metropolitan
Authorities
35 Great Smith Street
LONDON
SW1P 3BJ
Tel: (020) 7 222 8100

Chief Leisure Officers Association
Stevenage Borough Council
Daneshill House
Danestrete
STEVENAGE
Hertfordshire
SG1 1HN
Tel: 01438 356177, ext. 234

Department of National Heritage
2–4 Cockspur Street
LONDON
SW1Y 5DH
Tel: (020) 7 211 6000

Northern Ireland Office
Stormont Castle
BELFAST
BT4 3ST
Tel: 01232 763255

The Scottish Executive
New St Andrew's House
EDINBURGH
EH1 3TD
Tel: 0131 556 8400

Welsh Office
Cathays Park
CARDIFF
CG1 3NQ
Tel: 01222 825111

Department for Education
Sanctuary Buildings
Great Smith Street
LONDON
SW1P 3BT
Tel: (020) 7 925 5000

Home Office
Queen Anne's Gate
LONDON
SW1H 9AT

International agencies

Clearing House (Council of
Europe)
Espace du 27 Septembre
Boulevard Leopold II 44
BRUSSELS
1080
Belgium
Tel: 2 413 28 93
Fax: 2 413 28 90

Comité International Oympique
Château de Vidy
LAUSANNE
1007
Switzerland
Tel: 21 25 32 71
Fax: 21 24 15 52

The Council of Europe
Avenue De l'Europe
STRASBOURG
67006
France
Tel: 33 88 41 20 00
Fax: 33 88 41 27 81

Fédération Internationale de Sport
Universitaire
56 Avenue Franklin Roosevelt
BRUSSELS
Belgium
Tel: 2 640 6873
Fax: 2 640 1805

General Association of
International Sports Federations
Villa Henri
7 Boulevard de Suisse
MONTE CARLO
98000
Monaco
Tel: 93 50 74 13
Fax: 93 25 28 73

International Association for
Sports Information
Clearing House
Espace du 27 Septembre
Boulevard Leopold II 44
BRUSSELS
1080
Belgium

World Leisure and Recreation
Association
PO Box 309
SHARBOT LAKE
Ontario
KOH 2PO
Canada
Tel: 613 279 3172
Fax: 613 279 3130

Sports councils

Northern Ireland Sports Council
House of Sport
Upper Malone Rd
BELFAST
County Antrim BT9 5LA

Sport England
16 Upper Woburn Place
LONDON
WC1H 0QP
Tel: (020) 7 273 1500

Sports Council for Northern
Ireland
House of Sport
Upper Malone Road
BELFAST
BT9 5LA
Tel: 01232 381222

Sport Scotland
Caledonia House
South Gyle
EDINBURGH
EH12 9DQ
Tel: 0131 317 7200

Sports Council for Wales
National Sports Centre
Sophia Gardens
CARDIFF
CF1 9SW
Tel: 01222 397571

UK Sport
Walkden House
3/10 Melton Street
LONDON
NW1 2EB
Tel: (020) 7 380 8000

National Association for Sports
Development
Giffard House
36/38 Sherrard Street
Melton Mowbray
LEICESTERSHIRE
Tel: 01664 565531

National sports centres

Bisham Abbey National Sports
Centre
NR MARLOW
Buckinghamshire
SL7 1RT
Tel: 01628 476911

Crystal Palace National Sports
Centre
Ledrington Road
Norwood
LONDON
SE19 2BB
Tel: (020) 8 778 0131

Holme Pierrepont National Water
Sports Centre
Adbolton Lane
Holme Pierrepont
NOTTINGHAM
NG12 2LU
Tel: 01159 821212

Lilleshall Hall National Sports
Centre
NR NEWPORT
Shropshire
TF10 9AT
Tel: 01952 603003

Plas y Brenin National Centre for
Mountain Activities
CAPEL CURIGG
Gwynedd
LL24 0ET
Tel: 0169 04 214

Plas Menai National Watersports
Centre
Llanfairisgaer
CAERNARFON
Gwynedd
LL5 1UE
Tel: 01248 670964

The Welsh Institute of Sport
Sophia Gardens
CARDIFF
CF1 9SW
Tel: 01222 397571

The Scottish National Water
Sports Centre
Cumbrae
LARGS
Inverclyde
KA40 8RW

The Scottish National Sports
Centre
Glenmore Lodge
AVIEMORE
PH22 1QU
Tel: 01479 86256

The Scottish National Sports
Centre
LARGS
Inverclyde
KA30 8RW
Tel: 01475 674666

The Northern Ireland Centre for
Outdoor Activities
Tollymore
BRYANSFORD
County Down
Northern Ireland
Tel: 01396 722158

English sports councils

East Midland Region
Grove House
Bridgeford
NOTTINGHAM
NG2 6AP
Tel: 0115 982 1887/2586

Eastern Region
Crescent House
19 The Crescent
BEDFORD
MK40 2QP
Tel: 01234 345222

Greater London and SE Regions
Crystal Palace National Sports
Centre
PO Box 480
Ledrington Road
LONDON
SE19 2BQ
Tel: (020) 8 778 8600

North West Region
Astley House
Quay Street
MANCHESTER
M3 4AE
Tel: 0161 834 0338

Northern Region
Ayukley Heads
DURHAM
DH1 5UU
Tel: 0191 384 9595

South West Region
Ashlands House
Ashlands
CREWEKERNE
Somerset
TA18 7LQ
Tel: 01460 73491

Southern Region
51a Church Street
Caversham
READING
RG4 8AX
Tel: 01734 483311

West Midlands Region
Metropolitan House
1 Hagley Road
Five Ways
BIRMINGHAM
B16 8TT
Tel: 0121 456 3444

Yorkshire and Humberside Region
Coronet House
Queen Street
LEEDS
LS1 4PW
Tel: 01532 456 3444

Other official organizations

The Arts Council
14 Great Peter Street
LONDON
SW1P 3NQ
Tel: (020) 7 333 0100
Fax: (020) 7 973 6590

British Amputee Sports
Association
Bridge Way
ST LEONARDS ON SEA
East Sussex
TN38 8AP

The Association of Playing Fields
Officers & Landscape Managers
19 Oakfield Rise
Longfield
DARTFORD
DA3 7PA
Tel: 01322 21644

British Association of Advisers and
Lecturers in Physical Education
Nelson House
3–6 The Beacon
EXMOUTH
Devon
EX8 2AG
Tel: 01395 263247

British Association of Golf Course
Constructors
2 Angel Court
Dairy Yard
High Street
MARKET HARBOROUGH
Leicestershire
LE16 7NL
Tel: 01858 464346

British Association of Sport and
Medicine
51 Main Street
Bishopstone
AYLESBURY
Buckinghamshire
HP17 8SH
Tel: 01296 748186

British Association of Sports
Science
4 College Close
Beckett Park
LEEDS
LS6 3QH
Tel: 01132 784113

British Colleges Sports Association
11 Allcock Street
BIRMINGHAM
B9 4DY
Tel: 0121 766 8855

The British Council
10 Spring Gardens
LONDON
SW1A 2BN
Tel: (020) 7 930 8466

British Council for Physical
Education
PO Box 6
Woolton Road
LIVERPOOL
L16 8ND
Tel: 0151 737 3461
Fax: 0151 737 3664

British Blind Sport
67 Albert Street
RUGBY
Warwickshire
CV21 2SN
Tel: 01788 536142

British Broadcasting House
Portland Place
LONDON
W1A 1AA

British Deaf Sports Council
7A Bridge Street
OTLEY
West Yorkshire
LS21 1BQ
Tel: 01934 850214

British Institute of Management
Africa House
64/78 Kingsway
LONDON
WC2 6BL

British Institute of Sports
Administrators
24 Southfield
EAST MOLESEY
Surrey
KT8 0BP
Tel/Fax: (020) 8 224 0712

British and International Golf
Greenkeepers Association
Aldwark Manor
Alne
YORK
YO6 2NF
Tel: 01347 833 800
Fax: 01347 833 801

British Institute of Golf Course
Architects
The Pheasantry
Tandridge Golf Club
OXSTEAD
Surrey
RH8 9NQ
Tel: 01883 712072

British Les Autres Sports
Association
29 Gloucester Road
Walthamstow
LONDON
E17 6AE

British Olympic Association
1 Wandsworth Plain
LONDON
SW18 1EH
Tel: (020) 8 871 2677

British Paralympic Association
Delta Point
Room G13A
35 Wellesley Road
CROYDON
Surrey
CR9 2YZ
Tel: (020) 8 666 4556

British Red Cross Society
9 Grosvenor Crescent
LONDON
SW1X 7EJ
Tel: (020) 7 235 5454

British Safety Council
National Safety Centre
70 Chancellor's Road
Hammersmith
LONDON
W6 9RS
Tel: (020) 8 741 1231

British Sports Association for the
Disabled
Solecast House
13–27 Brunswick Place
LONDON
N1 6DX
Tel: (020) 7 490 4919

British Sports and Allied Industries
Federation
23 Brighton Road
SOUTH CROYDON
Surrey
CR2 6EA
Tel: (020) 8 681 1242
Fax: (020) 8 681 0012

British Standards Institution
2 Park Street
LONDON
W1A 2BS
Tel: (020) 7 629 9000

British Student Association of
Sport and Medicine
National Sports Medicine Institute
c/o St Bartholomew's Medical
College
LONDON
EC1M 6BQ

British Students Sports Association
11 Allcock Street
BIRMINGHAM
B9 4DY
Tel: 0121 766 8855

British Tourist Authority
Thames Tower
Blacks Road
Hammersmith
LONDON
W6 9EL

British University Sports
Federation
28 Woburn Square
LONDON
WC1H 0AA
Tel: (020) 7 580 3618

British Waterways Board
Greycaine Road
WATFORD
WD2 4JR
Tel: 01923 226422

Central Bureau for Educational
Visits and Exchanges
Seymour House
Seymour Mews
LONDON
W1H 9PE
Tel: (020) 7 486 5101

Central Council of Physical
Recreation
Francis House
Francis Street
LONDON
SW1P 1DE
Tel: (020) 7 828 3163

Centre for Sports Science &
History
Main Library
University of Birmingham
Edgbaston
BIRMINGHAM
B15 2TT
Tel: 0121 414 5843
Fax: 0121 471 4671

The Companies Register for
England
Companies House
Crown Way
Maindy
CARDIFF
CF4 3UZ

The Charities Commission and the
Central Registrar of Charities
St Albans House
57/60 Haymarket
LONDON
SW1Y 4QX

Chartered Society of Physiotherapy
14 Bedford Row
LONDON
WC2N 4HH
Tel: (020) 7 242 1941

Chief Leisure Officers Association
E L Harris
20 Essex Road
STEVENAGE
Herts
SG1 3EX
Tel: 01438 356177

Child Accident Prevention Trust
4th Floor
Clerks Court
18–20 Farringdon Lane
LONDON
EC1R 3AU
Tel: (020) 7 608 3828

The Commonwealth Games
Federation
Walkden House
Melton Street
LONDON
NW1 2EB
Tel: (020) 7 383 5596

The Companies Register for
Scotland
Companies House
102 George Street
EDINBURGH
EH2 3DG

Convention of Scottish Local
Authorities
Roseberry House
9 Haymarket Terrace
EDINBURGH
EH12 5XE
Tel: 0131 474 9200

Countryside Commission
John Dower House
Crescent Place
CHELTENHAM
GL50 3RA
Tel: 01242 521381

Countryside Recreation Network
Department of City and Regional
Planning
University of Wales
College of Cardiff
PO Box 906
CARDIFF
CF1 3YN

Department of Trade and Industry
123 Victoria Street
LONDON
SW1E 6RB
Tel: (020) 7 215 5000

The Directory for Social Change
Stephenson Way
LONDON
NW1 2HD

Disabled Living Foundation
380–384 Harrow Road
LONDON
W9 2HU
Tel: (020) 7 289 6111

Duke of Edinburgh's Award
Gullivery House
Madeira Walk
WINDSOR
Berkshire
SL4 1EU
Tel: 01753 810753
Fax: 01753 810666

Duke of Edinburgh's Award
(Scottish Office)
69 Dublin Street
EDINBURGH
EH3 6NS
Tel: 0131 556 9097

EDEXCELL
Central House
Upper Woburn Place
LONDON
WC1H 0HH
Tel: (020) 7 413 8400

English Nature
Northminster House
Northminster Road
PETERBOROUGH
PE1 1UA
Tel: 01733 340345

English Tourist Board
Thames Tower
Blacks Road
Hammersmith
LONDON
W6 9EL
Tel: (020) 8 846 9000

Forestry Commission
231 Corstorphine Road
EDINBURGH
EH12 7AT
Tel: 0131 334 0303

The Foundation for Sport and the
Arts
PO Box 666
LIVERPOOL
L69 7JN
Tel: 0151 524 0235

Girl Guides Association
17–19 Buckingham Palace Road
LONDON
SW1W 0PT
Tel: (020) 7 834 6242

Health and Safety Executive
Education National Interest Group
Maritime House
Linton Road
BARKING
Essex
IG11 8HF
Tel: (020) 8 594 5522

Health and Safety Executive
Belford House
59 Belford Road
EDINBURGH
EH3 3UE
Tel: 0131 247 2000

Health Education Authority
Hamilton House
Mabledon Place
LONDON
WH1H 9TX
Tel: (020) 7 383 3833

Heritage Coast Forum
Manchester Metropolitan
University
St Augustine's
Lower Chatham Street
MANCHESTER
M15 6BY
Tel: 0161 247 1067
Fax: 0161 236 7383

The Independent Television
Commission
70 Brompton Road
LONDON
SW3 1EY

Institute of Leisure and Amenity
Management (ILAM)
ILAM House
Lower Basildon
READING
Berks
RG8 9NE
Tel: 01491 874800
Fax: 01491 874801

Institute of Sport and Recreation
Management (ISRM)
Gifford House
36/38 Sherrard Street
MELTON MOWBRAY
Leicestershire
LE13 1XJ
Tel: 0166 465531

Leisure Studies Association
Bradford & Ilkley Community
College
Ilkley Campus
Wells Road
ILKLEY
West Yorkshire
LS29 9RD
Tel: 01943 609010

Local Government Training Board
Arndale House
Arndale Centre
LUTON
LU1 2TS
Tel: 01582 451166
Fax: 01582 412525

Motoring Organisations Land
Access and Recreation Association
Millar House
Corporation Street
RUGBY
Warwickshire
CV21 2DN
Tel: 01788 541137

Mountain Leader Training Board
Crawford House
Precinct Centre
Booth Street East
MANCHESTER
M13 9RZ
Tel: 0161 273 5835

National Association of Boys
Clubs
369 Kennington Lane
LONDON
SE11 5QY
Tel: (020) 7 793 0787

National Association for Outdoor
Education
12 St Andrews Churchyard
PENRITH
Cumbria
CA11 7IE
Tel: 01768 65113

National Association for Outdoor
Education (Scotland)
Scottish Centres
Loaningdale House
Carwood Road
BIGGAR
ML12 6LX

Sportscoach UK
114 Cardigan Road
Headingly
LEEDS
LS6 3BJ
Tel: 01132 744802

National Council for Schools
Sports
21 Northampton Road
CROYDON
CR0 7HB

Qualifications and Curriculum
Authority
222 Euston Road
LONDON
NW1 2BZ
Tel: (020) 7 387 9898

National Council for Voluntary
Organisations
Regents Wharf
9 All Saints Road
LONDON
N1 9RL
Tel: (020) 7 713 6161

National Council of YMCAs
640 Forest Road
LONDON
E17 3DZ

National Outdoor Events
Association
7 Hamilton Way
Wallington
SURREY
SM6 9NJ

National Playing Fields Association
25 Ovington Square
LONDON
SW3 1LQ
Tel: (020) 7 584 6445

National Rivers Authority
Rivers House
Waterside Drive
Aztec West Business Park
Almodsbury
BRISTOL
BS12 4UD
Tel: 01454 624400

National Sports Medicine Institute
c/o St Bartholomew's Medical
College
Charterhouse Square
LONDON
EC1M 6BQ
Tel: (020) 7 251 0583

Nature Conservancy Council
Northminster House
PETERBOROUGH
PE1 1UA
Tel: 01733 40345

Northern Ireland Council of
Physical Education
House of Sport
Upper Malone Road
BELFAST
BT9 5LA
Tel: 01232 381222

Outward Bound Trust
Chestnut Field
Regent Place
RUGBY
Warwickshire
CV21 2PJ
Tel: 01788 560423

Performing Rights Society Ltd
29/33 Berners Street
LONDON
W1P 4AA
Tel: (020) 7 580 5544

The Physical Education
Association of Great Britain
Ling House
162 Kings Cross Road
LONDON
WC1X 9TH
Tel: (020) 7 278 9311

Princes Trust and Royal Jubilee
Trusts
8 Bedford Row
LONDON
WC1R 4BA
Tel: (020) 7 430 0524

Royal Society for the Prevention
of Accidents (ROSPA)
Water and Leisure Safety
Department
Cannon House
The Priory
Queensway
BIRMINGHAM
B4 6BS

Royal Life Saving Society
Mountbatten House
STUDLEY
Warwickshire
B80 7NN
Tel: 01527 753943

Recreation Managers' Association
of Great Britain
5 Balfour Road
WYBRIDGE
Surrey
KT13 8HE
Tel: 01932 841583

RSA
Westwood Way
COVENTRY
CV4 8HS
Tel: 01203 470033

Running Sport (Publishing)
PO Box HP 86
LEEDS
LS6 3XW
Tel: 0113 279 1395

Scottish Accident Prevention
Council
Slateford House
53 Lanark Road
EDINBURGH
EH14 1TL
Tel: 0131 455 7457

Scottish Mountain Leader Training
Board
Caledonia House
South Gyle
EDINBURGH
EH12 9DQ
Tel: 0131 317 7217

Scottish Natural Heritage
12 Hope Terrace
EDINBURGH
EH9 2AS
Tel: 0131 447 4784

Scottish Sports Association
Caledonia House
South Gyle
EDINBURGH
EH1 3TD
Tel: 0131 339 8785

Visit Scotland
23 Ravelston Terrace
EDINBURGH
EH4 3EU
Tel: 0131 332 2433
Fax: 0131 459 2434

Scottish Youth Hotels Association
7 Glebe Crescent
STIRLING
FK8 2JA
Tel: 01786 451181

The Scout Association
Baden-Powell House
Queen's Gate
LONDON
SW7 5JS
Tel: (020) 7 584 7030
Fax: (020) 7 581 9953

Scottish Qualifications Authority
(SQA)
Hanover House
24 Douglas Street
GLASGOW
G2 7NQ
Tel: 0141 242 2211

SPRITO
24 Stephenson Way
LONDON
NW1 2HD
Tel: (020) 7 388 7755
Fax: (020) 7 388 9733

SPRITO Scotland
1 Colinton Court
GLENROTHES
Fife
KY6 3PE
Tel/Fax: 01592 743948

Sports Aid Foundation
16 Upper Woburn Place
LONDON
WC1H 0QN
Tel: (020) 7 387 9380

Sports Documentation Centre
Main Library
University of Birmingham
Edgbaston
BIRMINGHAM
B15 2TT
Tel: 0121 414 5843, ext. 2312

Sport and Recreation Information
Group
College of St Paul and St Mary
Francis Close Hall
Swindon Road
CHELTENHAM
Gloucestershire
GL50 4AZ
Tel: 01242 528111

Sports Retailers of Great Britain
20 Costello Edge
Scaynes Hill
HAYWARDS HEATH
RH17 7PY
Tel: 01444 831410

Sports Turf Research Institute
BINGLEY
West Yorkshire
BD16 1AZ
Tel: 01274 565131
Fax: 01274 561891

Sports Writers Association
c/o Sports Council Press Office
16 Upper Woburn Place
LONDON
WC1H 0QP
Tel: (020) 7 388 1277

St Andrew's Ambulance Association
St Andrew's House
48 Milton Street
GLASGOW
G4 0HR
Tel: 0141 332 4031

St John's Ambulance
1 Grosvenor Crescent
LONDON
SW1X 7EF
Tel: (020) 7 235 5231

Swimming Pool and Allied Trades
Association
Sparta House
1A Junction Road
ANDOVER
Hampshire
SP10 3QT
Tel: 01264 332628

The Training Agency
Muirfoot
SHEFFIELD
S1 4PQ
Tel: 0142 2753275

Travel Advice Unit
Consular Department
Foreign and Commonwealth Office
Clive House
Petty France
LONDON
SW1 6HD
Tel: (020) 7 270 4129/4179

United Kingdom Sports
Association for People with
Learning Disabilities
Solecast House
13–27 Brunswick Place
LONDON
N1 6DX
Tel: (020) 7 250 1100

United Kingdom Sports
Association for People with a
Mental Handicap
30 Philip Lane
Tottenham
LONDON
N15 4JB
Tel: (020) 8 885 1177

Universities Athletic Union
Suite 36 London Fruit Exchange
Brushfield Street
LONDON
E1 6EU
Tel: (020) 7 247 3066

Voluntary Service Overseas
317 Putney Bridge Road
LONDON
SW15 2PN
Tel: (020) 8 780 2266
Fax: (020) 8 780 1326

Welsh Sports Association
Sophia Gardens
CARDIFF
CF1 9SW
Tel: 01222 397571

Women's Sports Foundation
Wesley House
4 Wild Court
LONDON
WC2B 5PN
Tel: (020) 7 831 7863

Youth Clubs UK
11 St Bride Street
LONDON
EC4A 4AS
Tel: (020) 7 353 2366

Youth Hostels Association
(England and Wales)
Trevelyan House
8 St Stephen's Hill
ST ALBANS
Hertfordshire
AL1 2DY
Tel: 01727 55215

Media addresses

When writing to any media outlet, please try to ensure that all correspondence is personally addressed to the relevant individual, usually the sports editor.

Association of Independent
Producers (AIP)
Paramount House
162–170 Wardour Street
LONDON
W1V 4LA

BBC
Bush House
The Strand
LONDON
WC2B 4PH
Tel: (020) 7 240 3456

BBC
Broadcasting House
Langham Place
LONDON
W1A 1AA
Tel: (020) 7 580 4468

BBC Radio
Broadcasting House
Portland House
Portland Place
LONDON
W1A 1AA
Tel: (020) 7 580 4468

BBC Television Current Affairs
Television Centre
Wood Lane
LONDON
W12 7RJ
Tel: (020) 8 743 5588

BBC Television Sport & Events
Kensington House
Richmond Way
LONDON
W14 0AX
Tel: (020) 8 895 6161

BBC TV Northern Ireland
Broadcasting House
Ormeau Avenue
BELFAST
BT2 8HQ
Tel: 01232 338000

BBC TV Scotland
Broadcasting House
Queen Margaret Drive
GLASGOW
G12 8DG
Tel: 0141 330 2345

BBC TV Wales
Broadcasting House
Llandaff
CARDIFF
CF5 2YQ
Tel: 01222 572888

BBC World Service
PO Box 76
Bush House
The Strand
LONDON
WC2B 4PH
Tel: (020) 7 240 3456

British Sky Broadcasting
6 Centrairs Business Park
Grant Way
ISLEWORTH
Middlesex
TW7 5QD
Tel: (020) 7 782 3000

British Telecom International TV
Distribution Services (TVDS)
Room 723
Holborn Centre
LONDON
EC1N 2TE
Tel: (020) 7 492 2626

The Cable Authority
Gillingham House
38–44 Gillingham Street
LONDON
SW1V 1JU
Tel: (020) 7 821 6161

Carlton Television
101 St Martin's Lane
LONDON
WC2N 4AZ
Tel: (020) 7 240 4000

Ceefax
Room 7059
BBC Television Centre
Wood Lane
LONDON
W12 7RJ

Channel Four News &
Independent Television News
200 Gray's Inn Road
LONDON
WC1X 8XZ
Tel: (020) 7 833 3000

Channel 4 TV Co.
60 Charlotte Street
LONDON
W1P 2AX
Tel: (020) 7 927 8640

GMTV
London TV Centre
Upper Ground
LONDON
SE1 9LT
Tel: (020) 7 827 7000

European Sports Network
(Screensport)
Craven Hall
33–43 Fouberts Place
LONDON
W1V 2BH
Tel: (020) 7 439 1177

European Telecommunications
Satellite Organisation
(EUTELSAT)
Tour Maine, Montparnasse
33 Avenue du Maine
75755 PARIS
France
Tel: 010 331 45384747

Independent regional television

Eurosport UK
9 Gower Street
LONDON
WC1A 6HA
Tel: (020) 7 916 4113

Independent Broadcasting
Authority (IBA)
70 Brompton Road
LONDON
SW3
Tel: (020) 7 584 7011

Independent Programme Producers
Association (IPPA)
50–51 Berwick Street
LONDON
W1A 4RD
Tel: (020) 7 439 7034

Oracle Teletext
Craven House
25/32 Marshall Street
LONDON
W1V 1LL
Tel: (020) 7 434 3121

Super Channel
New Media Sales Limited
25 Soho Square
LONDON
W1V 5FJ
Tel: (020) 7 631 5050

Teletext
101 Farm Lane
Fulham
LONDON
SW6 1QJ
Tel: (020) 7 386 5002

Anglia Television
Anglia House
NORWICH
Norfolk
NR1 3LG
Tel: 01603 615151

Border Television
Television Centre
CARLISLE
Cumbria
CA1 3NT
Tel: 01228 25101

Central Independent Television
(East)
East Midlands TV Centre
Lenton Lane
NOTTINGHAM
NG7 2NA
Tel: 01602 863322

Central Independent Television
(West)
Central House
Broad Street
BIRMINGHAM
B1 2JP
Tel: 0121 643 9898

Channel Television
Television Centre
St Helier
JERSEY
Channel Islands
JE2 32D
Tel: 01534 73999

Grampian Television
Queens Cross
ABERDEEN
AB9 2XJ
Tel: 01224 646464

Granada TV
Granada TV Centre
Quay Street
MANCHESTER
M60 9EA
Tel: 0161 832 7211

HTV Wales
TV Centre
Culverhouse Cross
CARDIFF
CF 6XJ
Tel: 01222 597183

HTV West
Television Centre
Bath Road
BRISTOL
Avon BS4 3HG
Tel: 01272 778366

ITV Sport
200 Grays Inn Road
LONDON
WC1X 8HF
Tel: (020) 7 843 8000

Meridian Broadcasting
Television Centre
SOUTHAMPTON
Hants
SO14 0PZ
Tel: 01703 712122

S4C
Parc ty Glas
Llanishen
CARDIFF
CF4 5DU
Tel: 01222 754444

Scottish Television
Cowcaddens
GLASGOW
G2 3PR
Tel: 0141 332 9999

Tyne Tees Television
City Road
NEWCASTLE UPON TYNE
NE1 2AL
Tel: 0191 261 0181

Ulster Television
Havelock House
Ormeau Road
BELFAST
BT7 1EB
Tel: 01232 328122

West Country Television
Western Wood Way
Langage Science Park
PLYMOUTH
PL7 5BG
Tel: 01752 333333

Yorkshire Television
Television Centre
LEEDS
LS3 1JS
Tel: 01532 438283

Newspapers

Allsport (UK)
3 Greenlea Park
Prince Georges Road
LONDON
SW19 2JD
Tel: (020) 8 685 1010
Fax: (020) 8 648 5240

Courier & Advertiser
7 Bank Street
DUNDEE
DD1 9HU
Tel: 01382 23131

Daily Express/Sunday Express
Ludgate House
254 Blackfriars Road
LONDON
SE1 9UX
Tel: (020) 7 928 8000

Daily Mail/Mail on Sunday
Northcliffe House
2 Derry Street
LONDON
W8 5TT
Tel: (020) 7 938 6000

Daily Mirror/Sunday Mirror &
The People
1 Canada Square
Canary Wharf
LONDON
E14 5DT
Tel: (020) 7 510 3000

Daily Record
Anderston Quay
GLASGOW
G3 8DA
Tel: 0141 248 7000

Daily Star
Ludgate House
245 Blackfriars Road
LONDON
SE1 9UX
Tel: (020) 7 928 8000

Daily Telegraph/Sunday Telegraph
Peterborough Court, South Quay
181 Marsh Wall
LONDON
E14 9SR
Tel: (020) 7 538 5000

The European
200 Gray's Inn Road
LONDON
WC1X
Tel: (020) 7 418 7777

Evening Standard
Northcliffe House
2 Derry Street
Kensington
LONDON
W8 5EE
Tel: (020) 7 938 6000

Financial Times
1 Southwark Bridge
LONDON
SE1 9HL
Tel: (020) 7 873 3000

The Guardian
119 Farringdon Road
LONDON
EC1R 3ER
Tel: (020) 7 278 2332

The Herald
195 Albion Street
GLASGOW
G1 1QP
Tel: 0141 552 6255

The Independent/Independent on Sunday
1 Canada Square
Canary Wharf
LONDON
E14 5DT
Tel: (020) 7 293 2000

The Morning Star
1–3 Ardleigh Road
LONDON
N1 4HS
Tel: (020) 7 254 0033

The Observer
119 Farringdon Road
LONDON
EC1R 3ER
Tel: (020) 7 611 9000

Saturday Telegraph Magazine
1 Canada Square
Canary Wharf
LONDON
E14 5DT
Tel: (020) 7 513 2507

The Scotsman
20 North Bridge
EDINBURGH
EH1 1YT
Tel: 0131 225 2468

Sport & General Press Agency
68 Exmouth Market
LONDON
EC1R 4RA
Tel: (020) 7 278 1233
Fax: (020) 7 278 8480

Sun/News of the World
1 Virginia Street
LONDON
E1 9XR
Tel: (020) 7 782 4000

Sunday Post
Courier Place
DUNDEE
DD1 9QJ
Tel: 01382 23131

Sunday Sport
19 Great Ancoats Street
MANCHESTER
M60 4BT
Tel: 0161 236 4535

Press agencies

Associated Press
12 Norwich Street
LONDON
EC4A 1BP
Tel: (020) 7 353 1515

Hayters Sports Reporting
1st Floor
Humatt House
146–148 Clerkenwell Road
LONDON
Tel: (020) 7 353 0971

Press Association
85 Fleet Street
LONDON
EC4P 4BE
Tel: (020) 7 353 7440

Reuters Limited
85 Fleet Street
LONDON
EC4P 4AJ
Tel: (020) 7 250 1122

Sport and General Limited
68 Exmouth Market
LONDON
EC1R 4RA
Tel: (020) 7 278 5661

Sporting Pictures UK Limited
7a Lamb's Conduit Passage
LONDON
WC1R 4RG
Tel: (020) 7 405 4500

United Press International
408 The Strand
LONDON
WC2R 0NE
Tel: (020) 7 538 5310

Sports photographic agencies

Action Images
74 Willoughby Lane
LONDON
N17 0SP
Tel: (020) 8 885 3000
Fax: (020) 8 808 6167

All Sport UK Limited
3 Greenlea Park
Prince Georges Road
LONDON
SW19 2JD
Tel: (020) 8 685 1010

Bob Thomas Sports Photography
19 Charnwood Avenue
Westone
NORTHAMPTON
NN3 3DX
Tel: 01604 4144144

Coloursport
44 St Peter's Street
LONDON
N1 8JT
Tel: (020) 7 359 2714

Professional Sport Photography
8 Apollo Studios
Charlton Kings Road
LONDON
NW5 2SA
Tel: (020) 7 482 2311
Fax: (020) 7 482 2311

Sporting Pictures
7a Lamb's Conduit Passage
LONDON
WC1R 4RC
Tel: (020) 7 405 4500
Fax: (020) 7 831 7991

Useful websites

www.sportscotland.org.uk – **sport** Scotland
www.sportengland.org.uk – Sport England
www.sports-council-wales.co.uk – Sports Council for Wales
www.sportni.org – Northern Ireland Sports Council
www.ilam.co.uk – Institute for Leisure & Amenity Management (ILAM)
www.culture.gov.uk – Department of Culture, Media & Sport (DCMS)
www.scotland.gov.uk – Scottish Executive
www.isrm.co.uk – Institute for Sport & Recreation Management
www.open.gov.uk – CCTA Government Information Service
www.detr.gov.uk – Department of the Environment, Transport and the Regions
www.hmce.gov.uk – HM Customs & Excise
www.scotland.gov.uk – Scottish Office
www.cabinet-office.co.uk/quango – quango website
www.cabinet-office.gov.uk/seu – Social Exclusion Unit

www.hlf.org.uk – DCMS National Lottery site
www.nesta.org.uk – National Endowment for Science, Technology and the Arts
www.nof.org.uk – New Opportunities Fund
www.kidsclubs.com – Kids Clubs Network
www.museums.gov.uk – Museums and Galleries Commission (MGC)
www.nls.uk – National Library of Scotland
www.sac.org.uk – Scottish Arts Council
www.horticulture.demon.co.uk – Institute of Horticulture
www.iog.org – Institute of Groundsmanship (IoG)
www.rtpi.org.uk – Royal Town Planning Institute
www.snh.org.uk – Scottish Natural Heritage
www.sportscoachuk.org – Sportscoach UK
www.nsmi.org.uk – National Sports Medicine Institute of the UK
www.olympics.org.uk – British Olympic Association
www.bha-online.org.uk – British Hospitality Association
www.hcima.org.uk – Hotel & Catering International Management Association
www.visitbritain.com – British Tourist Authority
www.world-tourism.org – Word Tourism Organisation
www.visitscotland.com – Scottish Tourist Board
www.sportsonline.co.uk – Sports Online
www.sprito.org.uk – Sport & Recreation Industry Training Organisation
www.bsi.org.uk – Audit Commission Reference Page
www.cipfa.org.uk – Chartered Institute of Public Finance and Administration
www.rospa.co.uk – Royal Society for the Prevention of Accidents
www.the-stationery-office.co.uk – The Stationery Office
www.ipf.co.uk/sis – Institute of Public Finance
www.mintel.co.uk – Mintel

Bibliography

Abdullah, M.S., Saad, J.M., Zakaria, A.A. and Selvaraj, O. (eds) (1998) *Sport Sciences into the Next Millennium: Bridging the Gap (Proceedings of the 11th Commonwealth & International Scientific Congress)*, Kuala Lumpur: University of Malaya.

Adair, J. (1986) *Effective Teambuilding: How to Make a Winning Team*, Aldershot: Gower.

Adair, J. (1988) *Effective Leadership: a Modern Guide to Developing Leadership Skills*, London: Pan.

Adams, I. (1990) *Leisure and Government*, Sunderland: Business Education Publishers.

Allan, J. (1990) *How to Develop Your Personal Management Skills*, London: Kogan Page.

Amis, J., Slack, T. and Berret, T. (1995) 'Structural antecedents of conflict in voluntary sports organizations (VSOs)', *Leisure Studies* **14**, January.

Anon (1989) *Management of Voluntary Organisations*, London: Croner.

Anon (1992) *The British Health and Fitness Club Guide 1993: the Definitive Management Guide to Commercial Health and Fitness Facilities in Clubs and Hotels*, Harlow: Longman.

Argyle, M. (1972) *The Psychology of Interpersonal Behaviour*, Harmondsworth: Penguin.

Armstrong, M. (1990) *The Management Process and Functions*, London: Institute of Personnel Management.

Audit Commission (1989) *Sport for Whom? Clarifying the Local Authority Role in Sport and Recreation*, London: HMSO.

Audit Commission (1993) *The Quality Exchange: Leisure Services, Sport and Recreation*, London: HMSO.

Audit Commission for Local Authorities in England and Wales (1990) *Local Authority Support for Sport: a Management Handbook*, London: HMSO.

Badmin, P. (1992) *Leisure Operational Management, Volume 1 – Facilities*, Harlow: Longman.

Badmin, P. (1993) *Leisure Operational Management, Volume 2 – People*, Harlow: Longman.

Bale, J. (1989) *Sports Geography*, London: E & FN Spon.

Bass, B.M. (1990) *Bass and Stogdill's Handbook of Leadership: Theory, Research and Managerial Implications*, New York: Free Press.

Bennington, J. and White, J. (1988) *The Future of Leisure Services*, Harlow: Longman.

Bischert, R., Taylor, J. and Fitzsimons, M. (1992) *A Practical Approach to the Administration of Leisure and Recreation Services*, 4th edn, London: Croner.

Borrett, N. (1991) *Leisure Services UK*, London: Macmillan.

British Quality Association Leisure Services Quality Committee (1990) *Quality Assurance for Leisure Services*, London: British Quality Association.

British Standards Institution (1987) *Quality Assurance (BSI Handbook 22)*, London: British Standards Institution.

Brodie, M.B. (1967) *Fayol on Administration*, London: Lyon, Grant & Green.

Brown, P. and Hackett, F. (1990) *Managing Meetings*, London: Fontana.

Bucher, C.A. and Krotee, M.L. (1992) *Management of Physical Education and Sport*, St Louis, MO: Mosby Year Book.

Buswell, J. (ed.) (1993) *Case Studies in Leisure Management Practice*, London: Pitman.

Catterall, P. (ed.) (1990, 1991, 1992, 1993, 1994) *Contemporary Britain: an Annual Review*, Oxford: Blackwell.

Central Council of Physical Recreation. Wolfenden Committee on Sport (1960) *Sport and the Community*, London: CCPR.

Central Council of Physical Recreation (1991) *Fair Play in Sport – a Charter*, London: CCPR.

Central Office of Information (1994) *Aspects of Britain: Sport and Leisure*, London: HMSO.

Centre for Leisure Research (1993) *Compulsory Competitive Tendering: Sport and Leisure Management – National Information Survey Report*, London: Sports Council, 1993.

Chartered Institute of Public Finance and Accountancy (1991) *Compulsory Competition for the Management of Sport and Leisure Facilities*, occasional paper, London: CIPFA.

Chaudhry-Lawton, R., Lawton, R., Murphy, K., Terry, A. (1993) *Quality: Change Through Teamwork*, London: Century Business.

Coakley, J. (1994) *Sport in Society: Issues and Controversies*, London: Mosby.

Coalter, F. (1993) 'Sports participation: price or priorities?', *Leisure Studies* **12**, no. 3, 171–82.

Coalter, F. (1998) 'Leisure studies, leisure policy and social citizenship: the failure of welfare or the limits of welfare?', *Leisure Studies* **17**, no. 1, 21–36.

Cochrane, A.J. (1990) *Science and Golf: Proceedings of the First World Scientific Congress of Golf*, London: E & F Spon.

Collins, V. (1993) *Recreation and Law*, London: E & FN Spon.

Cooke, A. (1994) *The Economics of Leisure and Sport*, London: International Thomson Business Press.

Council of Europe (1990) *European Sport for All Charter*, Strasbourg: Council of Europe.

Council of Europe (1992a) *European Sports Charter*, Strasbourg: Council of Europe.

Council of Europe (1992b) *Code of Sports Ethics*, http://cm.coe.int/ta/rec/1992/92r14rev.htm

Council of Europe Committee for the Development for Sport (1991) *Workshops on Sports Management*, Strasbourg: Council of Europe.

Covey, S.R. (1992) *The Seven Habits of Highly Effective People*, London: Simon & Schuster.

Crowther, J. (1993) *Managing your Golf Club: the Facts and Skills of Golf Club Management*, Bakewell: Crowther.

Dale, B.G. and Oakland, J.S. (1991) *British Standards Institution: Quality Improvement through Standards*, Cheltenham: Stanley Thornes.

Davis, K.A. (1994) *Sports Management: Successful Private Sector Business Strategies*, Madison, WI: Brown & Benchmark.

Department of Culture, Media and Sport (2001) *A Sporting Future for All: the Government's Plan for Sport*, London: DCMS.

Department of Education and Science (1989a) *Safety in Outdoor Education*, London: HMSO.

Department of Education and Science (1989b) *Building on Ability: Sport for People with Disabilities*, available from Department of National Heritage, London.

Department of Education and Science (1991) *A Sporting Double: School and Community*, London: HMSO.

Department of National Heritage (1995) *Sport: Raising the Game*, London: DNH.

Dickinson, J. (1976) *A Behavioural Analysis of Sport*, London: Lepus Books.

Drowatzky, J. (1984) *Legal Issues in Sport and Physical Education Management*, Champaign, IL: Stipes.

Druce, R. and Carter, S. (1988) *The Marketing Handbook: a Guide for Voluntary and Non-Profit Making Organisations*, Cambridge: National Extension College.

Dumfries and Galloway Council (2001) *A Leisure and Sport Strategy for Dumfries and Galloway, 2001–2005*, Dumfries: Dumfries and Galloway Council.

Eady, J. (1993) *Practical Sports Development*, Harlow: Longman.

Eastern Council for Sport and Recreation (1979) *Sports Centre Design with Management in Mind*, Bedford: ECSR.

East Midland Regional Council for Sport and Recreation (1979) *Managing for Results: Report of the Sports Centre Management Seminar*, Nottingham: Sports Council, East Midland Region.

Edwards, H. (1973) *Sociology of Sport*, Homewood, IL: Dorsey Press.

Elvin, I.T. (1993) *Sport and Physical Recreation*, Harlow: Longman/ILAM Leisure and Management.

Evans-Platt, C. (1992) *Health and Fitness Centres: a Guide to their Management and Operation*, Harlow: Longman in association with Baths and Recreation Management.

Forbes, D., Hayes, R. and Reason, J. (1994) *Voluntary, but Not Amateur: a Guide to the Law for Voluntary Organisations and Community Groups*, London: London Voluntary Service Council.

Fyfe, L. (1994) *Careers in Sport*, London: Kogan Page.

Gerson, R.F. (1989) *Marketing Health/Fitness Services*, Champaign, IL: Human Kinetics.

Gibson, R. (ed.) (1997) *Rethinking the Future: Rethinking Business, Principles, Competition, Control & Complexity, Leadership, Markets and the World*, London: Nicholas Brealey.

Gilson, C., Pratt, M., Roberts, K. and Weymes, E. (2000) *Peak Performance: Business Lessons from the World's Top Sports Organizations*, London: HarperCollins.

Glatter, R., Preddey, M., Riches, C. and Masterson, M. (eds) (1989) *Understanding School Management*, Buckingham: Open University Press.

Glyptis, S. (1989) *Leisure and Unemployment*, Buckingham: Open University Press.

Goffman, E. (1959) *The Presentation of Self in Everyday Life*, Harmondsworth: Penguin.

Goldblatt, J.J. (1990) *Special Events: the Art and Science of Celebration*, New York: Van Nostrand Reinhold.

Goldblatt, J.J. (1997) *Special Events: Best Practices and Modern Event Management*, New York: Van Nostrand Reinhold.

Goodale, T.L. and Godbey, G.C. (1988) *The Evolution of Leisure: Historical and Philosophical Perspectives*, State College, PA: Venture Publishing.

Gratton, C. and Henry, I.P. (eds) (2001) *Sport in the City: the Role of Sport in Economic and Social Regeneration*, London: Routledge.

Gratton, C. and Taylor, P. (2000) *The Economics of Sport and Recreation*, London: E & FN Spon.

Gratton, C. and Tice, A. (1989) 'Sports participation and health', *Leisure Studies* **8**, 77–92.

Gratton, C. and Tice, A. (1994) 'Trends in sports participation in Britain', *Leisure Studies* **13**, 49–66.

Grayson, E. (1994) *Sport and the Law*, London: Butterworth.

Haggerty, T.R. and Paton, G.A. (1984) *Financial Management of Sport-Related Organizations*, Champaign, IL: Stipes.

Hall, C.M. (1992) *Hallmark Tourist Events: Impacts, Management, and Planning*, London: Belhaven.

Hammer, M. (1997) 'Beyond the end of management', in Gibson, R. (ed.) *Rethinking the Future: Rethinking Business, Principles, Competition, Control & Complexity, Leadership, Markets and the World*, London: Nicholas Brealey.

Handy, C. (1985) *Understanding Organizations*, Harmondsworth: Penguin.

Handy, C. (1988) *Understanding Voluntary Organizations*, Harmondsworth: Penguin.

Handy, C. (1997) 'Finding sense in uncertainty', in Gibson, R. (ed.) *Rethinking the Future: Rethinking Business, Principles, Competition, Control & Complexity, Leadership, Markets and the World*, London: Nicholas Brealey.

Haywood, L. (1994) *Community Leisure and Recreation*, Oxford: Butterworth-Heinemann.

Haywood, L., Kew, F. and Bramham, P. (1989) *Understanding Leisure*, London: Hutchinson.

Health & Safety Executive (1988) *The Essentials of Health and Safety at Work*, London: HMSO.

Health & Safety Executive (1993) *A Guide to Health, Safety and Welfare at Pop Concerts and Other Similar Events*, London: HMSO.

Health & Safety Executive (1999) *The Event Safety Guide*, London: The Health & Safety Executive.

Heathcote, K. (1988) *The Gym Business*, Newton Abbot: David & Charles.

Henry, I.P. (1990) *Management and Planning in the Leisure Industries*, London: Macmillan.

Herzberg, F., Mausner, B. and Snyderman, B.B. (1993) *The Motivation to Work*, New Brunswick, NJ: Transaction Publishers.

Hill, T. (1993) *The Essence of Operations Management*, Englewood Cliffs, NJ: Prentice Hall.

Hodgkin, R.A. (1985) *Playing and Exploring: Education through the Discovery of Order*, London: Methuen.

Hodgson, P. and Hodgson, J. (1993), *Effective Meetings*, London: Century Business Books.

Hoggett, P. and Bishop, J. (1985) *The Social Organisation of Leisure: the Study of Groups in the Voluntary Sector Context*, London: The Sports Council/ESRC, 1985.

Houlihan, B. (1991) *The Government of Politics and Sport*, London: Routledge.

Hylton, K., Bramham, P. and Jackson, D. (eds) (2001) *Sports Development: Policy, Process and Practice*, London: Routledge.

Institute of Baths and Recreation Management (1992) *Practical Leisure Centre Management*, vols 1 and 2, Melton Mowbray: IBRM.

Institute of Leisure and Amenity Management (1989) *Competitive Tendering: Management of Sports and Leisure Facilities*, Harlow: Longman.

Institute of Leisure and Amenity Management (1995) *ILAM Guide to Good Practice in Leisure Services Management*, vol. 4, Harlow: Longman.

Isaac-Henry, K. Painter, C. and Barnes, C. (1993) *Management in the Public Sector: Challenge and Change*, London: Chapman & Hall.

James, S. (1990) *Chambers Sporting Quotations*, Edinburgh: Chambers.

Jarman, C. (1990) *The Guinness Dictionary of Sports Quotations*, London: Guinness Publishing.

Jarvie, G. (ed.) (1991) *Sport, Racism and Ethnicity*, London: Falmer.

Jubenville, A., Twight, B.W. and Becker, R.H. (1987) *Outdoor Recreation Management: Theory and Application*, State College, PA: Venture Publishing.

Kelley, D.R., Beitel, P.A., DeSensi, J.T. and Blanton, M.D. (1994) 'Undergraduate and graduate sport management curricular models: a perspective', *Journal of Sport Management* **8**, no. 2, 93–101.

Koehler, R.W. (1988) *Law, Sport Activity and Risk Management*, Champaign, IL: Stipes.

Koski, P. (1995) 'Organizational effectiveness of Finnish sport clubs', *Journal of Sport Management* **9**, no. 1, 85–95.

Langmuir, E. (1995) *Mountaincraft and Leadership: a Handbook for Mountaineers and Hillwalking Leaders in the British Isles*, Edinburgh: Sport Scotland; Manchester: Mountain Leader Training Board.

Lee, M. (ed.) (1993) *Coaching Children in Sport: Principles and Practice*, London: E & FN Spon.

Leisure Futures Ltd (1989) *Marketing Leisure Services*, London: Leisure Futures.

Leith, L.M. (1990) *Coaches Guide to Sport Administration*, Champaign, IL: Human Kinetics.

Levant, J. and Cleeton, D. (1993) *Marketing the Training Function*, London: Kogan Page.

Liddle, B. (1987) *Dictionary of Sports Quotations*, London: Routledge & Kegan Paul.

Lock, D. (1992) *Project Management*, 5th edn, Aldershot: Gower.

Lynam, D. and Teasdale, D. (1994) *The Sporting Word*, London: BBC Books.

McCallum, C. (1995) *How to Raise Funds and Sponsorship*, Oxford: How To Books.

McCarville, R. and Copeland, R. (1994) 'Understanding sports sponsorship through exchange theory', *Journal of Sport Management*, **8**, 102–114.

McClelland, D.C. (1985) *Human Motivation*, Glenview, IL: Scott, Foresman & Co.

McFee, G. and Tomlinson, A. (1993) *Education, Sport and Leisure: Connections and Controversies*, London: Chelsea School Research Centre.

McPherson, B.D., Curtis, J.E. and Loy, J.W. (1989) *The Social Significance of Sport*, Champaign, IL: Human Kinetics.

Manser, M.H. (1987) *Chambers Book of Business Quotations*, Edinburgh: Chambers.

Marsden, A.K. (1992) *First Aid Manual: the Authorised Manual of St John's Ambulance, St Andrew's Ambulance Association and the British Red Cross*, London: Dorling Kindersley.

Maslow, A. (1954) *Motivation and Personality*, New York: Harper

Masteralexis, L.P. and McDonald, M.A. (1997) 'Enhancing sport management education with international dimensions including language and cultural training', *Journal of Sport Management* **11**, no. 1, 97–110.

Mikalachki, A., Leyshon, G.A. and Zeigler, E.F. (1988) *Change Process in Sport and Physical Education Management*, Champaign, IL: Stipes.

Mills, P. (1992) *Quality in the Leisure Industry*, Harlow: Longman.

Mullin, B., Hardy, S. and Sutton, W.A. (1993) *Sport Marketing*, Champaign, IL: Human Kinetics.

Naisbitt, J. (1995) *The Global Paradox*, London: Nicholas Brealey.

Newell, S. and Swan, J. (1995) 'The diffusion of innovations in sport organizations: an evaluative framework', *Journal of Sport Management* **9**, 317–37.

Nygaard, G. and Boone, T.H. (1985) *Coaches Guide to Sport Law*, Champaign, IL: Human Kinetics.

Ogilvie, K.C. (1993) *Leading and Managing Groups in the Outdoors*, Sheffield: National Association for Outdoor Education.

Orlick T. (1980) *In Pursuit of Excellence*, Ottawa: Coaching Association of Canada.

Outhart, T. and Taylor, L. (2000) *Leisure and Tourism for Intermediate GNVQ*, London: Collins.

Parkhouse, B. (1991) *The Management of Sport: Its Foundation and Application*, St Louis, MO: Mosby Year Book.

Parks, J.B. and Zanger, B.R.K. (1990) *Sport and Fitness Management: Career Strategies and Professional Content*, Champaign, IL: Human Kinetics.

Parks, J.B., Zanger, B.R.K. and Quarterman, J. (eds) (1998) *Contemporary Sport Management*, Champaign, IL: Human Kinetics.

Passingham, S. (1993) *Organising Local Events*, London: Directory of Social Change in association with the Institute of Charity Fundraising Managers.

Public Administration Research Centre (1988) *Supporting the Council: an Investigation into the Organisation, Charging and Costing of Professional Support Services in Local Authorities*, Bolton: PARC.

Pugh, D.S. (1971) *Organisation Theory*, Harmondsworth: Penguin.

Pyke, J. and Barners, R. (1994) *TQM in Action*, London: Chapman & Hall.

Ray, R. (1994) *Management Strategies in Athletic Training*, Champaign, IL: Human Kinetics.

Rodgers, B. (1978) *Sport in Its Social Context*, Strasbourg: Council of Europe, Committee for the Development of Sport.

Sayers, P. (1991) *Managing Sport and Leisure Facilities: a Guide to Competitive Tendering*, London: E & FN Spon.

Sceats, A. (1985) *Sports and Leisure Club Management: a Handbook for Organisers*, Plymouth: Macdonald and Evans.

Scott, J. and Rochester, A. (1984a) *Effective Management Skills, Vol. 1 – Managing Work*, London: Sphere in association with the British Institute of Management.

Scott, J. and Rochester, A. (1984b) *Effective Management Skills, Vol. 2 – Managing People*, London: Sphere in association with the British Institute of Management.

Scott, M. (1993) *Law and Leisure Service Management*, Harlow: Longman in conjunction with ILAM.

Shaw, R. (1993) *Spread of Sponsorship in the Arts, Sport, Education, the Health Service and Broadcasting*, Newcastle upon Tyne: Bloodaxe Books.

Shoebridge, M. (ed.) (1992) *Information Sources in Sport and Leisure*, East Grinstead: Bowker-Saur.

Slack, T. (1997) *Understanding Sport Organizations: the Application of Organization Theory*, London: Human Kinetics.

Smithson, S. and Whitehead, J. (1990) *Customer Care in Leisure Organisations: Guidelines for Managers and Staff*, Reading: ILAM in conjunction with Farnborough College of Technology.

Sport England (1996) *Getting it Right – Running Sport*. Wetherby: Sport England Publications.

Sport England (1999) *General Household Survey – Participation in Sport in Great Britain 1996*, Wetherby: Sport England Publications.

Sports Council (1990) *Managing Sport and Recreation under CCT: the Future Client Side Role*, London: Sports Council.

Sports Council (1994–5) *Recreation Management (Facilities – Fact File 1)*, London: Sports Council.

Stayte, S. and Watt, D.C. (1998) *Events from Start to Finish*, London: Institute of Leisure and Amenity Management.

Stier, W.F. (1994) *Fundraising for Sport and Recreation*, Champaign, IL: Human Kinetics.

Tancred, B. and Tancred, G. (1992) *Leisure Management*, London: Hodder & Stoughton.

Taylor, W.J. and Watling, T.F. (1988) *Basic Arts of Management*, London: Random House Business Books.

Thibault, L., Slack, T. and Hinings, C.R. (1994) 'Strategic planning for nonprofit sport organizations: the empirical verification of a framework and location of strategic types', *Journal of Sport Management* 8, 218–33.

Thomas, D.G. (1988) *Competitive Swimming Management*, London: Human Kinetics.

Thomas, E. and Woods, M. (1992) *The Manager's Casebook*, London: Duncan Petersen.

Thomson, I. (1992) *Alternative Approaches to Sports Development*, Stirling University.

Tilling, R. (past chairman, Birchfield Harriers Athletic Club) (2001) Presentation at Scottish Athletics Conference, Glasgow.

Torkildsen, G. (1993) *Torkildsen's Guides to Leisure Management*, Harlow: Longman.

Torkildsen, G. (1999) *Leisure and Recreation Management*, 4th edn, London: E & FN Spon.

Turner, J.B.W. (1989) *Henley: the Best Organised Picnic in Europe!*, Shrewsbury: Management Update.

Walker, M.L. and Seidler, T.L (1992) *Sports Equipment Management*, USA: Jones and Bartlet.

Watt, D.C. (1992) *Event Management in Leisure and Tourism*, Harlow: Longman.

White, A. (1995) *Managing for Performance: How to Get the Best out of Yourself and Your Team*, London: Piatkus.

Wilson, N. (1988) *The Sports Business: The Men in the Money*, London: Piatkus.

Wright, J. (1994) *Recreation and Leisure: City and Guilds Course 481, parts 1 and 2*, Kingston upon Thames: Croner.

Yiannopoulos, C.T. (1996) *Sport and Management: in Search of Common Language*, Athens: Medoussa.

Yule, W. and Gold, A. (1993) *Wise Before the Event*, London: Calouste Gulbenkian Foundation.

Zeigler, E.F., Bowie, G. and Paris, R. (1988) *Competency Development in Sport and Physical Education Management: a Primer*, Champaign, IL: Stipes.

Journals, periodicals and magazines

The ACHPER, Australian Council for Health, Physical Education and Recreation

Active/Women in Sport Newsletter, Australian Sports Commission

All Sport and Leisure Monthly, Graphic House

Anglo American Sports, Direct Access

Arena, The Scottish Sports Council
Arena Review, Centre for Study of Sport in Society, North-Eastern University, Boston
British Journal of Physical Education, Physical Education Society
Coaching Today, HHL – Consumer Magazines & Marketing Services
Event Organiser, Event Suppliers Association
Football Management, Portman Publishing & Comm
Golf Club Management, Harper Trade Journals
The Groundsman, Adam Publishing
Harpers Sport and Leisure, Harpers Publishing
Harpers Guide to the Sports Trade, Harpers Publishing
Health and Fitness, Hudson Brothers Publishers
Health and Physical Education Project, Health Education Authority
IFPRA Bulletin, International Federation of Park and Recreation Administration
International Journal of the History of Sport, Frank Cass
International Management, Reed Business Publishing Group
International Play Journal, Chapman & Hall
Journal of Sport and Social Issues, Centre for the Study of Sport in Society, USA
Journal of Sports Management, Human Kinetics Publishers, USA
Leisure Futures, The Henley Centre for Forecasting
Leisure Management/Leisure Opportunities, Dicestar
Leisure Manager, Institute of Leisure and Amenity Management
Leisure, Recreation & Tourism Abstracts, CAB International
Leisure Sciences, Taylor & Francis
Leisure Studies (Journal), Chapman & Hall
Leisure Week, Centaur Publishing
National Playing Fields Association Newsletter, NPFA
New Zealand Journal of Health, Physical Education & Recreation, New Zealand Association of Health and Physical Education and Recreation
Parks, Golf Courses and Sports Grounds, Clarke and Hunter
Peak Performance, Sport & Leisure Magazines
Recreation, ISRM
Recreation, Canadian Parks/Recreation Association
Sociology of Sport Journal, Human Kinetics Publishers, USA
Sponsorship Insights, Hobsons Publishing
Sponsorship News, Charterhouse Business Publications
Sport, The Sports Council
Sport Development Officers Association, SDOA
Sport Place, Black Oak Press, USA
Sporting Traditions, Australian Society for Sport History
Sports Club Management, The Association of Sports Club Managers
Sports Documentation Monthly Bulletin, Sports Documentation Centre
Sports Information Bulletin, Council for Europe, Belgium
Sports & Leisure Equipment News, Peterson Publishing Co.
Sports Report, National Indoor Arena
Sports Teacher, National Council for School Sports
Sports Turf Bulletin, Sports Turf Research Institute
Sportsnews, The Regional Sports Council
Sprig Bulletin, Sport and Recreation Information Group
Swimming Pool News, MGS Publishing

Times Higher Education Supplement, The Times Supplements
Water and Leisure, Royal Society for the Prevention of Accidents
Waterways, Inland Waterways Association
Women's Sports Foundation Newsletter, Women's Sports Foundation
World Leisure and Recreational Association Newsletter, World Leisure and Recreation
   Association
Workout, Wharncliffe Publishing

In addition, the sports councils (local and national) commission and publish many useful reports, documents, etc. relating to sports management and administration. The Central Council for Physical Recreation has a number of publications that would be of use to the sports manager/administrator (obtainable from the Publications Department, CCPR, Frances House, Frances Street, London SW1P 1DE).

Texts specific to a single sport may include useful information for the administrator; these are not listed here because they are so numerous.

Index